NOR MEEKLY
SERVE MY TIME

Nor Meekly Serve My Time

The H-Block Struggle 1976 – 1981

Edited by
Brian Campbell
Laurence McKeown
Felim O'Hagan

Compiled by
Brian Campbell

First published 1994
by
Beyond the Pale Publications
PO Box 337
Belfast BT9 7BT
Tel: +44 232 645930

British Library Cataloguing-in-Publication Data
A catalogue record for this book is available from the British Library.

ISBN 0 9514229 5 2

Typeset in 10 on 13pt Times
Printed by
Colour Books Ltd, Dublin

Acknowledgements

The publishers would like to thank the following for assisting in the production of this book: Sal Brennan, Jim Collins, Jason Doran, Mary Mullan, and Fran Webber.

Cover design by INSIDE OUT, Derry

Contents

Acknowledgements

T his book began as a project to commemorate the 10th anniversary of the 1981 hunger strike. It was envisaged then that a small pamphlet would be produced, but very quickly it became clear that there was material for a full-length book.

Because of the practical difficulties of producing a book from jail, it was decided to limit the contributions to those imprisoned in Long Kesh at the time. The stories of other ex-Blanketmen, of the relatives, activists and the republican prisoners in Armagh Jail remain to be told.

Dozens of prisoners were involved in compiling their memories, typing the many hundreds of pages and correcting errors and omissions. We would like to thank them all, in particular Joe McQuillan.

By its very nature, it was impossible to include everyone's accounts, many of which overlapped or were similar. We would especially like to thank the following whose accounts could not be included: Jimmy Burns, Gerard Clarke, John (Sleepy) Devine, Willie Doherty, Marty Kelly, Brendi McClenaghan, Paddy McCotter and Eamon (Doc) McDermott.

Others outside the jail very generously gave their time and resources to the project. A very special debt of gratitude is due to Róisín.

Our manuscript was offered to several publishers who, for various reasons, turned it down. We would therefore like to thank Beyond the Pale Publications for recognising that this is a book that deserves to be published.

Glossary

AG – Assistant Governor. The administration in Long Kesh is headed by a Governor (Grade 1), known colloquially as the No. 1, who has overall responsibility for the jail and is directly responsible to the NIO. Under him are Assistant Governors (Grade 2-5), around 25 in number, who delegate various areas of responsibility. Below the managerial level are the uniformed screws: Principal Officer (PO), Senior Officer (SO) and Ordinary Grade, the lowest rank. The complement of jail staff attached to an individual H-Block typically consists of an AG, PO, SO and 25-30 Ordinary Grade screws.

Bangle – The term used by the Blanketmen to describe the act of hiding contraband within their bodies. To 'bangle' was to insert a beart (see below) into the rectum.

Bear – Alternative nickname for a screw, often used by the Blanketmen. The name derives from the 1970s song 'Convoy' by CW McCall, which referred to the US cops as bears. One phrase in particular, 'bear in the air' (referring originally to a police surveillance helicopter), was used as a warning shout to let everyone know that a screw was coming down the wing. In fact, many Blanketmen refused to use the alternative nickname on the reasonable grounds that it was insulting to genuine bears.

Beart – An Irish word meaning parcel. A beart was a tightly packed parcel of tobacco wrapped in cling-film and smuggled in during visits; it also often contained pens, pencil leads, flints, cigarette papers and a few comms (see below). As Blanketmen were not allowed tobacco, a beart was the most precious commodity in the H Blocks.

Big cell – Cell 26 or, in Irish, an cillín mór. In each wing cell 26 is a double cell and during the protest it was used to store prison uniforms which men wore only to go on visits, and prison trousers which were worn to attend mass. However, cell 26 is significant in the memory of Blanketmen because mirror searches were regularly conducted there, and so it was the scene of much brutality.

Boards – The punishment cells, so called because they contained no beds, only wooden boards on a raised concrete platform. The boards were located beside the old internment cages in a separate phase of Long Kesh camp.

BOV – Board of Visitors. An NIO-appointed body of supposedly independent people from churches, trade unions, business and voluntary sectors whose task is, in theory, to monitor the prison regime and to make representations on behalf of the prisoners in respect of abuses of their rights. In practice, the BOV is at best totally ineffective and at worst (which is most of the time) simply another arm of the jail administration. BOV members were aware of the countless instances of brutality yet did nothing – not surprisingly, the BOV was detested by the Blanketmen.

Catwalk – A narrow caged walkway for the screws, alongside the exercise yard.

CC – cellular confinement. Originally CC referred solely to solitary confinement in the punishment cells for 'breaches of prison discipline'; prisoners could be so confined for up to 70 days. During periods of CC all bedding was removed from the cell between 7.30am and 8.30pm. In the first three years of the protest, each Blanketman was sentenced to three days CC and loss of all remission every 28 days. As numbers on the protest soon outstripped the capacity of the punishment cells, the screws contented themselves with keeping men in their own cells in the Block and removing their bedding. The practice of CC was discontinued for Blanketmen in 1979, but they continued to lose remission and all privileges (books, newspapers, educational facilities, radios, access to TV, etc).

Cell 26 – See 'big cell' above.

Cillín mór – See 'big cell' above.

Circle – The administrative area within each H-Block, containing offices, medical room, control room and screws' mess. It is located in the crossbar of the H (the legs being four wings). The area is in fact rectangular; the name is a legacy of Victorian prisons where the administration area was literally circular and wings radiated from it like spokes of a wheel.

Class officer – The Ordinary Grade screw in charge of the day-to-day running of a wing.

Comm – Abbreviation of 'communication'. A note written on cigarette paper or prison-issue toilet paper and wrapped in cling-film (such a note is also known as a teac – see below). Comms were the lifeblood of the Blanket protest, vital both for inter-block communication and communication with outside.

Craic/crack – A peculiarly Irish term meaning fun or good time. It also occurs in the phrase 'What's the craic?', meaning 'What's happening?'

Fáinne – Irish for ring or circle (see above).

Maggie Taggart – Nickname for smuggled crystal radio set. Maggie Taggart was a newsreader on a local radio station in the 1970s. (See 'Mrs Dale' below.)

Meat Wagon – A large van used to transport prisoners.

Mixes – Practical jokes, stunts and traps for the gullible and unwary, particularly those new to prison.

MO – Medical Officer. A screw attached to the prison hospital – most MOs had a very basic medical training.

Monkey suit – Nickname for the prison uniform.

Mrs Dale – Nickname for smuggled radio. 'Mrs Dale's Diary' was a long-running serial on BBC Radio 4. (See 'Maggie Taggart' above.)

NIO – Northern Ireland Office. The Stormont parliament was prorogued in 1972 and since then the NIO, under a British Secretary of State, has been responsible for the administration of the Six Counties.

No. 1 – Governor with overall responsibility for the jail. (See 'AG' above)

OC – Officer Commanding. Each wing and Block has its own OC, while the Blocks' OC is in overall charge of Republican prisoners in the jail. In spite of its militaristic overtones, the position of the OC is very much that of 'first among equals' in the prison community.

Pluid – Irish for blanket.

PO – Principal Officer (See 'AG' above).

POA – Prison Officers' Association. Ostensibly a trade union for the screws which negotiates terms and conditions of employment. During the period of the protests the POA had a strong influence on prison policy and was dominated by those most closely identified with the beatings of prisoners in the Blanket Blocks.

Rang(anna) – Irish for class(es). Ranganna Gaeilge were a part of life on the Blanket and, in spite of the adverse conditions, they were so successful that Irish soon became the everyday language of the Blocks.

Scéal – Irish for news or story. Next to tobacco, scéal was the thing upon which Blanketmen thrived.

Scéalaí – Irish for storyteller – that is, the man who told the nightly 'book at bedtime' out the door.

Sin é – Irish for 'that's it'. It was shouted by the OC whenever he wanted to get some attention in a noisy wing, so it came to mean effectively 'Quiet'.

Skin – A cigarette paper.

Snout – Tobacco.

SO – Senior Officer (see 'AG' above).

Squeaky-booter – Pejorative term for anyone who left the Blanket. It originated in the early days of the protest; one man decided to leave the protest quietly but as he made his way up the wing in the prison uniform and brand new boots, the squeak of the rubber soles on the polished floor gave him away.

Stailc – Irish for strike: stailc ocrais is hunger strike.

Stailceoir(í) – Striker(s).

Teac – Abbreviation of teachtaireacht, an Irish word meaning message; a teac is a comm (see above).

Wack – Slang for prison sentence. Someone who is getting his time hard is said to be 'doing heavy wack'.

Yippees – YPs, Young Prisoners – official prison jargon for those under 21 years of age.

The H-Block Song

I

I am a proud young Irishman.
In Ulster's hills my life began;
A happy boy through green fields ran;
I kept God's and Man's laws.
But when my age was barely ten
My country's wrongs were told again
By tens of thousands marching men
And my heart stirred to the cause.

So I'll wear no convict's uniform
Nor meekly serve my time
That Britain might brand Ireland's fight
Eight hundred years of crime.

II

I learned of centuries of strife,
Of cruel laws, injustice rife;
I saw now in my own young life
The fruits of foreign sway:
Protestors threatened, tortured, maimed,
Divisions nurtured, passions flamed,
Outrage provoked, right's cause defamed;
That is the conqueror's way.

Chorus

III

Descended from proud Connacht clan,
Concannon served cruel Britain's plan;
Man's inhumanity to man
Had spawned a trusty slave.
No strangers are these bolts and locks,
No new design these dark H-Blocks,
Black Cromwell lives while Mason stalks;
The bully taunts the brave.

Chorus

IV

Does Britain need a thousand years
Of protest, riot, death and tears,
Or will this past decade of fears
Of eighty decades spell
an end to Ireland's agony,
New hope for human dignity;
And will the last obscenity
Be this grim H-Block cell?

Chorus

Francie Brolly,
Dungiven, 1976.

Foreword

I was no stranger to death when the hunger strikes began in October 1980. My father died suddenly, without explanation or warning, when I was nine. Within the next 10 years both my mother and grandmother died slowly and painfully of cancer.

On 16 October 1972 John Paddy Mullan, OC Tyrone Brigade, Irish Republican Army, was taken prisoner by members of the Staffordshire Regiment, together with Hugh Herron, Quartermaster, and a young Volunteer in a car park in Ardboe. Hugh Herron was shot with his hands above his head. John Paddy was slain as he moved to save his own life and that of his young comrade.

This war had claimed the first of too long a list of people who were, and still are, part of my being. By 1980, death, and prison, grief, pain and loss were part of everyday existence for the whole community.

A good friend, the mother of a life sentence prisoner and a patriot in her own right, once said that we are all marked, indelibly marked by this struggle and our children would carry that mark for three generations.

I think she was right. Nothing, however, has marked me in all that long sorrow as indelibly as the deaths of 10 young men whom I didn't know personally. No deaths have been harder for me to come to terms with than the deaths of the hunger strikers.

Even now, 12 years later, I hold that period at arm's length. I don't want to address the question of why. Perhaps it provides a focal point by which the weight of pain might finally crush a heart too often broken. Perhaps it would unleash too much anger, too deep a sense of betrayal for effective work to continue. Perhaps the enormity of the sacrifice is too great to weigh against the human frailty of those of us who remain.

John Donne once wrote in a poem, 'Good Friday - Riding Westward', the words, "What a death were it, to see God die". I often think of that poem and the hunger strike together; maybe God died somewhere in the middle of it.

I wonder sometimes how many people stop to count how many seconds make up the minutes that made up the hours of the 66 days of Bobby Sands's dying, or the 73 of Kieran Doherty's, or the 46 of Martin Hurson's.

How many seconds did it take all 10 to die? I think of the power of such love as will lay down its life so resolutely, and I am in awe and perhaps fear of it, and I wonder what transforms ordinary young people into such universal defenders of human integrity.

I wonder if I were the mother, the sister, the comrade, the lover of such a person, how should I have survived the pain of his loss. And I close my mind to the thought.

I have struggled to write the foreword to this book because it is written by those who shared the lives of the hunger strikers in prison - those who struggled with them, suffered with them, starved with them, who sat and waited and watched as the clock ticked out the ebbing life of each in turn, whose pain of necessity is much deeper than mine.

Intellectually, politically, analytically, I know there is an evaluation to be made of the hunger strike in relation to the war, to the political struggle, to the emancipation of humanity. I know there are political lessons to be learned. I know all these things.

I also know that a train of events was set in motion when political status was withdrawn from the prisoners in 1976 that it was inevitably heading for a conflict that resulted in young men dying of hunger in 1981, and we couldn't stop it happening. Five years passed and we couldn't stop it happening.

The young men who have contributed to this book paid the price of that inability. They too are indelibly marked. They are incredibly brave, and mercifully forgiving of our weakness.

"Greater love than this no man hath than he lay down his life for his friend." Maybe I'm not sure how to deal with that degree of love. Maybe I wonder why they died for us, and we didn't die for them.

Bernadette McAliskey,
Coalisland, July 1993.

Editors'
Introduction

"I am dying not just to attempt to end the barbarity of the H-Blocks, or to gain rightful recognition as a political prisoner, but primarily because what is lost in here is lost for the Republic and those wretched oppressed whom I am proud to know as the 'risen people'."

The words of Bobby Sands on the first day of his hunger strike did not immediately echo in the ranks of the risen people. But when he died on 5 May 1981, they reverberated round the world, bringing an international focus on the Irish struggle and releasing a welled-up anger in Ireland.

Bobby Sands was right. The hunger strike was about ending the years of barbarity in the H-Blocks and it was about gaining recognition as political prisoners. But those were reasons pushed to the surface by the underlying tide of history that was the opposition to British rule in Ireland. The hunger strike was the latest battlefield on which republicans met the British. The weight of republican tradition and the prisoners' instinctive sense of struggle drove them to resist attempts at criminalisation until, with each option of struggle exhausted, a hunger strike to the death was inevitable.

It is difficult to imagine how the slow agonising tactic of a hunger strike could be seen as inevitable, but that was how it was in the H-Blocks in 1980-81. The resort to hunger strike was a measure of the intensity of the battle for the Republic. The desire for justice, the courage and the undiluted determination never to give in were awe-inspiring. The memory of the 10 men who gave their lives over those 217 days provokes a sadness and anger which remains a call for action.

As the hunger strikes unfolded, they changed the Republican Movement by heralding electoral intervention and mass political involvement, they transformed wider politics and they rocked the British into a dual strategy of increasing repression and building a wide anti-republican coalition. Garret FitzGerald and Margaret Thatcher, the signatories of the Hillsborough Agreement, have conceded that their motivation in drawing up the Agreement was to defeat a resurgent Republican Movement. The historical significance of the hunger strikes is clear when one considers how Anglo-Irish politics in the 1980s had their reference point in the changes brought about by the deaths in Long Kesh.

Just as the forces of Irish history produced the hunger strikes, so they in turn have affected subsequent history. This is why there is a need to understand what happened in the H-Blocks between 1976 and 1981.

The participants in those events are the witnesses best able to leave an historical record. This book is the Blanketmen as historians, people who not only changed history but were themselves changed by it.

No one who has grasped the enormity of what the Blanketmen experienced can fail to appreciate how deep are the reserves of resistance or how much this group of men has been steeled by what they came through. It is safe to say that the legacy of the hunger strikes has yet to be exhausted.

Brian Campbell
Laurence McKeown
Felim O'Hagan
Belfast, July 1994.

1

From Crumlin Road to the H-Blocks

March 1976 – April 1977

When a British government commission recommended in January 1975 the phasing out of political status (officially termed special category status), few realised the full significance of the recommendation, and fewer still guessed its lethal consequence. 1975 was after all a time of seemingly fundamental shifts in the political landscape of the North. The British government had been engaged in talks with the Republican Movement, and a truce agreed between the IRA and British forces was to last into the latter part of that year.

As months passed, however, it became clear that the British were not interested in peace. They had exploited the truce while preparing counter-insurgency measures whose objective was to isolate those engaged in the resistance struggle and to 'normalise' life in the Six County state. A major part of British policy was the criminalisation of Republican prisoners.

Political status had been won in May 1972 following a 35-day hunger strike in Crumlin Road Jail in Belfast. Since then, thousands had served their time under a regime which recognised them as political prisoners. Now the British government was telling the world that the national liberation struggle was nothing more than a criminal conspiracy led by 'Mafia-like Godfathers', yet the reality of the prison regime stood in stark contradiction to British propaganda claims. Special category status had to be withdrawn.

The British government declared that those convicted of charges occurring after 1 March 1976 would be treated as common criminals and serve their sentences not in the Cages of Long Kesh, but in the purpose built cellular accommodation in a separate phase of Long Kesh camp: the H-Blocks.

NIO spokespersons invariably referred to the H-Blocks as 'the most modern prison in Europe' and spoke in glowing terms of the facilities available. The media dutifully reported these statements. What went unreported was the brutality of a regime designed to beat prisoners into submission. The accounts of those first Republicans denied political status, the majority in their late teens and early 20s, detail the degradation, fear and confusion of the early days of the Blanket protest. Above all, the accounts show the conviction and solidarity of the prisoners, and their determination that neither they nor the liberation struggle were ever to be criminalised.

JACKIE McMULLAN ...

I was arrested in May 1976 and taken to Crumlin Road Jail where I was held on remand. I was aware that political status had been removed two months earlier and I remember looking for indications of how this was going to work out in practice. But I was also somehow hoping there'd be no meaningful difference. In June, the remaining Republican remand prisoners with status moved from Crumlin Road's A wing to Long Kesh and, since C wing was almost full, A wing was used to house the stream of new men coming in. So, two wings held remand prisoners, both Republican and Loyalist.

Although we didn't know what the Brits had planned for us, it was becoming apparent they had something in mind. Already we knew that they would try to make us wear 'monkey suits' and we had decided that, whatever we were going to do, part of it would be to refuse to wear convict uniforms. We had no idea where we'd be going after being sentenced. We had heard some talk of them building something in Long Kesh. We weren't too concerned about that because it would be all over in a short while – possibly even before any of us would be sentenced – or so we thought.

There was a vague awareness that we were heading for some sort of confrontation, but it wasn't something which preoccupied us. I think this was partly because most of us were young and hadn't the inclination to think too far into the future. The attitude was one of taking each day as it came and it would be time enough to worry about courts and sentences and political status when they started to affect us directly. The average age was around 19 or 20, and we were more concerned with the craic and pulling 'mixes' on each other than anything which might happen to any of us in the long distant future.

1976 was a glorious summer; the courts were closed until September and that seemed a lifetime away. Some of us even entertained notions of being out of jail by then because, as always, there were some mad – and some not so mad – schemes for escape.

Right through July and into August the number of prisoners built up. There were three men to each cell and between A wing and C wing there must have been over 150 Republicans by the end of August. The courts were due to start at the beginning of September, so our thoughts were more and more being turned in that direction. Protests were being held outside and I remember one being addressed by Máire Drumm (Sinn Féin Vice President; she was shot dead by Loyalists on 28 October 1976 in the Mater Hospital, Belfast, while recovering from an operation) in which she said they would tear the Crum down brick by brick. We were lifted and excited by this; it was always good to know we had support outside.

On 14 September Ciaran Nugent was the first Republican to be sentenced since the removal of political status. We were eager to hear where they had taken him and what had happened to him after court. Then we heard that he was in the punishment cells in B wing in the Crum and that he was naked. Over the next few days we heard little else but confirmation of this original story and then he disappeared. They took him away – we hadn't a clue where.

NED FLYNN . . .

Three weeks after Ciaran Nugent was sentenced, my solicitor came unexpectedly and told me I was due in court the next morning. I refused to recognise the court and before I knew it, I was sentenced to three years. It was only then that the realisation dawned on me that I was entering a system that intended to bring me to my knees. I knew that our strength lay in unity, and it was vitally important for the first handful of men who were sentenced to remain steadfast and resolute.

When I returned from the court, I was granted a visit with my mother and father. It was very solemn. They knew without asking what road I was going to take and they were behind me 100%. My mother cried a lot during the visit, so I was glad when the screw said 'time up'. We hugged and said our goodbyes. Little did I know that it would be 19 months before I would see them or any of my family again.

Two hours later I was in a 'meat wagon' on my way to Long Kesh. There were five Loyalists in the van along with me who had been sentenced that same day. They told me they were going to abide by the prison rules. I felt as if I was on my own, completely isolated from the whole human race. I was about to enter the unknown and I was very nervous and frightened of what lay ahead. One of the things I remember clearly from that day was the weather; it was the coldest October I could ever remember.

When the van reached the reception area, I was taken out, put into a cubicle and told to put the prison uniform on. I refused. A screw told me he didn't care what I did but I had to leave the clothes I was wearing in reception. So I told him I would wear the coat and trousers until I went into the Block and then take them off. This I did.

I was brought into H1 and put into a cell along with non-political prisoners. I immediately took everything off, sat on the floor and told the screw that I was a Republican POW and I would not be wearing any prison uniform or conforming to any prison rules.

They made me walk naked from C wing to B wing, where I was put into an empty cell. They threw me in one blanket and told me to sleep well. When I told them I hadn't eaten since 11.30am (it was then about 6.30pm), they just laughed and said that I could have all the food I wanted if I put the prison uniform on. The door was slammed shut and, with the sound of rattling keys fading in the distance, I stood at the door to try and detect any kind of noise coming from the wing, but there was none. I shouted out to Ciaran Nugent but there was no answer. The silence told me I was the sole occupant of both wings. At about 10.30pm I hit the alarm button in my cell and asked the screw to give me some water to drink; all I got was verbal abuse. So I curled up in the corner of the cell and put the blanket around me to try and keep warm. I didn't sleep because at hourly intervals during the night the screw battered the hell out of the door.

A new day dawned and with it a more intense effort by the screws to break me. I had no less than 20 visitors to my cell that day and each one had the same message: my protest was futile; I was on my own because Ciaran Nugent had put the uniform on after a few days (in fact, he hadn't); and if I put the gear on, I could eat all the food I wanted. They sent orderlies down to shout through my door that Nugent had put the uniform on. I was now beginning to believe that I was on my own, but it didn't matter. I knew that some of my comrades were coming behind me and they would take the same road that I had taken. For my food that day I got two sandwiches and a cup of cold tea.

This procedure lasted for four days: very little food to eat and very little water to drink, no exercise, no reading or writing material. All my personal property had been taken away from me: tobacco, lighter, personal letters and washing items. I still had to sleep on the floor of the cell. That Sunday I asked to go to mass but this request was refused.

On the fifth morning, I was taken out of the Block, put into a van and driven to the punishment Block. All I had to cover me was a blanket. I was brought before a governor who sentenced me to 14 days loss of remission, 14 days loss of all privileges and 3 days' solitary confinement in the punishment Block. This last punishment was laughable since I had been in solitary confinement since I came. I was put into a cell with just a raised wooden board in it and a screw threw the prison uniform in and told me, if I didn't have it on by the time he came back, I'd be sorry. True to his word, he came back 15 minutes later with three other screws and they beat me with their fists and boots; all I could do was crawl up into a ball on the floor. When they eventually left, my body and legs were covered in bruises. Before my three days were up, I was to receive another beating, but not as bad as the first.

The cold and the constant droning noise from the air vent was much worse than the beating. I was in a concrete cell measuring nine by six feet, with no heating and just a blanket around me to keep me warm. The cold was so intense that when my bedding was put in at 8.30 that night it took me at least three hours to get some kind of heat into my feet. It is not surprising I ended up with a mixture of the cold and the flu. I felt really miserable. Those three days were the worst I've ever had to endure; my only consolation was having the Bible in the cell. I read it from cover to cover.

I was brought back to H1 where I was once again put into a wing on my own. Nothing had changed; I was still receiving the same treatment. By now I was convinced that Ciaran Nugent had put the uniform on. This did have an effect on my morale, but when I was feeling low and sorry for myself, I sang rebel songs and this always seemed to perk me up.

Two days later I was moved to C wing and I couldn't believe my ears when I went on the wing: a friendly voice after all this time. It wasn't that long, but to me it seemed like an eternity. Six of my comrades were in cells beside me; the six (known as the ABC bombers) were sentenced together. My stay with my six comrades was short-lived; two days later I was on the move again.

The next phase of the plan to break the protest was directed at Republican prisoners who were under 21. They obviously thought we were very weak and vulnerable and as such, would be more likely to succumb to the system. So it was that Ciaran Nugent, Paul McAnearney and myself were moved to H2. I went to D wing, Paul to C wing and Ciaran to A wing.

In a wing there are 24 cells; 12 on each side of the landing. There were two non-political prisoners in each cell on one side; on the other side all the cells were empty, and I was put into the third last cell on that side. By doing this the administration was showing us what we could get if we put the gear on, and they were going to degrade and humiliate us in front of these other prisoners in the hope that we would capitulate.

I was now getting three meals a day, but together they wouldn't add up to one meal, and what there was was inedible. The usual routine was to leave my food on a table in the canteen for 30 minutes and when it was cold enough, the screws got an orderly to bring it to me in my cell. When you are locked up 24 hours a day and deprived of the basic necessities that most human beings in the western world take for granted, you have to have something in your day to look forward to. With all Blanketmen it was food, inedible as it was and small as the portions were. It was a means of survival.

After a few days, I was allowed to leave my cell with a blanket wrapped round me to collect my food and bring it back to my cell. This progressed to the stage where I was actually allowed to go out to the yard for exercise with a blanket wrapped round me. The yard was full of small stones and it was sore on the feet, but it was a small price to pay for getting out of that tomb for a whole hour. Eventually I was allowed out for five minutes every morning to get a wash. After three or maybe four weeks on my own (I lost all sense of time) I was joined by two comrades.

JACKIE MCMULLAN . . .

In late October-early November they began taking batches of men out of the Crum to the Kesh. These were men who were nearing the time of their trial and who no longer had to go to the remand courts every week. At first it was thought they might be going to one of the Cages, but word soon filtered back that they were going to a H-Block. Everything was changing rapidly now. A lot of the old faces were disappearing and just as many new ones were coming in. The relatively laid-back, easy atmosphere of the summer months was now replaced by a new buzz.

I was awaiting trial myself and in early November I was taken with five or six others to Long Kesh. We knew by then we were going to 'H-Block', but that was all we knew. We didn't know if H-Block was the name of a new jail, what sort of structure it might be or the sort of regime it might hold for us – not a very friendly one, we suspected, and we were right.

One of the men with us had been in Long Kesh before and when we arrived there, he recognised some of the buildings. He was baffled though as we drove into a yard with a single-storey brick structure on either side of us. We were baffled too. This was it: H-Block.

The first thing I noticed going into this place was the hostility of the screws. There was a reception committee of about 20 of them, some with their batons out, slapping them into their hands. They made us stand spreadeagled against a wall and barked out questions about names, addresses and so on. One of them then ranted about how we were to behave here, follow orders, no OCs, hard way, easy way, blah, blah, blah. From here we were taken to the cells and locked up for the night.

At this time only two of the four wings in this Block (H1) housed remand prisoners. In the wing facing me – C wing – were the Blanketmen. There were about 10 of them at this stage and I was able to shout over to them at night. They were doing OK. They had no radios, so we gave them the news every night. They weren't allowed newspapers or books either. All they had in their cells was the furniture and a Bible. They had been allowed to keep the tobacco they had had with them when they were sentenced but had been told they would be allowed no more when it ran out. We, of course, were making efforts to ensure that it would never run out. One of the orderlies who had access to their wing was prepared to smuggle over tobacco for us, so we got that organised.

The H-Blocks were designed to afford the screws maximum control. They were built to accommodate between 90-100 men in four self-contained wings. The reduction in the numbers, so the principle goes, allows the screws greater scope in running the wings. This is especially so if, in a wing of 20 men, there were only seven or eight Republicans, the rest Loyalists and non-politicals. From the outset the screws in the H-Blocks tried to impose a strict control and to run the wings along almost military lines. They wanted us to address them as 'mister' and to stand for them each time they opened our cell doors. There were certain areas of the Block in which prisoners weren't allowed to smoke, certain areas of the wing into which they weren't allowed at certain times – all sorts of petty restrictions designed to aid control and discipline.

Fortunately for me, I was there only six days before I was sent back to the Crum for trial. After a further two weeks there I was tried, convicted and sentenced to life, all within 45 minutes. When I was in the court, I met Sleepy Devine who was already on the Blanket and who was down on further charges. He told me that in the two weeks since I had left H1, those Blanketmen who were under twenty-one had been moved to H2 and things weren't just as rosy there as they had been in H1. In fact it was a horror picture. He said that they weren't allowed any tobacco and the screws were beating them regularly. This wasn't the sort of scéal I wanted to hear.

I was kept in B wing awaiting transport to the Blocks. I'd been a bit surprised at getting a life sentence but, to be honest, my immediate concern was what was facing me in H2. I was able to shout out to the lads in C wing and pass on to them the scéal I got from Sleepy. They were all standing under my window having a laugh at my expense; they thought my newly-acquired life sentence a big joke. That's one thing that struck me in those days; there was no sympathy to be got from your comrades. I don't know how it developed or if it has always been a feature of jail, but every misfortune was treated as a huge joke. Looking back on it now I think it was no bad thing in as much as it prevented men from feeling sorry for themselves and it established a devil-may-care attitude.

The following day I was brought, along with four others, to the Kesh. One of the four was a Loyalist who had been sentenced to three months for assaulting an RUC man. One was a man from Lurgan who'd been given six years for holding firearms in his house for the IRA. He wasn't going on the Blanket. The other two I didn't know, but they said they were INLA, in for armed robbery, and that they'd be going on the protest. At least I wouldn't be on my own.

When we reached the Kesh, I was taken into reception and put into a cubicle. After a few minutes a screw opened my door and told me to hurry up and get the uniform on; they hadn't all day to wait. I started telling him I wasn't going to wear it, but he closed the door before I could get it out. Shortly after this a van arrived to take us to the Blocks. Two of us, because we were under 21, were going to H2, the others to H1. The screw tried one more time to get me to put the uniform on. I told him 'no'. He said I would have it on the next day, 'make no mistake about it'. I told him not to bet on it, but inside I was very apprehensive.

On the journey from reception to H2 I was very nervous. When we got into the Block, a crowd of screws came out of a room to greet us; they were glaring and growling. It was total hostility right from the start and I was very, very frightened. They looked like giants; I'd never before seen such a crowd of big, burly men and they were all going to attack me. I think I was shaking. First they gathered round the other lad who had put the uniform on and who they'd made stand about 20 feet away from me. One of them asked him a question – his name or something – and when he answered, he immediately got a heavy slap on the face. They asked him something else and slapped him again, almost knocking him down. This was repeated three or four times, each time ending with him getting slapped or thumped. He was in tears before they sent him down the wing. Then they came over to me. I wish they'd started on me first.

About seven or eight of them gathered round me as if jockeying for the best position to get a swing at me. I knew I was in for a beating; it was only a question of how bad it would be. The screw in charge, the PO, told me to put the uniform on. I said 'no' and got a whack across the face. He started screaming and cursing, told me again to put it on; I refused and got thumped again. Each time he ordered me to put it on, I said 'no' and got a slap on the face or a punch. I was knocked to the ground a couple of times but was dragged back up by the screws who were all the time yelling and screaming insults at me. They were also trying to make me address them as 'sir' and each time I refused, I was thumped.

The entire thing couldn't have lasted more than a few minutes. By the end of it I was thoroughly terrified, but there was no way I was going to put on the monkey suit and I saw the screws had now accepted this. They ordered me then to take my clothes off right there in front of them. I stripped down to my under-clothes, but they insisted I take off everything. I did.

From there I had to walk naked to the wing I was allocated to. All the way down to the cell I was burning with humiliation as I had to walk past other prisoners and, worse, more screws, who stood glaring at me. For me, that was the worst experience of the whole time I spent on the Blanket protest.

When I got into the cell, I grabbed a blanket and held it around me. I was shivering, so I huddled close to the heating pipes which ran through the cells. It's a strange thing; we're so accustomed to the heat of our clothes that it took me weeks to adjust to the loss of them, even though the temperature in the cells was quite normal. I was forever shivering and freezing and couldn't get heat into me at all, even at night in bed.

I was in D wing, H2. There were three other Blanketmen in the wing, each of us in a cell of his own, and another six or seven in the rest of the Block. All the other prisoners were conforming – mostly non-politicals. As I had just found out, brutality was the order of the day. All prisoners in the Block were under 21, a lot of them only 17 or 18, and the screws took great delight in bullying and terrorising us all. There were numerous petty rules which were enforced through fear and beatings. We had a bed, a table, a chair and an empty locker in the cell. We weren't allowed to sit or lie on the bed until permission was given each night. Anyone caught lying on his bed would be beaten up; that was clearly understood. Similarly, any of us caught talking, or any of the ordinary prisoners caught talking to us, was liable to get slapped about or worse.

We weren't allowed to smoke. I've often thought this one of the most cruel aspects of prison: denying people cigarettes. I don't smoke now myself, but I know what it's like to crave for a smoke for weeks on end, to be able to think of little else. It's torture. Sometimes one of the other prisoners would push a lit cigarette in under the door but it was a dangerous business for them and, since there were four or five smokers amongst us, it was difficult for anyone brave enough to go round us all. Some men persevered and waited all day at their cell door for a fag to be pushed in. On a good day you'd get two, but more often than not it was none.

We tried other methods of getting smokes. There were other Republicans on the wing who weren't on the Blanket and they gave tobacco and a lighter to a prisoner whose cell was beside one of ours. When the screws left the wing that night after lock-up, he was to pass them on to us by swinging them from his window to his neighbour's. Just as he was doing this, however, a patrol of screws came round and caught him. Next morning he was taken from the wing to another part of the Block and given a bad beating which we were able to hear from our cells. The message was clear to all those not on the protest: they weren't to help us in any way. The screws even used to stop outside their cells at night and tell them to keep their radios low in case we might hear some music or snatches of news.

We weren't allowed any books, newspapers, magazines or reading material of any kind. The idea was to deny us stimulation in the hope that the solitude and boredom would drive us off the protest. The worst thing though was the constant fear. From half-seven in the morning when the screws came onto the wing until half-eight at night when they left again, we never knew the moment our door would open and two or three of them would come in to slap and punch us about. Usually it would be under the pretext of a 'cell search'. We all wore a blanket wrapped around our waist and at some point during the search they'd ask for the blanket as if to search it too. Then, as we stood naked, they'd invent some excuse to hit us. There's an awful feeling of defencelessness when you're standing naked in front of people who are hostile to you. The screws were aware of this and took full advantage of it.

It was always a great relief at night to hear the screws leaving the wing. It was as if we could start to breathe again, at least until the next morning when we heard the keys jingle and knew they were back. It wasn't as if we were each getting beaten up every day. In the four months I was there I was assaulted only about four or five times. The beatings themselves weren't the worst thing; it was the ever present fear of them, not knowing when you'd be next. Often the worst thing was listening to someone in a neighbouring cell get a hiding, hearing the groans and the thumps against the wall, or witnessing someone being brutalised out on the landing. We could see out the side of the door and the screws hit the conforming prisoners as often and as gratuitously as they did those on protest.

The screws had power and, like the bullies they are, they abused it to the full. We often speculated as to the type of people they were. What sort of men would devote time and energy to inflicting so much misery on young prisoners, some of them naked and confined to a cell all day? Possibly they had been bullied themselves all their lives. They took such enjoyment out of it too. They laughed and joked as they recounted the various instances of brutality they had been involved in. They loved it, loved the power the NIO had vested in them. For most of them it must have been the first time in their lives they had experienced power; they were so filled with it.

We were locked in our cells virtually the whole day, getting out only to wash, slop out and collect our food from the canteen which we brought back to eat in our cells. All of these we were forced to do naked, not being allowed to wear our blankets outside the cell. Once every two weeks we had to walk to the doctor's room and then to the governor's to be adjudicated for our refusal to obey orders (to wear prison gear or engage in prison work). I was amazed that a doctor faced with a young lad naked, shivering and obviously frightened could routinely ask if everything was alright and on receiving the uneasy reply 'yes', return to whatever he was doing beforehand and completely ignore the very evident fact that everything was not alright. Before I came into jail I had nothing but respect for doctors and priests, but there were doctors and priests during the Blanket protest who saw a lot of what was going on and turned a blind eye to it. This was another major lesson in the education I received in the H-Blocks.

NED FLYNN . . .

Not long after Jackie and Sleepy came into the wing, the screws came round and told us that from this day forward, if we wished to wash, go to the toilet, collect our food, go for exercise, or go to mass, we would have to go naked. So it was that we had to undergo the humiliation of having to leave our cells naked to do the things which were essential to our day-to-day living.

At this stage of our protest, November 1976, our numbers were few and, because we were refused visits with our families, we had no contact with the outside world. The atmosphere at the time was so highly intimidating that we had no alternative but to leave the cell naked.

We discussed going to mass naked but decided not to, although one of my comrades from the other wings did go. The chaplain of the jail at this time was Father Toner – the bishop's secretary – and his feeling towards us was one of indifference. The following week none of us went to mass; the priest came into our cells and gave us communion. We eventually did go to mass wearing only the prison trousers.

Sickness was always a constant problem, but the three of us suffered whatever sickness we had rather than go out of the cell naked to have lewd remarks and verbal abuse shouted at us. We tried to go out to the toilet or to slop out as infrequently as we could and we asked the screws to let the orderlies bring the food to our cells, but they told us, if we wanted food, we had to leave our cells naked and get it ourselves.

Every time we left the cell naked, it was to a tirade of every kind of abuse you could think of. The screws came up with a new nickname for us – the Streakers – and that was the way they always greeted us now when we left our cells: 'Here come the streakers'. If I was embarrassed by the screws or the other prisoners seeing me naked, I made sure they weren't aware of it because it would have given them a moral victory over me. Not once did I try and cover my nakedness with my hands. I always kept them by my sides and ignored the sneers and jeers. They had taken so much from us already but they could never take away our dignity or self-respect.

Walking up and down the wing was bad enough, but being forced to go out to the circle to see the governor and the doctor was an absolute nightmare. It was usually at 9.30am when there were at least 60 prisoners lined up in the circle ready to go to work and maybe 20 to 30 screws. They would drag this out for as long as they possibly could; some of the lads spent 30 minutes standing in the circle. One morning in December, as the other prisoners with their uniforms were waving their arms about and jumping up and down to keep warm, one of the Blanketmen was standing there naked. A welfare woman then came into the circle. This was highly embarrassing for the welfare woman as well as for my comrade, but the screws did absolutely nothing to stop the woman from seeing him standing there.

Christmas 1976 came and for us it was just a day like any other: 24 hours solitary confinement, with the exception of going to mass. We got a Christmas dinner and it was the usual: cold with very small portions. For the Blanketmen there was to be no Christmas spirit from the screws or the administration.

For the five or six months I spent in H2, the screws were always pushing the line that ours was a lost cause, nobody gave a damn about us and we were more or less abandoned by our families and supporters. They backed this up by pointing out that we were receiving very little mail. By right we were allowed to write one letter a month and allowed one back. I received one letter in this six month period; it was four pages written by my father and three sisters. When the censor was finished with it there was hardly a page left. They said my family wrote things that I wasn't allowed to read. (When I was released in 1979, I found out what they had been doing with my letters; they had sent them down to reception to go into my property. When I eventually saw my family for a visit in 1978, they told me that they had only received one letter, yet for that six month period I had written them one every month. This was a common experience among Blanketmen.)

JACKIE McMULLAN . . .

Hunger was a constant companion in those days. It's amazing; I had never known real hunger in my life before – at least, not for any length of time. Now the days were filled by waiting from one meal to the next, seemingly always hungry. The ordinary prisoners could at least supplement the prison fare with extra bread and maybe some chocolate from the tuck shop. We could do neither and the hunger was made worse by our craving for cigarettes. To add to this, whenever the kitchen sent less food to the wing than it was supposed to, the shortage was shared by the Blanketmen. We were at the bottom of the pile and if anything was short, it was our loss.

But I think life was even worse for the ordinary prisoners. They could watch TV for a couple of hours each day and they had radios, reading material and tobacco but, as well as the humiliation of having to wear a monkey suit and do prison work, they got a very bad time from the screws. They were out of their cells most of the day, always under the eye of the screws who would lash out at them for any misdemeanour or for no reason at all. I saw screws hitting them for giving 'dirty looks', for not addressing them as 'sir', for smoking in the wrong place and even for whistling. Most of these reasons of course were inventions and the real reason would be that the screw didn't think the prisoner cowed enough, or maybe he just felt like hitting someone.

They used to have cell inspections. These had to be seen to be believed. The screws would go into the cells at any time of the day and either search them or just look about to see if there was anything out of place; but cell inspections took place perhaps once every two or three weeks on a Saturday morning. When it was announced that one was to take place, there was immediate and total panic. Men ran for brushes, mops and cloths and we could see the fear on their faces. All the furniture, beds included, was taken out of the cells onto the landing and dusted, scrubbed and polished, all at a frenzied pace.

The cell itself was subjected to the same process; every inch of it cleaned, all the surfaces, corners and spots you wouldn't even know existed made immaculate, walls washed, floor polished and made to shine, all within an amazingly short time. Then the furniture was put back and everything replaced exactly as it should be. 'Exactly' was the operative word. There were unbelievably precise directions for every single item in the cell. Shoes and boots had to be pointed in a particular way, books had to be ordered in a certain manner (only three books per prisoner) and a 'bedpack' of blankets, sheets and pillow had to be made as if carved out of stone.

After an hour or so of this frantic activity, word was sent down the wing that the SO was coming and the tension and fear rose to an incredible level. The men stood military fashion outside their doors and, like a field marshal inspecting his troops, the SO looked them up and down, checked their uniforms and boots, and then entered their cell. Sometimes he wore a white glove and ran his finger along surfaces to check for dust. If he found nothing wrong in a cell, he left and went to the next one. If there was the least thing out of place – a fag end or even ash in an ashtray – he went berserk, or pretended to. Bedpacks were flung out into the landing; books, chairs and everything else was overturned and he came rushing out to scream abuse and threats at the terrified occupants of the cell. We were excluded from these cell inspections because we weren't conforming, but we could see what was going on through the side of our cell doors. There was no greater incentive for us to stay on the protest.

NED FLYNN . . .

The screws got two breaks a day and during those everybody in the H-Blocks was locked up. The breaks were from 12.30pm to 2.00pm and from 4.30pm to 5.30pm. There is a bar in the camp for the screws. During their breaks they can go to the mess for food or to the bar; most of them choose the latter. After the lock-ups was always a bad time for us, because that was when the screws, with drink taken, were at their most aggressive.

There was one screw in particular at this time given a free hand by the administration to do as he wished with us. He was very aptly named Jack the Maniac. He had the mentality of a child but physically he was very broadly built and his most outstanding feature was his hands; they were like shovels. The first night he ever came onto the wing, himself and two other screws came down to my cell. I had a fair idea what was coming. He asked me what I was in jail for and, when I told him, he slapped and punched me about the cell. The two screws with him thought this was hilarious. By no means was this a severe beating, but I remember quite clearly when they left the cell I was shaking from head to foot. I was fortunate in a sense that my cell was the first he went to; my two comrades had heard quite clearly what happened, and waiting for the inevitable was probably worse than the beating. When he went to each of their cells, I could hear the usual noises that were associated with a beating: furniture being up-ended, keys rattling, moans and groans, walls being thumped, more than likely by one of my comrades who had been slammed against it.

Things just went from bad to worse. We were getting just enough food to keep us alive. Screws coming into the cell and slapping us about was becoming more regular and so the threat of violence was with us every minute of the day. With the lack of food, the beatings, the intimidation and harassment, we decided enough was enough: we'd go on hunger strike; we didn't seek clearance from the leadership or our camp staff. And so it was on a Sunday night at teatime we ate our last meal. Our demands were simple: 1) a substantial rise in the portions of food we were getting; 2) an end to the beatings.

On Monday morning, when we refused our breakfast, the class officer came to my cell and asked me why we were refusing our food. I told him we were on hunger strike and wouldn't be coming off it until we got an assurance that the brutality would stop and that we got the same amount of food as the other prisoners who weren't on the Blanket. He cursed at me, went out and slammed the door. I've no doubt that from the outset the screws were of the opinion that we'd last out until we got really hungry and that would be the end of it, so initially they weren't unduly worried.

Tuesday came and we were still refusing food. It was now plain to them that this wasn't a minor token protest. The food was being left in our cells and, not surprisingly, the portions were much bigger than usual. After mealtimes the screws came into our cells and said, 'McMullan ate half his stew,' or 'Flynn ate one of his potatoes,' or 'Devine ate some of the vegetables,' but we ignored them.

By Wednesday, the administration was becoming very worried; most notable of all was the class officer who wasn't as cocky as he had been three days before. It was a hive of activity on the wing that day; SOs, POs, doctors, chiefs and even the Number One governor paid us a visit. The No 1 was the same as all the governors I'd come into contact with; surrounded by his foot soldiers, he came into the cell with an air of superiority about him. He gave you a look which, if translated, would have said, 'you are lower than the vermin in the sewers', and when he spoke, his tone relayed the same message. It was he and his sidekicks who had introduced the policies which we were now on hunger strike against. He knew why we were taking this course of action, so when he started questioning me about it, I refused to answer him and he just walked out of the cell.

Thursday was the fourth day and once again there was a lot of activity about the wing. The class officer was being called out to the circle more than usual, which made me think that the administration was more worried than they were letting on to be. By this time the prison chaplain, Father Toner, was aware of the hunger strike and that night about 6 o'clock he paid us a visit. When I explained the reasons why we were on hunger strike, he told me that the over-21s had sent a message with him telling us to stop the hunger strike. I told him that this was not possible and that it would just make our situation worse and my two comrades were of the same frame of mind. Father Toner approached the class officer and that night we got a guarantee that the food would change dramatically and the brutality would stop. So we ended our hunger strike. We felt quite relieved but also quietly jubilant that we had got a moral victory over the regime. They had tried everything possible to break us, but we were still there, and we had now shown them that we wouldn't just lie back and take everything that they threw at us. For a while after that the food was brilliant and it was warm – it was the first time since I embarked on the Blanket protest that I didn't feel hungry – and for a while the brutality also stopped.

It became obvious after this that the screws were growing anxious. There was no sign of our protest ending; we had established a solid base and our numbers were slowly but surely getting bigger. They had implemented a policy in H2 which was meant to break the back of the Blanket protest but it was failing and they were running out of time. So they decided to intensify their efforts. The food got worse again and the harassment and intimidation intensified.

JACKIE McMULLAN . . .

We weren't allowed to close the windows of the cells and I remember snow coming in. I was freezing but I didn't really care. By that time we were getting used to it and, to an extent, you soon learn to compensate for the hardship. We weren't allowed to talk; it would have resulted in a beating had we been caught, but we got to know the screws' routines and we talked to each other where the heating pipes ran through the walls between our cells. It was risky but there was a certain pleasure to be got out of taking the chance. We even laughed and joked about the ridiculousness of our situation. It was like something from a horror story; locked in a cell all day, starving, freezing, naked, terrified and watched over by a bunch of thugs who enjoyed making us suffer. Who would believe it? Sleepy Devine was in the cell on one side of me and Kevin Campbell on the other side. We had great craic talking about it all and swopping yarns. Then I'd get up from the pipes and pace the floor, maybe smiling or laughing to myself about what had just been said.

The screws didn't let up any, but with the increasing numbers we were starting to become more assertive and began challenging them on rules and conditions. According to their own rules we were entitled to one hour of exercise per day, yet they had never offered it to us. We asked about this and they said that the exercise was available to us but we weren't prepared to wear the prison uniform in order to get it. Our argument was that this wasn't specified in the rules. This seemed to carry a bit of weight because next day they came to us and offered us exercise – in the nude. They thought we wouldn't take it but Sleepy and I went out and walked around the yard as if there was nothing unusual. There was sleet coming down and the gravel was sore on the feet, but we knew we were being watched in the hope that we would give up, so we didn't. However, after about 15 minutes they brought us back in. Next day and for a few days afterwards they offered us exercise inside an empty wing. We initially accepted this but then refused it on the grounds that we were entitled to fresh air.

KEVIN CAMPBELL . . .

On Sundays we were allowed to go to mass as long as we wore the prison trousers. The mass was in A wing canteen and we were escorted over two at a time. They had four rows of chairs specially for us to sit on: one at the back, one at the front and one at each of the walls. They then put the ordinary prisoners between us to avoid contact and around eight screws would gather at the back of the canteen, creating an atmosphere of tension. Sunday was always a big day for us as we were able to count the numbers and exchange a few words with our friends.

As the weeks rolled by, the numbers increased. After I was there two months the number of Blanketmen rose to 30 and we knew that the numbers in H1 were probably the same. Our morale was climbing with the numbers. The harassment and degrading treatment continued. They introduced a system whereby men had to get washed in three minutes, saying they hadn't got the time to work with us. If anyone was still washing when the three minutes was up, he was dragged back to his cell. They continued with the cell searching every day, even though we were always locked up and had no contact with anyone. We were forced to stand naked outside the cells while they conducted the search. We knew this was all geared to degrade us. During these raids someone was always knocked about creating an air of tension and fear in the wing.

When the number of Blanketmen in the Block climbed above 30, we decided to take a stand on these issues, especially standing outside the cell naked, going to the canteen naked for our food and slopping out naked. At mass that Sunday word was spread about the Block that from Monday we would be refusing to leave the cells naked. We all keyed ourselves up for what would happen next morning.

The next day, when we refused to leave the cells naked, the screws were furious. They knew it was an organised effort for every Blanketman in the Block had refused to go naked to the canteen to get his breakfast. At first they refused to bring it down to our cells but come half-ten, they relented. The breakfast had been put out at 8.00am and the tea and porridge were freezing. No one complained as we knew this would give them the excuse to tell us to go and collect it ourselves, naked.

That evening they started cell searching and they were very aggressive. When they told us to stand outside the cell door naked, we refused. Most of us were dragged from our cells by the hair and punched and slapped about. We were then thrown against the wall while they wrecked the cells. We knew that they were upping the harassment to try and get us to back down and go about naked. After about four days of this, they broke and decided to give us towels to go about in. We viewed this as a major victory; even though it was only to get a towel, it helped to break their efforts to degrade us.

JACKIE McMULLAN . . .

The increase in our numbers meant greater contact with the ordinary prisoners, which led to more cigarettes and a greater flow of scéal. Our confidence also began to grow at this time and we spent more and more time talking to each other, down at the pipes and even out the doors. It was harder for the screws to handle the increased numbers, and the less committed among them became less diligent in enforcing the countless petty rules. But, for the most part, it was still a very fear-filled experience.

We weren't allowed any visits. We were entitled to one visit per month according to their rules, but they insisted we wear the prison gear to get them. We refused. So we were very much cut off from the world outside that one H-Block. The only scéal we got was from the new men coming onto the protest and whatever bits and pieces we could elicit from the other lads in the wing. The screws at all times made a conscious effort to prevent us from getting any news, ensuring we heard no radio and that no newspapers were left about the wing while we were out of our cells. They hated us, either because they were bigots – and a lot of them were – or because they saw us spoiling their new jail. Before we came along they were having it their own way; they could dish out orders and slap people about when they felt like it. Now here we were threatening their power. We also hated them. I can honestly say that the screws in H2 taught me to hate. I had never hated anyone in my life before going there, but I learned to hate them.

Throughout February and March there was a steady stream of men coming onto the protest. By the end of March it was clear that they were under pressure for space and would soon need to do something about it. All the other prisoners were doubled up – two to a cell – but we were kept on our own. We were speculating that they would be forced to double us up too and when, just after Easter, on 12 April, they brought in bunk beds for our cells, we thought we were about to acquire cellmates. When they opened our doors at two o'clock however, we were told we were moving to a new Block.

They took us naked out of the Block and put us into vans. It was all hustle and bustle: screws rushing around and dogs barking. It was disorientating. For the first time in four months some of us were out of the Block; we were very apprehensive and once again our nakedness added enormously to our sense of vulnerability. It only added to our confusion, therefore, when, on arrival at the door of the new Block, we heard men cheering and shouting out our names. I remember seeing a crutch waved from one of the cell windows; it was like some mad dream.

If we were going to get beaten – as we fully expected we would – it would happen just as we entered the Block, before we went down the wings. We were made to face the wall. I stood like that for a while, then a screw touched me on the shoulder. I nearly jumped out of my skin, thinking, 'this is it'. But he told me not to worry, no one would touch us here. A friendly screw? I could hardly believe it.

From here we were allocated to different wings. I went to B wing and as I was walking down to the cell, I heard men calling out my name from behind the cell doors. I couldn't take it all in, but as soon as the door was locked behind me I got talking to one of the men I knew and he filled me in on it all. We were in H5, which had only opened that day. All the prisoners in it were Blanketmen: almost 100 of us. Two wings – A and D – were for those over 21 and the other two – B and C – were for the under-21s. My cell door was opened and a screw asked me if I wanted to brush my cell out – he actually asked me; I could hardly believe it. This was already like Butlins compared to the last place.

It immediately became apparent that this was going to be a completely different setup from the one we had just been through in H2. We could talk out the doors all day, we had singsongs at night and after those we talked to our neighbours into the small hours of the morning. On Sunday when we went to mass, all four wings of us were together and it was like a madhouse: almost every one of us with skinheads, wearing only prison trousers and all talking together, swopping scéal, renewing acquaintances and meeting new comrades. It was brilliant.

2

Consolidation of the Protest

April 1977 – March 1978

Altogether in H5, the Blanketmen were now better able to assess their situation. Each week saw their numbers grow as the inexorable conveyer belt shunted Republicans from the RUC interrogation centres, through the Diplock courts and on to the H-Blocks. It was realised that numerical strength alone would not force the British government's hand and much time was spent in discussing tactics to make the protest more effective.

Meanwhile, day-to-day life in the enclosed world of the Blocks had to be endured. The immediate enemy was the screw on the wing and a continual battle of wits was played out as the prisoners' resourcefulness ensured that their quality of life was as high as it could be in the severely limited circumstances. 'Beating the system' was the watchword of the Blanket protest. As newly sentenced men joined the protest, they quickly adapted to the bizarre lifestyle and became absorbed into the culture of the Blocks.

By early 1978 upwards of 250 Republicans were on the Blanket and the prison administration was forced to open H3 as a second non-conforming Block. With the new year came a marked increase in the brutality and harassment by the screws, and the protest escalated.

KEVIN CAMPBELL . . .

When we got to H5, we discovered that there were about 90 of us on the Blanket. The first few days were taken up exchanging stories and catching up on the news. Now with the Block full of Blanketmen we were able to set up our own structures, get an OC and Adjutant and organise in a proper manner. Our first task was to try to get some reading materials, books and magazines, to help break the monotony of solitary confinement. But we were met with a blank refusal. 'Wear the uniforms and you will get them', they said. Then a week later they refused to allow us out to the sinks to wash or shower, saying there were too many of us and we'd only be allowed out two at a time. This was a lame excuse. They only wanted us out of our cells to slop out and shower once a week. They now expected us to wash and shave, without a mirror, in the same basin of water. We refused to do this and, before long, we all had beards. This became a symbol of the Blanketman.

After we settled in H5 we held discussions out the doors and assessed our progress. It was from these discussions that we realised we were facing an uphill struggle, so we dug our heels in for a long wait. We came to the realisation that we weren't going to attain political status from the Blanket alone. We would have to build the numbers up and make the people outside more aware of the situation.

As the weeks turned into months and the numbers climbed higher, they were forced to start doubling us up in the cells. The prison chaplain added his voice to our requests for reading materials and in the end, they gave us religious books and magazines – no books of educational value or newspapers were permitted. However, we accepted what they offered as it helped to break down the boredom. The only time we got out from the cells was to slop out, go to mass and take a shower once a week. The mass was the highlight of the week as we could get talking with our comrades and get the scéal.

Ned Flynn . . .

We were now able to make contact with other cells by 'swinging the line'. Swinging the line from cell to cell originated in the Crumlin Road Jail and it was very efficient for passing things from one cell to another. For the Blanketmen in the H-Blocks it was a lifeline. The process was simple. We tore a strip of blanket about 6 foot long and half an inch wide. On one end we tied a dead weight – a bar of soap or a tube of toothpaste – to give enough power to get a swinging action. We put it out the window and told the man in the next cell to put his hand out. Then we started swinging. When he grabbed the dead weight, the stuff – anything from a religious magazine to tobacco – was tied on at the other end of the line.

The swinging took place mainly at night when most of the screws had left the Block. The screws knew about the swinging and were always trying to catch us. So one night they set a trap and unfortunately for me and my cellmate, Zack Smith, we were caught. Unknown to us, a screw had been sitting in the yard with a two-way radio at a blind spot where none of us could see him. Mackers (Gerard McAreavey) swung tobacco and newspaper clippings in to Martin 'Archie' Livingstone. Just as Archie started swinging them into me we heard the screw in the yard speaking into his radio and, before we knew it, the shout went up from the look-out at the bottom of the wing, 'Bears on the air!'

I wasn't unduly worried because it was unheard of for the screws to open anyone's door after 8.30 pm, but we were in for a shock. The door was opened and five or six screws came into the cell and immediately began attacking us. I was pulled out of the cell and made to stand in the corridor naked while they gave big Zack a body search and beat him. Once they were finished he was taken out and I was taken in. They told me to bend down and touch my toes. I refused. They beat me; then three of them grabbed me and bent me over while one of them spread my legs as far apart as he could get them. When he had a clear view of my back passage, he let me go. Sadly for the lads on the wing we didn't have time to hide any of the stuff – it was all caught.

Swinging the line gave us access to everybody on our side of the wing, but not to the lads on the other side. That was the case until someone came up with the ingenious idea that would enable us to pass stuff from one side of the wing to the other. It consisted of a button taken from a prison shirt and 10-15 feet of fine wool which was used to stitch the top of the prison blankets. We tied one end of the wool onto the button. At the bottom of every cell door was a small gap through which the button would pass. It was then flicked with a plastic comb, making it shoot across the wing with the string travelling behind. After a couple of attempts we always managed to get it close enough to the cell opposite for the man in the cell to be able to fish it in using a folded mass sheet as a hook. Contact was made. We shot the line at the bottom of the wing because the chances of it being caught were much less.

There was always a battle of wits going on between us and the screws over shooting the line. After 8.30 pm, when the screws had left the wing, we would start. A screw often sat at the top of the wing and watched contact being made. (The screws often gave themselves away by their aftershave and soap: we quickly picked up these alien smells.) He wouldn't move until the stuff (tobacco, cigarette papers, newspaper clippings, comms) started to go across, hoping to catch it. We were well aware of this, so the man in the cell at the very top of the wing would be posted as look-out. When the stuff was attached to the string the look-out was told that it was to be passed in 30 seconds or whatever; then, when it went under the door, the fella on the other side was told to pull gently, unless there was a threat. As soon as the screw saw it emerge from the cell door he would tiptoe up the wing, but our eagle-eyed look-out always spotted him and the shout went up, 'Bear on the air! Pull the gear in quick!' Automatically the screw took a mad charge up the wing. By this stage most of the lads were at the door cheering on the man pulling the stuff in. He was nearly always successful; a big cheer would go up and the screw went back down the wing with his tail between his legs.

To counteract us shooting the line across the wing the screws would flood the landing with a fireman's hose. But we found a way round this. Instead of shooting it under the door we shot it out the gap at the top. The man on the other side did the same, the lines got tangled up and contact was made.

Shooting the line was developed even further and we could link up with the wing facing us across the yard, a distance of about 30 metres. We used a longer piece of thread and made a ball from the sponge of the mattress. We tied the ball to the line and the other wing did the same; then we threw the ball across the yard with the line on it, and the other wing threw their line over ours, tangling them together.

Our numbers were steadily rising and yet the protest was having no effect. The administration was happy to keep us contained in the one Block, shut off from the outside world and they hoped the Blanket protest would fizzle out. They had time on their side.

Kevin Campbell . . .

By October 1977 H5 was full and every cell was doubled up, so they opened H3. A number of men from each wing in H5 were taken out to start the new Block and reports from the Crum left us in no doubt that it wouldn't be long before it would also be full. There were hundreds of men on remand.

Leo Green . . .

When I was on remand (March 1977-April 1978), the Blanket protest didn't seem to be taken too seriously. Discussions on its implications or analysis of the emerging situation never figured at all. Optimistic rumours and naive political presumptions about the future course events would take both inside and outside the jails were the order of the day then. A report from Long Kesh, for example, of a problem in the foundations of one of the newly-built Blocks had, by the time it reached Crumlin Road, become a rumour that the H-Blocks were all sinking. Further proof, we readily believed, that the whole exercise was something of a sham and nothing more than a phase or fit of pique the Brits were going through. It was presumed that everyone on remand would join the protest and eventually force of numbers alone would ensure a speedy abandonment of Brit attempts to have us do prison work and wear prison uniform.

An awareness of the conditions endured by those already on protest gained a little definition once we were moved to the Blocks, still on remand and awaiting trial. Apart from experiencing the physical structure of the H-Blocks first hand, we came into contact with a few of the Blanketmen at the visits area of the jail. I remember thinking after meeting two of them how gaunt they looked. I noticed also that both had a nervous way with them and how all this contrasted starkly with their much repeated assurances to ourselves on remand that the protest was something of a 'gift' or 'no problem'. [Editors' note: Gradually, from 1977 onwards an increasing number of Blanketmen, especially married ones, took visits.]

SEAN LENNON . . .

For the period I spent on remand I was involved in various types of protest to highlight the crisis. There were two objectives: to try and get segregation while on remand; and to bring to the attention of the public the problems in the H-Blocks. The types of protest we were conducting were very physical and resulted in lots of us being beaten up by the screws. I psyched myself up and developed a mentality of 'not an inch' in order to build a defence around myself to sustain me throughout the struggle. I accepted fully that no matter what, I would not wear the prison uniform or do prison work.

At this time my ideas were based on the centuries old Republican tradition which had been handed down from generation to generation and finally our own generation whose turn had come to carry on the struggle. When I was thinking or giving views on how we should tackle the problems, the overriding factor in deciding what to do was heavily influenced by the Republicans of the past and their stance while in jail – in every phase of struggle Republicans had to fight the jail system to maintain their identity as POWs. It was a case of 'the heart ruling the head', but that was the diet I was fed on and it was made up of highly principled stands and militaristic tactics. All of us who were involved from the early days saw things in the same light. Losing wasn't a part of our language. My thinking would have been summed up in the immortal words of Terence MacSwiney: 'It is not those who can inflict the most, but those who can endure the most who will be victorious'. We had to confront them head on and take it on the nose.

PETER CUNNINGHAM . . .

I arrived in H3 after being sentenced. Walking up the wing for the first time was weird. To hear lads' voices from behind doors calling out, breaking the eerie silence of a second previous, asking and shouting questions – What's your name? Where are you from? What did you get? How many of you are there? – and their cheering, yelling and banging on cell doors had a sort of hypnotic effect. I went into the cell, took in its bareness and sat on the pipes hoping and praying that either Doc (Robert Doherty) or Mario McDowell (my co-accused) would follow me. No sooner had I sat down than I heard a voice whispering my name and it took me a minute or so to realise that it was coming from the cell next to me. Curley McQuaid was trying to get my attention through the pipes. In the middle of our conversation the lads started to yell, cheer and bang the doors, drowning us out; the cell door opened and Mario walked in.

Shortly after the screws left the wing the OC called us up to the doors and asked us our names, sentences and where we came from. After that we were asked to give the lads any scéal we had, which had us feeling as if we were newscasters on TV. We recalled news that had happened weeks and months before and from all over the world. I remember saying to Mario, 'These lads know virtually nothing and care for nothing other than news, any news, of the protest's effect outside.' We were soon to join them.

Kevin Campbell . . .

Christmas 1977 came and went and it was nothing special: just another day locked up. The administration was always looking for ways to break our morale. At Christmas they used the cards. We were expecting cards from family, friends, relations and people who were concerned, but the governor held them and would only permit us to have five each. We had no choice in picking the ones we wanted; the first five picked by the screw were thrown into our cells. We didn't allow it to bother us even though the screws ensured that the cards sent by our mothers, wives and girlfriends never reached us. Those were the ones we were all looking forward to getting.

Jaz McCann . . .

In the early stages of the protest the idea that we would fail to win our demand for political status was never a real possibility in my mind. Perhaps it was due to a strong feeling of righteousness, together with the naivety of youth. This secure little world of mine received a rude awakening just after Christmas 1977, however, when the OC, Sean McKenna, assessed our position as we entered another year's protesting and came to the conclusion that the Blanket was not effective enough. It was just like a kid being told there was no Santa Claus. The matter was not thrown out to the wing to discuss because Sean wanted first to raise it with the OC in H3. I only got to hear of it because I was next door to him. One of the suggestions he made was to stop washing. Personally, I had no ideas to offer. It was difficult enough accepting that the Blanket on its own was not enough. I gradually came to realise that we were in a rut. The screws and the administration appeared to accept the protest; what set H3 and H5, the Blanket Blocks, out from the rest of the Blocks was merely that there was a different routine. The different routine in H3 and H5 was becoming institutionalised and so was giving the administration no real cause for concern.

Nothing came of Sean's idea. He appeared to be having a communications problem with the OC in H3. Beatings, which had all but ended in H5, became a regular feature of H3 and later the H3 OC was removed to the boards for isolation. So perhaps the administration was not happy with the ever-growing Blanket protest after all. I remained confident that something would turn up.

SEAN LENNON . . .

Talk was centring on the need to do something else as the Blanket protest on its own wasn't enough and was going nowhere. Various options were talked about, and the options were very limited. We could put on the uniform and go into the system to try to break it down from within. We were very cagey about this. It didn't gather any momentum at all and died a sudden death. A second option was to sit on the Blanket and see if anything came along. Or we could embark on a hunger strike. This was a popular one, even though it was more out of gut reaction than logic. We all accepted that the protest would more than likely end this way, so some advocated it sooner rather than later. While these discussions went ahead, the lads began to reorganise ranganna out the doors. There were Irish ranganna, topical discussions from time to time and singsongs and quizzes. These were all used to break down the boredom and to demonstrate to the screws that we were far from beaten. Morale was very sound then and men were coming on the Blanket every day, with very few leaving.

My own thoughts were that we needed to do something to bring the whole thing to a head. The IRA was shooting screws outside in retaliation for the inhuman conditions under which we were being held. We had a Relatives' Action Committee on the outside trying their best to highlight the protest. Other than that things were still and it appeared that, as the Brits weren't under any pressure, they were happy to allow the situation to continue.

But I had not got the answer to what we should or could do. I was aware enough to accept that we needed a slow escalation and we needed to work hard to bring it to the attention of the people in Ireland and further afield. To embark on a hunger strike then would have been madness, because men would have been dead long before it was realised outside among the people what was happening. So I was in favour of escalating the protest and gradually building awareness among the people. There were lots of others on the Blanket at that time who would have been of the same line of thought, in particular those who had already done time in the Cages. I was interned for three years, and, as we had carried out numerous protests in the Cages, I had an insight into the workings of the jails and the Brits. Those of us who had this insight and some political awareness saw the need to build to a climax instead of diving headlong.

KEVIN CAMPBELL . . .

In the early months of 1978 there was an escalation in beatings. When men were slopping out or going to the toilet they were constantly harassed by the screws. It became a dreaded thing to slop out and go for a shower.

JOE McQUILLAN . . .

In March 1978, about two weeks after I was sentenced, I was moved from A wing H3 to C wing H3 to the YPs. I was doubled up with Brian McCool from Derry, who was the wing OC. At teatime the grub came around: no salt, sugar or sauce. I asked Brian what was the crack; he thought I was winding him up. Breakfast the next morning brought half a dozen cornflakes floating in 10% milk and 90% water. I soon realised life in C wing was a lot different from A wing. During the weekly shower, the class officer would come and lean on the half-door, talk effeminately and make lurid remarks – I was out of the shower in seconds. After we slopped out, which was twice daily, we would come back to our cells to find the screws going through our belongings, or we would find them scattered over the floor. The novelty of being on the Blanket was starting to wear thin.

The first incident I remember was when, during a cell search, the class officer pulled the towel off one of the other blokes and an argument broke out. Several other screws rushed to the cell and while some started to beat him, his cellmate, Greek Moran, was dragged up the wing. As they passed our cell, the screws used his head as a football against our door. I was white, trembling and also physically sick. My only comfort was that my new cellmate, Mario McDowell, was the same. Such an unmerciful kicking he got; then he was charged with 'assaulting an officer'. When he complained that he was beaten, he was further charged with 'making false allegations'.

JAZ McCANN . . .

Brendan Hughes, better known as the Dark, and several others arrived from the Cages. They had lost their political status as a result of a fracas after a visit. The Dark let it be known that he believed the protest was ineffective. I and many others were livid. I could just about take this from the OC who had spent a substantial amount of time on the Blanket, but not from someone who, despite his seniority in the Republican Movement, had not earned his spurs on the Blanket – an accolade only time could bring. In fact his seniority would not initially have been an asset to him. As far as his relationship went with our wing, it was a positive handicap.

Cynicism, I must admit, was never in short supply in our wing and I think the explanation for this could be traced back to the wing's disturbed 'childhood'. About a month or so after H5 opened, a senior member of the wing, who had been no less than the Blanket OC, 'squeaky booted' (this was the term used to describe someone who left the protest; the prisoner would put on the prison clothes, which included new boots, and, as he walked up the landing for the last time, the rest of the lads could hear the distinctive 'squeak, squeak, squeak', instead of the usual slap of bare feet). He informed us that he had to go to the hospital for an operation on his varicose veins, which was quite in order. However, later that afternoon the screws, with great joy, spread the news that our OC was in H8 (a conforming Block). We didn't believe them and dismissed it as another ploy to demoralise us.

For days the screws persisted with their taunts about the OC. Each of them claimed to have spoken to him in H8 and vouched for his happiness. The stories were similar – 'he has the feet up, smoking his brains out, feeding himself with Mars bars and watching the football'. We made a great laugh of what to us was an obvious fabrication and we wondered at the short-sightedness of the screws. Wouldn't they look foolish in a week or so when the OC arrived back from the hospital? After a few days some of the lads began to have doubts, probably inflamed by the fact that even some of the more moderate screws (they did exist) were touting the story. For over a week I kept faith with the ex-OC until, to my utter dismay, word came through of a definite sighting of him in prison clothes, confirming what most of us thought was unbelievable.

We overcame our disappointment by making a laugh of the situation, including our own naive response. From that day on we were prepared to believe the worst about anyone and anything. A bigger bunch of iconoclasts there never was.

It became a hobby of the wing to speculate on the chances of Republicans on remand joining the Blanket (if sentenced). The more senior the Republican the more the bets were heavily placed against him. These mock assessments ran like a serial, just like Coronation Street, and, just like Coronation Street, no one took it seriously, at least no one compos mentis. It was all an act. But I now recognise that it wasn't just a means of entertainment; it was also a way of preparing ourselves for big names letting us down. I remember the day one of the lads met Gerry Adams (who was on remand) on the visits. He told us that Gerry said that he was to tell the Dark that he (Gerry) would be joining him shortly on the Blanket. This news was greeted with raspberries and an assortment of other irreverent sounds and comments. The punters marked him down as a non-starter. Others gave odds that he would turn out because he would have to say that he at least tried the Blanket, but that he would fall at the first hurdle. It was all good craic, no one seriously believed the mocking predictions.

However, the legacy of cynicism that the squeaky booting OC had left did not help the Dark's cause. There was, from some quarters, an angry reaction to his statement that the Blanket was ineffective and, when the inevitable parallels were made between the squeaky booting OC and the Dark, it wasn't that easy to determine whether this was a part of the wing's usual sham or whether it was serious. In fairness, I would say that this ambiguity was not so much caused by doubts about the Dark as by irresponsibly making a joke out of an issue about which feelings were running high.

It became clear that the Dark had some very definite plans for the Blanket. He was not in our wing but his old friend Bobby Sands was and he used him to suss out the general feeling of the wing. When Bobby, instructed by the Dark, asked for opinions about putting on the prison clothes and fighting for political status within the system, there was a resounding and highly charged reaction against it. I suppose it was almost like asking the Free Presbyterians to join the Church of Rome: sacrilege! How could a Republican even contemplate wearing the badge of a criminal? Wouldn't he condemn himself? Wouldn't he besmirch the noble tradition of Republicanism?

Bobby tried to give some substance to the proposal by arguing that we could make their system unworkable through burning the workshops and disrupting their routine on the wings. I'm not sure whether he was converted to the idea of such a strategy or was just fulfilling the role of devil's advocate in order to give the Dark's views a fair hearing. I cannot recall one other person in the wing who said anything favourable about the idea. Many felt a strategy that involved wearing the gear was illegitimate and therefore didn't even warrant discussion. Some suspected that the suggestion there was a strategy behind it was just a sop to get us off the protest. Others felt it just wouldn't work, that we would lose our momentum for protest action and the prison administration would be better equipped to defuse, isolate and minimise our action. Wearing the prison clothes was an obvious mental block that no one wanted to step over. The idea, to my knowledge, was never discussed again openly in the wings until we were into the second hunger strike.

We knew the Dark was not going to be content to let things go as they were. A little bit of excitement began to generate as we anticipated his next move – how to make the Blanket effective. With the knowledge that plans were afoot to escalate the protest, the staleness of the Blanket became apparent and I grew impatient for action. Bobby was in regular contact with the Dark's wing. Messages were shouted back and forward in Gaeilge and code and it was obvious to us all that he was receiving the details of the next phase of action. Like many others, it was then that I decided that I must learn Gaeilge, because I was afraid of missing something.

SEAN LENNON . . .

Shortly after the arrival of the Cages men the Dark took over as OC of the Blanketmen and discussion was generated faster. The men were looking towards him for answers and the way forward. After long discussions and weighing up the ins and outs over the year that had slowly slipped away, the patience of the lads was running out. The pressure was on for movement. So we decided to escalate the protest and embark on the no-wash protest. On hearing this, morale rose again. The lads were on a high – myself included.

3

The No-Wash Phase Begins

March 1978 - July 1978

While their presence as non-conforming prisoners was itself an act of resistance to British criminalisation policies, the Blanketmen were not content simply to sit passively in their cells. As harassment and brutality increased, the protest gradually escalated. Beginning with a refusal to slop out, the prisoners then stopped washing, and finally they started to smear excrement on the cell walls.

To outsiders such tactics might have appeared extreme, even repulsive. To prisoners lacking other means to highlight their cause, they were the only effective tactics available. Utterly determined to win recognition as political prisoners, they used their bodies as weapons.

Outside the jail Relatives' Action Committees (RACs) had been set up in many areas. These comprised the families and friends of prisoners, and they were to be a key element in harnessing support in the next three years. It was largely due to their efforts that many organisations and individuals were moved to take an interest in what was happening in the H-Blocks.

By June 1978 increased numbers led to the opening of H4 as a third Blanket block. Almost 300 Republicans were on the protest. Various politicians, including DUP leader Ian Paisley and Fermanagh/South Tyrone MP Frank Maguire, visited the H-Blocks, and in July Archbishop (later Cardinal) Tomás Ó Fiaich described conditions as similar to 'sewer pipes in the slums of Calcutta'.

Joe McQuillan . . .

Coming towards the end of March 1978, the camp staff realised the petty harassment could not be allowed to go on and so we refused to wash and slop out. For the first day or two the screws took it as a laugh, coming around the cells and emptying the piss pots. Then they came around to slop out the urine and excrement and handed in our grub wearing the same rubber gloves. We had the contents of the pots spilled on the cell floors or our bedding, leaving no alternative but to empty the pots out the window. The screws and orderlies took to hosing down the yards with high pressure hoses and many cells were soaked because the lads didn't get their windows closed in time or the pressure smashed them. The screws, wearing protective clothing and face masks (looking like the Cybermen from Dr Who), would spray around the windows with disinfectant from back packs.

Jaz McCann . . .

The new phase of action became known as the 'no-wash, no slop out' protest. It was a gradual rather than a sudden escalation. It began with refusing to brush and mop out our cells. The following week, we refused to wash, then we refused a clean sheet change, and so it continued. Morale was sky high. We felt that we were winning and for a change we, not the screws, had control over our lives because we dictated the pace of events. The screws for their part were demoralised because they had no control over what happened next. They dreaded Mondays because that was the day that we kept upping the tempo of the protest by introducing something new.

Joe McQuillan . . .

Once a week there was a laundry change. Each man had two sheets and a pillow case, but the screws would only change one of the sheets for a clean one, and the pillow case once a fortnight. We decided this was senseless and asked that the two sheets and the pillow case be changed each week. When the weekly laundry came, we threw out the lot. The screws threw in one clean and one dirty sheet. The next time the screws opened the door, we threw the dirty sheets into the landing and the screws kicked them back in. This lasted several days until we threw out both sheets and said we wanted a full laundry change. That was that; the screws not only refused but never gave us the sheets back.

Peter Cunningham . . .

When we embarked on the no-wash protest and refused to slop out, I remember thinking, 'I hope this doesn't drag on'. But drag on it did and in those early weeks and months of escalating protest there was a sense of purpose which was missing beforehand.

SEAN LENNON . . .

The screws reacted very violently and beatings became the order of the day. But morale was at its highest. We were all talking about victory around the corner as we reckoned we had them on the ropes. We were starting to gather some support on the outside and the people on the streets were protesting for us and calling for a return to political status. This encouraged us to go at it even harder. But the reins were being applied by those who knew that the much talked about victory wasn't as close as we thought; it would be a long hard struggle.

KEVIN CAMPBELL . . .

After a few weeks of not slopping out or brushing out, the cells became filthy. Rotten food was piling up in the corners. It was around this time that the screws decided to take all the furniture out of the cells. They went to one wing and took all the beds, tables, lockers, and chairs from the cells, leaving them with nothing but a mattress, three blankets and a pillow. When word about what they were doing was shouted to the other wings, it was decided to smash everything in protest. So we wrecked up and put everything out the windows. When they reached our wing, we could hear the screws beating the lads in the top cells, so we keyed ourselves up for it.

When they came into my cell, the first two screws attacked my cellmate, Drew Forbes, punching him in the face. I was hyped up and knew what was next so I took the initiative and attacked the screws in self defence. I punched one of them a few times in the face, and he fell against the wall. Four other screws ran in and attacked me. They beat me until I fell. When Drew and I were lying on the floor, they ran out of the cell and on the way out, one of them jumped on Drew's back. They left and went to the circle. We both knew that they would be back. Fifteen minutes later 15 screws returned with the PO. They opened the cell door and ordered Drew to the boards. As he was leaving the cell, he was attacked again. He fell and was dragged up the wing by the ankles over broken furniture and beds that lay all over the wing, all the time being punched and kicked about the head and face.

I was ordered out of the cell. I'd seen what had happened to Drew, so I knew what was coming. As I walked out, I was attacked by about five screws, beaten to the ground, and one of them tried to grab me by the ankles. I struggled back to my feet but was grabbed by the hair and arms and was run up the wing, at the same time being punched. At the top of the wing I was dragged into the shower area and beaten again, then pulled to the circle by the hair. Drew was there and we were forced to face the wall. They continued to beat us. There were screws in the circle shouting, 'Kill the Fenian bastards'. After what seemed like ages, but was probably only a few minutes, they left us alone.

A van arrived to take us to the boards and we were told that the beating we had just got was nothing to the one we would get there. On the way to the boards I was terrified. When we got there, we were dragged from the van and banged against the fence. The screws who took us down said they were going to take us one at a time to the cell. But the one in charge of the boards said that we had had enough and pulled us down to the cells himself. I was that relieved, I could have kissed his boots. I don't think I could have taken any more because I was physically and mentally exhausted.

About an hour later a doctor came and examined us. He just looked me over, felt my ribs and nose and asked me a few questions about where the pain was. When I tried to explain to him what had happened, he refused to listen. That night Drew was taken to hospital with a suspected broken jaw. I had a black eye and a swollen nose and was bruised all over.

For the next 17 days we were held on the boards, 14 of them classed as a remand period. They used the excuse that the screws who charged us were out on the sick. In reality they were holding us there until the bruises had gone away.

The boards consisted of about 20 cells. They were small with frosted windows and grilles and no direct sunlight got in. The floor was concrete and the seat was concrete with a small board on top. Likewise the bed was concrete with boards along the top.

Fourteen days later, we were brought up in front of the governor and charged with assaulting two screws. We refused to recognise this kangaroo court and were found guilty and sentenced to three days solitary confinement, 14 days loss of remission and three days on No. 1 diet. The No. 1 diet consisted of two rounds of dry bread and a cup of black tea for breakfast, a bowl of soup and four rounds of dry bread for dinner, and four rounds of dry bread and a cup of black tea for tea. This diet was widely used to punish the Blanketmen when they were on the boards.

When we arrived back in the wing, it was in a shambles. There was no furniture in any of the cells – the only things left were two mattresses, blankets, piss pot and water gallon. The windows had been broken while we were away. They were broken to aid ventilation because the screws were throwing heavy disinfectant through the side of the doors and men had actually passed out with the fumes. It was worse than CS gas.

PEADAR WHELAN . . .

Don Mulholland, my cellmate, asked me if I thought the riot squad would come in once we were wrecking the place. I said I didn't know. I was very nervous and tense.

When the order came, it was almost a relief. We could hear the first rumbles of banging and smashing from across the yard in B wing. Whoever had the responsibility of shouting to D wing screamed 'Lean ar aghaidh' (go ahead), making sure he was heard and practically losing his larynx in the process.

We set about our task in a hurry because we wanted to make sure we had everything broken before the riot squad came in. I bashed the table off the wall. It didn't disintegrate as it was supposed to, but in time the legs and cross bar loosened until they came off; that left us with the plastic chair. I hit it one thump with a table leg and it bounced about two feet in the air. I jammed it against the wall and tried again; the job was a good one. I had a laugh at Mulsey; he took our 'hammer' to break the shelf from the wall. He had seen that my efforts on the table and chairs failed to get first time results, so he put everything into his swing. It was a sledgehammer to crack a nut. The plywood shelf just exploded in bits and we were showered with splinters and lumps of wood.

We got the order 'sin é' (that's it) before we broke the table top; we threw it under the bed out of the way. All the lumps and bits of broken furniture were to be thrown out the window. However, given our worry that the riot squad would be in to beat us, we considered keeping the table legs as weapons to defend ourselves. We had two lines of thought. We could keep the table legs and when the riot squad came into the cell, we'd get stuck into the first man. Then we thought that if they had the added anger and excuse of beating us because we had fought them, they would probably beat us within an inch of our lives. That was worrying. We worried that we might be the only ones fighting them, which would make us stand out. That swung our decision and the two table legs followed the other junk into the catwalk.

Afterwards, when everything quietened down, we felt there was nothing to do except wait for the riot squad. I got down to the pipes to have a yarn with my next door neighbour, Leonard Ferrin (the Wolf). I wanted to know what he thought about the night's events. Putting the wrecking into the context of our protest, what we had done was an act of rebellion and mutiny against the authority of the jail administration and NIO, so we felt excited about the importance and impact of it. But we also felt certain that the riot squad would be sent in. We wondered how long it would take before the Brits realised that trying to break the protest was, in the end, a waste of time, that they would have to do something because they couldn't run the jail in an orderly fashion. The wrecking up proved the strength and control we had; the protest was going to get bigger and we were prepared to endure hardship out of our commitment to fight for political status.

Leonard and I talked that night about the impact the no-wash protest was having on the international front. In Europe, Britain and America we were getting a lot of publicity and a lot of questions were being asked of the British about their treatment of the POWs. So to our minds in 1978 the logic was fairly straightforward. The prison authorities couldn't contain our protest; conditions were deteriorating continually while all over the world Britain, which delighted so much in criticising the Soviet Union for its treatment of prisoners, was now in the dock for refusing to deal justly with our situation. We couldn't imagine the protest lasting until Christmas, never mind going beyond it.

Sometimes we would talk until the early hours of the morning, but on this occasion we found it difficult to carry on a conversation. I think it was because we were always mindful of the riot squad threat. So, despite feeling we had a victory, we were nervous and decided to call it a night.

I don't know if deciding to talk to the Wolf was a wee bit of escapism, designed to take my mind off the consequences of what we had done, but as I lay in my bed, in the silence, it just brought home to me how isolated we were in our cells. I really was scared of what the screws would do to us when they came in. I couldn't really express my fears or deal with them, so by way of protection and comfort, I got my rosary beads and prayed.

Religion was very important to us then. It was something we turned to for comfort. We could take some hope in its being there and we believed in it. Before going into jail I went to mass and would have gone to communion and confession occasionally. My religious practice was largely perfunctory, done because I had to do it rather than wanting to do it. As time went on though, I began to take more of an interest in religion and I prayed more, went to communion on Sundays and confessions often. Being religious and being Republican went hand in hand, so I had a sense that religion and being religious made us better people and so gave an added sense of legitimacy to our struggle. Later as the screws became more systematically violent during wing shifts and cell searches, the pressure on us mounted steadily. I would have prayed for protection during the shifts. All the men who were doubled up with me prayed in the cell. They said novenas and rosaries all the time. It never occurred to me to talk about why we prayed, but I believe that as individuals we used religion at the time because we did get something out of it.

Religion was also important to us as part of our identity because of the screws' contempt for us as Catholics, as much as Blanketmen and

Republicans. Often they would vent their bigotry by breaking rosary beads during searches and wing shifts. When we said the rosary out the doors at night, the night guard screw would turn on the vacuum machine (used for sucking up the piss we'd slopped out the doors) to drown out our praying. Once, as the rosary was being said and the Hail Mary recited, in response to 'Hail Mary, full of grace', a screw walking in the wing said, 'She's only a fucking whore'. We were incensed. We were 'Fenian bastards', to the point where a screw on the Twelfth brought in his sash which he lent to an orderly who paraded around the wing wearing it, to wind us up.

After all the nervousness and tensions waiting for the riot squad to murder us, nothing happened. The next morning the usual complement of screws came onto the wing. One we called Steve the Greek checked all the cells. He walked in, checked beneath my bed, saw the table-top and took it out. That was it, we weren't even charged with destroying prison property.

LEO GREEN . . .

I was still on remand in March 1978 when the no-wash protest began. It quickly dispelled any rising doubts as to just how far off victory might be. The escalation seemed likely, we thought, to force the issue to a conclusion. I wondered for a few weeks if I would even make it onto the Blanket before it was successfully wound up and Republican POWs returned to the Cages. I listened one evening to a radio interview with a doctor about the possibility of an outbreak of disease as a consequence of the worsening hygiene situation in the H-Blocks. His assertion that the human body could survive indefinitely in such conditions free from serious disease convinced me to revise my estimate of how much longer the Blanket would last from a few weeks to a few months. I wasn't even disappointed. I would make it onto the Blanket after all.

I was sentenced in April 1978 and went on the protest in H3. After a month or so, the wing was moved to H4. Conditions were getting worse all the time. In contrast to this, the scéal, all rumours of course, was good and morale was consequently high. Some of the rumours arose from a cocktail of wild optimism and exaggerated truth. At one point it seemed that the American dockers could (and soon would) dictate all British policy in Ireland. They supported the men in the H-Blocks and the women in Armagh and would soon boycott all British goods until we were granted status, we heard. Alongside such fanciful notions were the deliberate 'mixes' by the numerous jokers among us. For days we pondered what seemed to be a rising-up of dockers all over the world on our behalf, until someone spiked the latest scéal that the Swiss dockers had joined the 'Smash H-Block' bandwagon with the revelation that Switzerland is land-locked.

BIK McFARLANE . . .

I arrived in H3 after a failed escape attempt from the Cages and I wasn't particularly enthusiastic at the prospect of not washing for an indefinite period. Neither was I cheered by the fact that lock-up was permanent – two men in a small concrete box-like cell with nothing to read or stimulate the mind. My first month there was difficult – I wanted out for a walk, a shower, a decent meal, to watch a programme on TV, to play a little music, to sit and yarn over a cup of coffee and a biscuit, to kick a ball, write a letter, smoke a pipe, so many things I had taken for granted which now became impossible luxuries. They all belonged to a different world and I had to force myself to come to terms with the severity of the situation – no creature comforts until we broke the Brits and dressed ourselves in our own clothing.

As weeks rolled into months, conditions deteriorated. The sole welcome aspect was the smashing of the windows in an attempt to get even a little fresh air into our putrid, maggot-infested cells. The prospect of having to endure a harsh winter without windows to ward off biting sleet and snow was far from our minds in the swelter of summer. There was a marked increase in brutality and degradation, liberally indulged in by willing screws, the majority of whom came from staunchly Loyalist communities. Attacks were frequent and vicious; men were scalded and battered.

KEVIN CAMPBELL . . .

After a lengthy debate, we decided to take a visit with our loved ones. By then most of us hadn't had a visit for almost 18 months. We knew our people were very worried about us, so we decided to put their minds at rest. In my first visit in almost 18 months my family were very shocked when they saw the state I was in. They nearly didn't recognise me when they came into the visit boxes. To them I looked like someone from an asylum. My eyes were staring and glazed over, with dark rings under them, and my face was deadly pale. I had lost a lot of weight by then and the beard I'd been growing for almost a year didn't help matters at all. Everyone who took visits that week came back with stories of how shocked their visitors were on seeing them.

We found out also that people outside didn't understand the situation inside. Because of our stance of refusing to take the monthly visit, we had in effect isolated ourselves. The people were only hearing the British government's lies and propaganda. After this we realised it was in our interests to continue with the visits. We realised we could be beaten to death and the people outside wouldn't know a thing about it.

LEONARD FERRIN . . .

I arrived that mid-March morning at the visits like a lost soul dressed in a horse-haired monkey suit with prison boots that would have undoubtedly fitted the biggest feet in Ireland. I felt dejected by the comments made by passing screws on my appearance and as I was just thinking to myself 'never again', Tom McElwee came on the scene. He shook my hand and, after introductions, gave me a run-down on the screws' surveillance and procedures on the visits. His escort – a fire and brimstone Christian – threatened to have him returned to his Block without receiving his visit if he didn't cease his conversation with me. Big Tom held firm until he was quite satisfied that I had understood the points raised and then, and only then, did he continue on his journey, oblivious to the utterances of the trailing screw.

JOE McQUILLAN . . .

During visits the screw stood directly behind us and sometimes at our side, in between us and our visitors. We sat at one side of the table and our visitors on the other side, so the screw, if he was at our back, looked straight at them. There was no privacy; even touching hands or kissing your loved ones ran the risk of the screws saying they had seen objects being passed. The prisoner would then be trailed out and given a strip search, and the visit would be terminated. But it was all worth it to see them and to hear their news. After the visit, several screws would stand at the door; one of them had the job of checking the prisoner's book. The standard question was, 'What's your number?' Not replying earned another kicking. Non - Blanketmen had to endure none of this. Outside the visiting area a portacabin was installed; it was used solely to strip Blanketmen. When we approached it we could see it sway from side to side and hear the shouts and thumps of a comrade being searched and stripped.

The short walk to and from the visit, although designed to keep Blanketmen separated from each other and as a further form of harassment, was great. During the walk the 'doggie men' would walk behind us and let the dogs jump and snarl only inches away from us, or van drivers would swerve their vans towards us to see our reaction. But the walk was the only form of exercise we had and the fresh air, come hail, rain or snow, was fantastic.

I remember at this time talking through the small expansion sleeve around the heating pipe to Blute (Gerry McDonnell) in the next cell, and he asked me what I thought of the suggestion that, instead of emptying the contents of our pots out the window, giving the screws the excuse to use the hose and soak us at the same time, we could empty the urine out the doors and put the excreta on the walls. I was horrified at the thought of it and was relieved when orders came that everything should be put out the door hatch.

Despite the deteriorating conditions, morale in the wing seemed to be gaining in strength. With the windows out, men talked more to each other during the day and, through the broken hatches, could see other prisoners facing them. At this time we were charged each fortnight with refusing to wear a prison uniform and do prison work. The governor would come into each cell with several screws and each prisoner was required to stand as he was adjudicated and sentenced to three days cellular confinement, 14 days loss of association, 14 days loss of privileges and 14 days loss of remission. For the next three days the bedding was removed from the cells, leaving only the Bible and one blanket. We refused to stand during adjudication as a further protest. Each night after the slop-out most men talked through the doors, told jokes, or had a singsong. Around this time there started what was to become a Blanket institution – the bedtime story. Most nights, when the general banter had finished, a man would relate a book he had read or a film he had watched. All this took place after the nightly decade of the rosary; 'Paidrín anois' (rosary now) was usually the first thing heard after the screws left the wing and before the slop-out.

As part of our protest we wrote some political slogans on the cell walls. Myself and my cellmate were very original: 'We are POWs' and 'Up the IRA'. We also started to throw our leftover food into the corners of the cell, and we splashed tea onto the ceiling, staining it dark brown. When the weather got warmer, the rotting food in the corner soon grew a 'beard' (a fungus mould). Eventually a slurping sound could be heard, and soon the pile began to move and maggots emerged. I was disgusted. I couldn't stand maggots and refused to walk up and down the cell because of them. I spent most of the day on my mattress watching them wriggle and climb the walls. One morning I decided to lift my mattress and put it against the pipes to dry out as the damp from the floor soaked it. I nearly went up the walls, much to my cellmate's amusement. The floor beneath my mattress was alive with maggots. We counted 97 and my cellmate kindly flicked them back into the corner for me. Later he would gather them up in handfuls and throw them out the window to feed the wagtail and other birds.

One Sunday while we were at mass in the wing canteen, the screws came in wearing protective clothing and shovelled the contents of the corner into bins. The stench was overpowering, even more so an hour later when we were returned to the cells. The empty corners soon returned to their former glory as most meals that day went straight into them, the men being unable to eat because of the smell. All I could do was huddle in the corner with the towel over my face and mouth, feeling as if I would be physically sick.

KEVIN CAMPBELL . . .

Some of the lads gathered up the maggots and put them under the doors out
onto the wings saying ,'If we have to live with them so will the screws'. At
times the wings were covered with them and the screws were hopping mad.

We were now throwing piss and excrement out the windows. During the
day screws came round the yards with a hose and pretended to be cleaning
the place, but in fact they were hosing our cells. We had no way of stopping
this and our cells, blankets and mattresses were soaked. We would spend all
day and half the night drying them out. At night they would come round
wearing rubber gloves, lift the shit and throw it through the broken windows
on top of us. We decided to stop throwing it out the windows. And seeing
that we couldn't let it lie in the cells, we had no other option but to put it on
the cell walls.

PEADAR WHELAN . . .

The Blanket was full of crises, which were mainly personal. Putting the shit
on the wall was one such personal crisis. We stopped using the toilet early
on in the protest. We used our chamber pots and slopped the contents out
into a bucket which the screws brought around the cells. I disliked that. I
think it is because going to the toilet is a very personal thing and so
slopping a pot out in front of an audience of screws made it public. To me it
was an embarrassment.

Despite the inevitability of putting shit on the walls, it wasn't any less a
conflict of conscience; after getting over the taboos we still had to come to
terms with living and eating in a small cell covered in shit.

We thought about it in terms of our health and on one occasion my
cellmate and I had a discussion about the possible effects of breathing in the
fumes and dust from the shite. We felt it could only generate germs and
poisons which in the long term might harm us.

We also thought about it in terms of the impact it might have on people
outside and in a way, I think, that sums up the real conflict. Over the whole
period of the protest we worried about our health through not washing,
living in dirt with germs and maggots and the screws' constant use of
concentrated disinfectants. We had spread shit on the outside walls, so what
we were going to do wasn't far removed from that. While we worried about
our health, we worried too about how people would see our going against
everything we had been taught and if they'd understand it.

The day came and, one after the other, men spread their shit on the cell
walls. They made it public by shouting out. Someone's cellmate got up to
the window claiming he was in need of fresh air as his cellmate was 'putting

one up'. We joked about the different techniques for spreading the shit: some used sponge from the mattress, some used their hands, others mixed it with piss in the pots to make it cover more wall. We folded the mattress to get up to the ceiling or sat on our cellmate's shoulders. When it was our turn my cellmate put our first shit on the wall; he spread it in a big streak down the middle of the wall and couldn't do it quickly enough. I was standing at the window getting air. When he finished he came over to the window to shout to Huck next door and boast about his work. But in truth he was very self-conscious because he was uncomfortable with what he'd done. But that was it from then on in.

When the screws opened the door, they behaved as if they were disgusted, and tried to provoke guilty feelings and embarrassment in us by saying that animals wouldn't even live in their own shit, so we must have been worse. This didn't really bother me because of how I felt about the screws. However, my human response was to think it was awful. According to my instincts I was doing something dirty. But when it came to it, I saw putting shit on the wall as an aspect of the struggle I was part of. At the time words and ideas about pride, dignity and principles were a large part of our vocabulary and thinking. I believe we were influenced by the images of past Republican heroes but as our struggle was going on in different circumstances, we had to use what methods we had. Putting shit on the walls was one such method and we had to come to terms with it in that light.

JOE MCQUILLAN . . .

Over the next several months the harassment continued. The screws had a new toy; they were issued with a squeegee to sweep the urine out the door at the bottom of the wing. As the floors were not always level, we used leftover food to build a 'dam' at the door to stop the urine flooding back into the cells. One night I was wakened by an uncomfortable feeling, a damp sensation on the mattress around my hip. Dear God, it couldn't be! I moved my hand down gingerly; it couldn't have happened but it had. I'd wet my bed. What was I going to do? It was still pitch black. Could I dry the mattress and the blankets against the pipes? Without my cellmate knowing? I had to do something quickly. I decided to get up. As my foot touched the floor, it was almost covered to the ankle in liquid. Ah God, I couldn't have done all that damage. It only dawned on me then that I could hear the sound of a piss pot being scraped on the floor, a bloke cursing and a squeegee being pushed. The screw had come around with a coat hanger and run it under the doors, destroying the dams, and then pushed the urine into the cells. The sounds of the pots being scraped on the floors soon became a nightly racket; bailing out the cells, trying to push the urine out as quickly as it was being pushed in. Many a night we spent playing this game with the screws, our bedding and our night's sleep coming off the worst.

The screws refused to hand us in our meals and took to leaving them on the floor outside our cells. Then, instead of opening the doors immediately, they delayed for five or 10 minutes, even up to half an hour, by which time the food was cold. We could turn the plates upside down without losing any of the food. If we got nine chips it was a good meal, but on average we would get half a dozen. These had to be literally prised off the plates. One particular screw whom we nicknamed Píopa (the Pipe) would walk up the yard on his way home, stop and out of his holdall produce a large plastic bag full of chips, to the laughter of his cronies. One night when he did this he proclaimed 'They're for the dog'.

In response to the screws leaving the meals outside the doors we refused to hand the plates out to them, and instead placed them at the bottom of the cell doors. The screws then set the meals further and further up the landing so that we had to leave the cell to collect them. We soon stopped this because of the abuse and the harassment. They took to kicking the meals in with their feet, or a particular favourite of theirs was to open the door, set the food on the ground and slam the door on it, sending the plates flying everywhere.

One morning a screw, the Francach (the Rat), came to the cell I was in. As usual when he opened the door, the food – in this case porridge for breakfast – was outside the cell door, so we refused to lift it in. To our amazement the screw picked up the two bowls and offered them to us. My cellmate, John Downey, moved towards him to accept them. As he reached out his hand, the screw threw one of the bowls at him, hitting him on the face. I turned and saw the porridge dripping off his chin and I didn't know whether I was sad, angry or amused. Then the other bowl bounced off the side of my head and almost immediately the cell door was slammed shut. I'm not a great porridge fan but I could've cried at the loss, I was so hungry.

On Friday at dinner time the usual meal came up: battered fish (minus the fish, just a slap of batter) and peas. For me it was the best meal of the week and I looked forward to it. The screw set the plates on the floor and slammed the door shut, and to our amazement the plates slid nicely into the cell without upturning. I lifted them off the floor, turned with a grin, tripped on the end of the mattress and lost the lot. The look on my cellmate's face told me that he had a few choice names to call me. Thank goodness we weren't on speaking terms.

Someone in administration had decided to put in new windows. The trade screws – mechanical bears as we called them – came around and replaced a row of windows with perspex-type sheets. One of the trades bummed that these windows could not be broken. He hit the window a friendly tap with his hammer to prove the point. It was well made – the window shattered, and out they all came. A later attempt to put in stronger perspex was also aborted. After the screws replaced them in one wing the lads somehow managed to burn them out, almost choking themselves in the process.

John Thomas . . .

One Sunday morning in H5 I was in a pretty good frame of mind as I looked forward to the mass. The mass was only incidental; I was looking forward to meeting the other men in our wing and the yippees from C wing. This was the only chance we got to associate, to exchange scéal and get a bit of tobacco from some of my comrades in the yippee wing who didn't smoke and had their monthly visit the previous week. The Block OC then shouted across from the wing opposite that there was a good chance that Frank Maguire, the MP for Fermanagh/South Tyrone, would be in to see conditions in our Block today. He decreed that we were to give all the rotten food in the corners of the cells a good stir up so Frank would get a good smell of the place.

We gathered in our groups before mass. The rubbish heaps had been well raked over and the consensus was that the smell was no worse than usual; in fact there was no real smell at all. One man said the screws had been complaining about it and because we lived in the cells with the stink, we wouldn't notice it.

We had a good bit of craic at mass and I was happy that I'd be smoking that day. There was no sign of Frank – another bit of 'bum scéal', we thought. Thankfully I didn't join the back-stabbing of the Block OC as from my window I saw Frank walking up the yard with a posse of prison officials around him. I then played a prominent role in back-stabbing the back-stabbers of the OC.

Sean Tracey, who was in a cell with Paddy O'Hagan (both were from Tyrone and were called the Malones of the wing), said that Paddy 'Malone' had just 'dropped one', so our OC told him to stick it on the back of his door, because if Frank came in he would go to their cell (they were constituents of his).

Sure enough, Frank went to the Malones. Frank was a Westminster MP and his vote was being increasingly sought by a crumbling Labour government to keep it in power. He was in a very strong bargaining position and, as he gave us 100% support, we wanted to know 'gach rud' (everything) about our position. The rest of the wing weren't too pleased because they reckoned the Malones would be talking about the price of pigs instead of getting the scéal. Anyway, the Malones' door no sooner opened than it shut and the quickly fading sound of steps could be heard going down the wing. Gerry (Nick the Devil) McConville shouted into the Malones, 'What did you say to him?' Sean Malone then described what happened; 'Me and Paddy were facing the door when Frank came in and he was ashen-faced and shaking. He just about managed to shake our hands and then his chest started heaving. Next thing he turned and ran down the wing'.

Sure enough we were all able to hear the 'booack booack' as poor Frank puked into the urinal at the end of the wing. So much for raking the rubbish in our cells. We couldn't smell it but it nearly killed oul Frank. Then we all got up to the door to back-stab the OC because we got no heavy scéal. Sure the place was smelly enough.

JOE McQUILLAN . . .

Around the start of June 1978 a comm told us that each dividing wall between the cells had two shackle holes that had allowed cranes to drop each pre-cast section into place when the Blocks were being built. These holes were then filled with cement. We were to knock them out on a certain night. Directions were ambiguous, to say the least. All sorts of measurements were given – seven-and-a-half novena books from the window, 12 from the door, or was it the other way around? Has anyone got a novena book? My cellmate and myself spent two hours looking at every tiny hole on the wall and wondering if this was it. Half the wing were in the same boat. Someone shouted that they had found the holes and that they were on the black paint mark around the bottom of the wall, six inches off the ground. They were about three inches in diameter, filled with light plaster and easily knocked out with a few wallops. We were still looking for a thin coat of plaster over a hole as we tapped the wall, hitting the tooth brushes with the bottom of cups. I soon stopped this when I saw my cellmate's tooth brush go clean through his cup. We never did succeed in getting those holes out. It turned out they were six inches deep and covered with plaster. However, most of the wing did succeed.

TOM HOLLAND . . .

In July 1978 we received word that the then archbishop, Tomás Ó Fiaich, would be visiting the H-Blocks to talk to the prisoners from his diocese. When the day eventually arrived, we were in C Wing, H3. Apparently there was a dispute within the administration as to how this visit could take place with the minimum amount of adverse publicity. Technically, the archbishop had the 'right' to visit each individual parishioner in the wing, but the screws wanted him to do as little travelling in the Block as possible and they didn't want him to view the prisoners' cells. The screws suggested that all prisoners entitled to see the archbishop should wear the prison uniform and go to the wing canteen as one single group. This was a blatant attempt to conceal our atrocious conditions and give some semblance of 'normality' to the situation. The lads refused to agree to this.

Because the administration did not want to be seen to be refusing the archbishop a visit, they eventually came to an agreement with the prisoners. Everyone Tomás Ó Fiaich wanted to see would gather in one cell but would not have to wear any part of the prison uniform. The archbishop arrived and was escorted by the screws to Martin Hurson's cell where all the men from his diocese were assembled. For nearly an hour the prisoners conversed with him, primarily about the protest. They confidently and proudly articulated the reasons why the British criminalisation policy had to be smashed, and expressed their determination to ensure that this happened. Tomás Ó Fiaich listened attentively to their opinions, taking in the circumstances of the surroundings and the commitment of the men.

Eventually the protesting prisoners were moved back to their own cells. Later that evening, a row developed among the screws – apparently the Block PO wanted to know why, of all cells available, the wing screws chose Martin Hurson's cell as the meeting point between the archbishop and the prisoners. Martin and his cellmate were two of the most diligent protesters in H5. The screws' public relations exercise had backfired. A few days later when Tomás Ó Fiaich released his 'Sewer pipes in the slums of Calcutta' statement, the administration was highly embarrassed:

> *'Having spent the whole of Sunday in the prison, I was shocked at the inhuman conditions prevailing in H-Blocks 3, 4 and 5, where over 300 prisoners were incarcerated. One would hardly allow an animal to remain in such conditions, let alone a human being. The nearest approach to it I have seen was the spectacle of hundreds of homeless people living in sewer pipes in the slums of Calcutta. The stench and filth in some cells, with the remains of rotten food and human excreta scattered around the walls, was absolutely unbelievable. In two of them I was unable to speak for fear of vomiting.*
>
> *The prisoners' cells are without beds, chairs or tables. They sleep on mattresses on the floor, and in some cases I have noticed they are quite wet. They have no covering except a towel or blanket, no books, newspapers or reading material except the Bible (even religious magazines have been banned since my last visit), no pens or writing materials, or TV, or radio, no hobbies or handicrafts, no exercise or association. They are locked in their*

cells for almost the whole of every day and some of them have
been in this condition for more than a year and a half.'

Archbishop (later Cardinal) Tomás Ó Fiaich, following his visit to the H-Blocks,
31 July, 1978.

JOE MCQUILLAN . . .

The doctor, who normally called into the cells for those men due for or
already on adjudication (to ask how they were keeping), now stopped this.
He walked down the centre of the wing, either looking straight ahead or
talking to a screw, completely ignoring those in the cells. The cell doors
would be opened and immediately shut. If we were quick enough we would
catch a glimpse of the doctor's white coat. And so we were passed fit for
punishment. For this he was branded a quack. From then on, once he come
onto the wing, the first person to see him would shout out 'Quack on the
air!' and the rest of the wing would quack like ducks. The governors were
called the Big Bear and the shout 'Big Bear on the air!' would mean all
those not on adjudication would bang their piss pots on the doors.

The three days CC were very exhausting as the cells were stripped of the
mattresses and each person left with only one blanket from around 8.00am
until 8.00pm. Sitting on the cold floor was very uncomfortable, as was
walking up and down an 9 by 7 feet floor on bare feet for 12 hours.

Around this time I broke my first cellmate, a term given to anyone whose
cellmate 'squeaky-booted'. The previous night one of the blokes on the
wing called a singsong out the doors. He said it was a farewell singsong. He
was asked who was leaving and he replied that he would be leaving in the
morning. Everyone had a laugh at this 'joke' and had the singsong anyway.
The next morning when the screws came around, he announced to them that
he was leaving. He went around several cells and shouted into them that he
was away. This was extraordinary. Normally most people leaving the
Blanket did so because the pressure was too much. They were broken men
who walked straight off the wings, said nothing to anyone and in many
cases covered their faces on the way out of the Block.

That same morning when the screws opened the door, my cellmate, who
had been walking the floor for half an hour, picked up the breakfast – some
cornflakes, watery milk, bread pushed down into the bowls to absorb the
milk, and the plastic knives and spoons pushed through the centre of the
bread. He started to verbally abuse the man who had just left: 'The bastard,
the stinking rotten bastard'. I asked him a few times why he was taking it so
badly, but he wouldn't answer me. At two o'clock the screws came back
after lock up and did the head count. This involved opening the cell doors

and looking into each cell. As the count started, my cellmate started the walking routine, and when the door opened, he made a beeline for it. I couldn't believe it. As he reached the door he turned and said, 'That bastard fucked up my plan, I wanted to leave this morning.' I took his leaving very personally. We hadn't really talked or got on in the cell together; I was always quiet and timid, not a conversationalist. Maybe it was my fault that he left, not the screws'. Almost ten years later when I met him I still couldn't ask him why he had left.

The protest was upped once more. This time the administration decided to cut back on our monthly parcels. Until this we were allowed to receive one bar of soap, three shampoos, three packets of tissues and two religious magazines. It was now limited to three packets of tissues. All the cells were searched and magazines, Bibles, toothbrushes and combs were removed. Some men also had their rosary beads taken, and anyone with more than one religious medal had the extra ones removed.

I remember receiving one letter from my mother. It began 'Dear Son' and from then on it was all blacked out. Not a single word in between was legible until 'your loving Mother'. My family can at best be called apolitical, the letters from my mother being almost identical: 'I'm keeping well; your father, brother and sisters are keeping well. Are you keeping well? Are you still going to mass? Everyone was asking. I'll go here. Take care.' Nothing that the prison security could class as a breach of security, no reason for censorship but pure harassment. There was no way to redress the issue: our only contact with the outside world read by the censor and then blacked out by him. It was soul destroying. Maybe it wasn't the standard letter; maybe someone in the house was sick; had something happened? It was always a terrible fear among men, worrying in case anything might happen to their parents, wives, children. Even if they did receive word somehow, they still could do nothing; they wouldn't even be considered for parole.

KEVIN CAMPBELL . . .

We had to do something to occupy our minds. So in every wing the ranganna Gaeilge were organised. Men who had acquired the language, either in the Cages or in school, took the classes. Since we had no writing materials, we had to write the ranganna on the cell walls. We would keep a patch of the wall clean to write on and, using a broken piece of a liberated toothpaste tube, we would scratch the Gaeilge on the walls. Within a year Irish became the first language within the Blocks. All the news and business was given out the doors in Gaeilge; it was not only a means of communication but became a weapon in our hands to use against the screws. They hadn't a clue what we were saying and this really got to them. It helped to isolate them.

4

Wing Shifts, Mirror Searches and Forced Washes

July 1978 – December 1978

B y the second half of 1978 there were over 300 prisoners on the Blanket in H3, H4, and H5. In August the prison administration introduced wing shifts – that is, all the men in one wing were moved to an empty wing in the same Block to allow for the cleaning of the cell walls. Once those cells were cleaned men from another wing were moved in, and so a continuous rota of cleaning and moving within each Block was established.

Wing shifts were not designed solely to facilitate the cleaning of cells, they also provided an opportunity for the screws to brutalise and degrade the prisoners, and the subsequent introduction of the mirror search refined the opportunities for inflicting brutality and degradation. As the efficiency of cell cleaning improved, wing shifts were soon taking place every 5-6 days and became a routine dreaded by all Blanketmen over the next two and a half years.

Further refinement in the prison administration's tactics was to come before the end of the year, and it was an episode which was to reflect shamefully upon the medical personnel within the jail. Men were kicked and beaten in the presence of a doctor who then sanctioned forced washes and haircuts. These the screws carried out with relish.

What the various tactics proved, if proof was necessary, was that the British government was far from conceding to the Blanketmen's demands. As a bitter winter set in they knew it was going to be a long haul.

JOE MCQUILLAN . . .

Around June 1978 the OC of the wing called everyone to the doors and said that he had a comm to read from the camp staff. Word had been received that the screws had from September to December to 'break' us. Nothing about how this was to happen, how they were to break us, was known, but the implications were that the harassment was to be stepped up. My stomach sank around my knees. I could only think of an increase in the beatings and the cell searches. I didn't know if I could take any more. The light at the end of the tunnel seemed to be that if the screws could not succeed by December, then by January 1979 we would be granted our status and moved to the Cages. Rumours about the refurbishment of the Cages ran rife for the next few months: reports that mechanical bears were seen going into and working on several empty huts; screws were seen fixing the wire; new beds were going into the huts. If I could bring myself to stick it out until Christmas, then it would all be over. New blokes coming down from the Crum were expressing their satisfaction that they had made it onto the Blanket as they had heard it was almost over and wanted to be able to say that they had taken part in it.

Not long after this we were given our first wing shift. This was a fairly relaxed affair, the cell doors being opened one at a time. The two occupants then picked up their mattresses, blankets and personal property and walked straight across to the wing that had been steam-cleaned.

During the second shift we were stopped at the top of the wing and the screws gave our bedding a quick once -over before we were allowed to continue on our way. On the third shift we set our bedding to one side and were directed to a table. Here we were asked to remove our towels, which we did, and we were then looked over. At the start of September we moved wing once again. On reaching the top of the wing, we were once again directed to put our bedding to one side and shown towards a table. I noticed more screws than normal but had no notion why. At the table I was asked to take off my towel, which I did, and was told to bend over. I was taken aback and was dumbfounded. I didn't believe what I was hearing. Suddenly four or five screws jumped on me, grabbing my arms and legs. One grabbed my hair, pulled my head down onto the table and repeatedly banged it off the table surface. The rest of my body was raised into the air until I was upside down. One ordinary screw (not an MO), the Albanach (the Scotsman), spread my legs and pulled my buttocks apart; his thumbs pushed at the entrance of my anus, pulling it open. The pain was bad, but nothing compared to the humiliation I felt at that moment. This couldn't be happening; it was nothing less than sexual assault.

I was then dropped on the floor where the same screw pulled at my hair, ears, nose and mouth while the rest held me. After several minutes, I was given back my towel and thrown into a toilet cubicle. A group of screws stood around the open door calling me a 'dirty bastard', making snide remarks about my privates, telling me that the 'Fenian parents are dirty tramps so we can expect little else from yous'. In the wing it was dead, not a sound. If a pin had been dropped, everyone in the wing would have heard it. So September had arrived. My cellmate arrived behind me. We didn't speak. I knew by the expression on his face how he felt. For months after, I bled every time I excreted.

LEO GREEN . . .

Once the wing shifts began, everything deteriorated at an accelerated pace. The wing shifts gave the screws an excuse for physical contact, an excuse for beatings. A shift would mean, at best, a rough body search or, at worst, a bad beating. My first experience of such a search was a shock. I was taken to an empty cell. There, six screws held my arms and legs, raised me from the ground, turned me upside down and opened my legs like a pair of scissors. After that, I knew they were capable of anything.

JOE MCQUILLAN . . .

The table search grew more frequent and more savage. We now came to dread the sound of the table being dragged across the concrete floor. Our stomachs churned and we literally shit ourselves, then smeared it on the walls as quickly as possible before the screws opened the doors for the move.

The wait was the worst, a shift could last an hour and if you were left to the last it meant having to listen to 44 men being beaten. The door would open and outside the cell we were greeted by half a dozen screws. We were no longer permitted to carry our bedding with us. The screws in the wing would grab, punch and kick us, running us to the top of the wing.

The worst shift was one across the circle which was about 60 yards longer. At the grille a second squad of screws was waiting to take over the beatings on the way to the table. At the table the ultimate humiliation: the PO, ever so polite, would say, 'May I have your towel please? Thank you. Would you bend over the table, sir? No? Grab the bastard!' Arms twisted up my back, legs in the air, head banged off the table, hands probing my buttocks and anus, all to their laughter and jeers. Ears, nose and mouth searched with the same hands, my towel thrown on the floor between two lines of screws, having to run the gauntlet to recover the towel to hide my nakedness and suffer the beating for it. The screws' favourite was a hard smack with an open hand on back or buttocks leaving a brilliant imprint: 'The glorious Red Hand of Ulster'. From here, the fourth team and then the final team, the fifth, would beat us down to the cells.

Sometimes these moves took place around 8.00am and the screws would put the bedding outside the cells until 8.00pm, leaving us with only a thin towel to wear all day. With the winter approaching, we would be blue with cold. When the bedding was finally put into the cells, we would find that the screws had deliberately mixed up all the belongings. Seldom did one get his own mattress or blankets, and what we did get was usually soaked in urine or had been rubbed in the excrement on the walls. As the cleaning screws got more proficient at their work we got shifts at 4-5 day intervals.

Oddly enough, morale heightened. As the last cell door closed, everyone in the wing banged on their doors: no orders, no directives, pure spontaneity; then someone would sing and most of the wing would join in. Bawling out the likes of 'Provos March On', finishing with wild cheers and yells, getting rid of the built-up tension and aggression. The screws would be raging. I remember one man being trailed along the ground naked, the screws pulling him by the hair. The man had one hand trying to hold the hand pulling on his hair, the other was trying to cover his privates. And I could hear him growl, 'If I had an M-60 now ya bastards.' For some reason that cheered me.

One particular governor boasted that the running, beatings and the table search were his personal initiatives and that these were only the beginning. The IRA executed him several weeks later. We got a wing shift on the day of his funeral. All the usual teams were in place but no one was touched, no one pushed, no one run. Our heads were slightly bent forward, but we were not put over the table. One screw, Jimmy Crocodile/Claw-hammer Head, growled at me on the way down the wing, 'We're not afraid of yous.'

During the wing shifts most of the men were marked. On Sundays one priest in particular, Fr Faul, would come in to say mass on a regular basis. At the start we all went to him as he was renowned for being outspoken about brutality. We would show him the marks and explain to him how they were caused. He received what must have amounted to thousands of complaints against the screws and in particular against the Block PO, Paddy Joe Kerr, under whose direction and eye the events occurred. Faul informed us that he had raised the matter to have the PO replaced. Several years later Kerr, who had since been decorated by the British government for services rendered, was executed by the IRA. Faul condemned the killers and said Kerr was a good decent family man who would harm no one. It was hard to believe this.

Along with the increased frequency of wing shifts came an increase in cell searches. Often the day after a wing shift where everyone had been table searched, our belongings gone through thoroughly and ourselves and our bedding checked with a metal detector, we would be subjected to a cell search. There was no security reason, nor was there any pretence; we all understood that it was harassment, part of the strategy to break and demoralise us. The cell searches always ended with the contents of the piss pots being poured over the bedding and the men in the cell being systematically beaten.

When the footsteps of the screws were heard approaching and the cell keys rattling, we knew we were in for a hard time. Each man could feel himself sink, trying to become so small that the screws would pass over him. Men would reach for their rosary beads and pray that God would not let it be them. Then they would pray that God would let the beating of the bloke in the next cell come to an end: the sickening thuds of fists, boots or batons on a naked man, who could do nothing but curl up in the foetal position in the corner to try and minimise the damage. When the screws replaced the squeegee as a means of getting rid of the urine from the landing with a vacuum water cleaner, they also learned to turn it on during these beatings, as its loud whining shrill would drown out the dirty deeds, but it fooled no one.

James Henry Brown, 'Susy' to everyone, got a bad beating from the screws and word was sent out to his family. They and the Relatives' Action Committee contacted the jail chaplain and asked him to call on Susy to find out the extent of the beating, with a view to taking a court case. The chaplain, Fr Toner, called into Susy's cell and asked him for an account and to see his bruising. The priest listened and looked, and on his way out said, 'Sure it's no more than you would have got in the school playground.' Thank goodness I didn't go to that school.

One wing we moved to still had the shackle holes in the walls and now someone discovered there was a rectangular hole around the heating pipes. This would have been to allow the heating to be installed and then the side sections of the wall to be lowered into place on top of them. The remaining gaps were then patched around later. We set to work digging out the plaster with a bent piece of wire that had been used to hold the window in place. It was hard going, but we eventually managed to dig out a hole about six inches wide and four to five inches high and through to the next cell. It made it a lot easier to talk to each other.

Some of the blokes had broken their cups. They had been using them to try to knock the holes through. Those with damaged cups were told by the OC to ask the screws for new ones. The screws threatened to charge them with damaging prison property. All decisions were taken by the camp staff and it took some time at this stage to get word back and forth. After a couple of days, word came back that we should break all our cups if the screws refused to replace the two or three broken ones without charging anyone. The staff asked the governor to replace these broken ones. The governor said that he would replace them only if the individuals concerned gave an undertaking not to damage them. The Block OC said he would give that undertaking on behalf of everyone. The governor refused this, so all the cups were smashed.

The next morning the screws gave the tea in disposable polystyrene cups. Once we drank the tea we disposed of them only to be told we would be given only one cup per day. This meant we only got one cup of tea a day, in the morning. Coming into October the issue still hadn't been resolved, so we broke the plates and cutlery. At meals we were given a paper plate, a disposable knife, fork and spoon and again told that these were to last all day. This went on for several weeks – we got a small cup of tea for breakfast and a dinner from which we were expected to keep the paper plate until tea time. As we didn't have the plates at tea time the food was put into our hands. Eventually the administration issued new cups to everyone. Three hundred new cups, plates, bowls, knives, forks and spoons, and goodness knows how many disposable ones in the interim, all because they refused to issue two or three cups at the start. There had to be a lesson in there somewhere.

NED FLYNN . . .

During the summer of 1978 the doctor came into each of our cells and, if he decided any of us needed a wash, he indicated this to the screws who then took us down to the boards and forcibly washed us. Joe Watson was the first to be taken out from H5 and I was taken down the next day.

The screws came to my cell and told me I was going to the boards to be washed. I sat on the cell floor with my blanket round me and told them I wasn't going. Four of them came into my cell and grabbed the blanket from me, then two of them caught me by the legs and dragged me naked down the landing and into the circle. I was lifted into a van and taken to the boards, all the time being slapped and punched.

When we reached the punishment Block, they carried me in and dropped me into a bath of cold water. One screw rubbed shampoo into my hair while two others scrubbed my body with deck scrubbers. No part of my body was left untouched – they used the deck scrubbers on my privates, which left me in pain for days afterwards. My whole body was covered in scrapes.

JOE MCQUILLAN . . .

Around November the table search was replaced by the mirror search. At first this was a mirror 14 inches by ten inches on the end of a stick so the screws could raise and lower it, while one shone a flash light on your back passage. The rest of the move remained as usual: the runnings, the beatings and so on. Only now at the search point we were asked to squat down over the mirror. We would stand straddling it, but refused to squat. Our arms would then be jerked out and back, our legs kicked from below us sending us crashing to our knees, all the while being punched and insulted. The third or fourth move of this type resulted in one man being knocked down so quickly that his backside hit the mirror and smashed it. He got even worse treatment for damaging prison property. On the next shift the stick was replaced and the mirror now rested on a piece of foam. Beatings became so routine that, when the OC would ask each cell in turn for an account of the shift, the reply became the standard 'Mar's gnath' (the usual).

JOHN THOMAS . . .

It was three weeks to Christmas, 1978. I was walking up and down the cell and it was a miserable day outside – and inside also, as there was no window in my cell. I had my mattress sitting on its edge against the wall and I was walking parallel to it. I had one of my three blankets doubled over and wrapped around myself, another one in which I had cut a slit fitted neatly over my head like a poncho, and my last blanket was folded four times (so it was about a foot wide and eight foot long) and laid on the floor to keep my feet from freezing. As I walked up and down, I was able to see another Blanketman, Roy Mallon, in a cell about four up from me in A wing opposite; he was dressed as I was and, for his sake, I hoped he wasn't any colder than myself. Seeing him had interrupted my thoughts of the latest IRA operation, the shooting dead of three Brits in South Armagh. I didn't know how the operation was carried out so I took a slight reddener in case he spotted my strange movements, because in my thoughts I had played a starring role in the operation. He said nothing and I hoped he wouldn't engage me in any conversation because it was so cold I needed to keep on the move to help the blood circulate. I then heard the front gate opening and some indistinct voices. Roy could see the gate and he shouted, 'JT, here comes the biggest man in the world.' Just then I got my first sight of him and I recognised him immediately as Don Concannon, the under-Secretary of State, a giant of a man. I shouted to the rest of the wing and immediately heard lots of different voices from other cells.

We hated Concannon as much as Roy Mason because these were the men who refused to grant us political status. So we were all up to the cell doors listening intently. He came to our wing and I heard him greeting the orderlies in the canteen with a 'How are you doing, lads?' I was trying to see further down the wing than possible through the cracks up the side of my door but I knew the man nearer the canteen would spot him first and give a shout that he was heading up the wing. Sure enough, Keegan in the end cell let up a roar, 'Lump of shit in the air' ('Bear in the air' means a screw is coming, but this was Concannon, so, 'Lump of shit in the air'). As he made his way up the wing, he was greeted with a crescendo of noise. Some of the men were banging the steel doors with piss pots while others were hollering, 'What about South Armagh, you bastard!' 'Up the 'RA!' was very popular too and my very politically aware cellmate, Jimmy B, was standing behind me gritting his teeth as other expletives became harder and louder. I then saw Concannon and he looked frightened to death. With that racket going on, he turned half way up the wing and went back from whence he came. Keegan roared again, 'Lump of shit off the air.'

Most of the men were laughing then with a general euphoria in the air and the noise lessened dramatically. Suddenly big Livvy's voice rang out with the words, 'Concannon, you bastard, I wish I'd your head full of thrupenny bits.' We all fell about laughing. Keegan shouted up that even the screws were laughing. Jimmy B and two other leading cadres in the wing took their places at the door and a political debate quickly ensued between them on the implications of Concannon's visit. This was interrupted as Concannon walked down the yard with the No. 1 Governor in tow, and the No. 1 was looking very embarrassed as Concannon had both arms raised in the air looking like a right plonker, and all of us shouting in unison, 'Big head! Big head!'

So ended the visit of Don Concannon to H5. Although it lasted only about 20 minutes, our wing got enough from those 20 minutes to keep us in conversation for two weeks. Because of his arm waving, we put him down as a bit of a corner boy, a big lout. We couldn't wait till wee Roy Mason paid us a visit.

Ciaran McGillicuddy . . .

On 8 December 1978 I was moved to Long Kesh. I was 16 years old. I went to H4. When I got between the main Block gates I said a wee 'Our Father' and asked my granny, who had died the day I was arrested, to help me stick it out. When the van pulled up at the door of the Block, I said my goodbyes to the lads going to the other Blocks and went to H4.

In the circle I saw the biggest screw in the world coming across to me and laughing and shouting, 'Look at the baby Provo!', which had everyone laughing but me. He told me to face the wall. As I stood facing the wall, I was waiting for a punch in the back of the head, but it never came. The PO called me into his office. Like all the screws, he didn't know how to react to someone as young as me. He offered me a clean cell with chairs, bed, table and so on, as I was too young to go in with all the men. But I said I wanted to do what all the rest were doing.

When I turned into B Wing, the smell hit me right up the face. It was unbelievably bad; it nearly made me throw up. It was like walking into an invisible wall. It was like the smell of bodies decomposing. But after a while on the Blanket I became used to the smell, though coming back from a visit I always hit that invisible wall again.

I was put into cell 4. I nearly died when I saw it only contained a mattress and a cup, no windows and very little paint on the walls. I could see men at the windows in the cells across from us. I hid down as I didn't want them to see me. But it didn't work, as they told the man in the next cell who banged my wall. I didn't know what to do; I wanted to pretend I wasn't there, but I had to answer. I gave him my name and he called it out the door in Irish. All I heard was my name and the men banging on the doors (this was my welcome). I thought I was in a wing full of Orangemen as I knew some of them were on the Blanket protest. I thought the banging was them telling me to get off the wing. I went to the window and all I could see was men waving fists and shouting out the windows. Once again I thought they were calling me names. But when all the shouting and banging was over, I was called to the pipe between the cells and everything was explained to me. The Blanketman next door then told me to get some shit up on the wall right away. I sat for 20 minutes trying to go to the toilet. I spread it on the wall in one big stroke and it felt degrading.

When I was on the Blanket about two or three days, the screws came and told me my mother had sent in word for me to come off the Blanket because I was breaking her heart. From that day until my first visit I felt bad. But once I saw my mother and found out it was all lies, I felt on top of the world. All the lads had told me not to listen to what they said but in the back of my mind I was worried. Once I knew my mother and father supported me and my family were all cheering me on, I knew I'd be OK.

THOMAS LOUGHLIN . . .

During the searches the screws began using a metal detector, much to the horror of Tom McFeely and John Thomas because they had a lighter and knew the screws would get it. So it had to be carefully concealed. 'You're going to have to bangle it,' Tom said. 'No way am I bangling that,' JT said, but he eventually did once the screws began to move the lads from wing to wing. As expected, the sweat was flying out of JT. 'Jesus, Tom, do you think they'll detect it?' 'Not if it's well up,' said Tom.

During the move they put the metal detector between JT's legs and the thing went berserk. 'He's got something up his rear end!', squealed the screws. At that he was taken into the MO's room. 'Right, what is it?', the screws asked. 'Fuck away off', said JT, 'There's nothing up my arse'. 'Right, get him up to the prison hospital and we'll use the tongs to get it out'. JT's heart nearly stopped. He shouted that he had a metal pin in his leg; there was nothing up his arse. But they took him up to the hospital where the good doctor asked him what he had hidden. JT kept saying 'nothing' and that no one was sticking tongs up his arse. 'OK,' said the doctor, 'in that case we'll have to take you to the outside hospital'. Again JT nearly collapsed. 'I'm not going to any hospital', he said. For a second there was a Mexican stand-off until JT said he had a lighter but it wouldn't come down. The doctor told him to sit on the table, pull his legs up to his chest, and don't worry. Within seconds the doctor had the lighter out. The next day he was up in front of the governor who seemed slightly bemused by it all. Sitting on the desk was a wee plastic bag and in it was the lighter covered in shite. 'Listen, Thomas,' said the governor, 'yesterday you were a nobody, today you are the talk of the camp and because of that I'm not going to sentence you. Now go on back to your cell'. At that, the governor burst out laughing.

Joe McQuillan . . .

Christmas was approaching fast but there was no easing up. At the end of November the screws came to the cells and dragged the men, one at a time, up to the wash house. Approaching the wash house, I saw the doctor standing talking; he was well aware of the men being dragged and beaten in front of him. I was dragged no closer than about 15 feet from him; he was standing with his side towards me talking to an MO and without turning to look at me, he pronounced that I had head lice. If I had, he would never have seen them from that distance. But the truth of the matter was that I didn't have them, nor had anyone in our Block. The doctor then ordered that everyone in the Block was to be washed and have their hair and beards cut 'on medical grounds'. It was to be another series of beatings, only this time they must surely do me some good; after all, it was to be no ordinary beating but a special medically approved beating.

A few days into December the blokes on the yard side of our wing saw five men from D wing being moved into the cells facing them in C wing. At first we thought that it was a wing shift but this was odd as it was our turn to move next. Several minutes after the last of the five were moved into the cells, the men in our wing watched in horror as groups of screws went into their cells simultaneously and kicked the sweet daylights out of them. All were later treated by the doctor for their injuries. Then, one at a time, their limp bodies were trailed out of the cells; they were bathed, shaved and had their hair shaved. They were returned to the same cells where they could relate their stories to us.

TOMBOY LOUDON . . .

On Sunday, 3 December 1978 we were told by a screw on night guard that a few men were to be force-washed the following morning. No names were mentioned, so any one of us could be picked. That night was a long one as men talked at pipes and out windows about who were going to be the unfortunate ones the next morning. Voices could still be heard in the early hours of the morning as men tried to ease each other's fears. I thought I was certain to be one of those picked as my hair was the longest in the wing and I had been taunted a few times by the screws during wing moves on how they would love to cut it. I didn't get much sleep that night and when morning came, I could feel a tightening in my stomach.

The tension in the wing was high – not a sound to be heard. At around 10am a total lock-up was called and we knew that this was it. The sound of heavy boots passed my cell and I heard a door open and a shout, 'Hurson, doctor' and Martin saying, 'I don't want to see him.' He was dragged by the hair from his cell and the sound of boots and fists thudding into Martin could clearly be heard. They dragged him to see a doctor (nicknamed Mengele by all the Blanketmen). I could feel the nerves in my body take hold; I wanted to shout something, but it just wouldn't come out. My cellmate, Hector McNeill, was wounded in the leg when he was caught and I could see the nerves in his bad leg twitching as we stared at each other.

Joe McNulty was next and he received the same treatment as Martin, if not worse. The tension was really bad and I could hear the fear in the voices of the lads as they shouted to each other, 'Whose cell was that?' The sound of heavy boots again stopped outside my cell and I heard a screw say, 'Loudon's in here'. I sat on the floor on top of my mattress as my door opened and the bolt was shot. A screw shouted, 'Loudon, doctor' and before I could even say anything, they all piled into the cell. I was dragged by the hair, face down, kicked and punched; a boot caught me full in the face and blood poured from my face and mouth. I was taken to cell 26 where the prison uniforms were kept and told to put on the trousers. When I refused, I was again punched and kicked and dragged, naked, by the hair to the doctor's room where I was held down on the floor. All I could hear was a voice say, 'Yes, lice'. I tried to get up off the ground to make a complaint to this so-called doctor but an MO said, 'Get the smelly bastard out of here'. I was then dragged to an empty wing and thrown into a cell.

As the door slammed behind me, I heard a voice shouting through the gap in the pipes; it was Martin Hurson in the next cell. He told me that his foot had stuck between the grilles as they dragged him out and the screws tried to break it, and that he thought that two of his toes might be broken. He told me that Joe was in the next cell to him and that he might have a broken nose and had lost a lot of blood. I told him that my own nose was bleeding but not broken and that one of my eyes was swollen. We heard another two being dragged and thrown into one of the cells. We all shouted encouragement to each other, which didn't go down too well with the screws.

I was then dragged from the cell and taken to the canteen where I was held in a chair while three screws set about cutting my hair and beard with scissors and shears. My head ached from being dragged about everywhere by the hair and I screamed every time the shears went over the lumps on my head. As I sat there held in the chair I could hear the bath being filled. My face and head felt raw from the nips of the shears. I was dragged to the toilet area and thrown into a cold bath and held down under the water for a while as the screws had their fun. I really thought I was drowning as I struggled to get my head above the water. They scrubbed my whole body with a scrubbing brush, which nearly tore the skin off my back. I was then pulled from the bath and held in another chair while they shaved my head and face with a blunt razor – I was a mass of cuts. All sorts of threats about cutting my throat were made and my nerves were on edge as the smell of drink came from them all. I was then asked was I going to walk back to my cell; I told them 'no' and was punched again in the face. I was dragged back to my wing and thrown into my cell.

As the door slammed behind me, the look on my cellmate's face told me he was totally shattered. He cursed the screws up and down and did everything he could to help me. Other lads were shouting to me, concerned about my health. My whole body was aching, my nose and mouth were very sore from the boot and punch in the face and I had a black eye.

When the screws came around to throw in our food, they all stood and laughed and joked about the great job they had done on me. I said to myself, if it took them three hours to do us five surely they didn't intend doing this to everybody. A few hours had passed and you could still feel the tension hanging in the wing. I was just starting to come down myself when I heard the sound of feet and my cell door opened again. My heart was beating fast; all that had happened that morning was going through my head. Three screws stood at my door and one said, 'Medical Officer wants to see you' and I replied, 'I don't want to see him'. I prepared myself for another beating, but this time they just dragged me out by the arms to the doctor's room and the medical officer put some kind of cream all over my body and said it was to stop the lice. I shouted back at him, 'I never had any lice', and he laughed and said, 'There is no chance of you catching them now'. I was then dragged back to my cell.

That night we got up to the door and gave the lads a full run-down on what happened. Martin Hurson had been taken to the prison hospital where it was found he had two fractured toes, and Joe McNulty was taken to the Royal Victoria Hospital in Belfast where it was found he had a broken nose. The feeling in the wing that night was one of fear but also determination to face head-on whatever the screws would throw at us. The beatings that morning had shattered a few of the lads in the YP wing beside us. Two of them left the protest because of what had happened.

JOE MCQUILLAN . . .

Over the 12.30-2.00pm lock-up we could hear the blokes in D wing shouting the scéal about the forced washes to the camp OC in H5. They asked for instructions – the reply from the camp OC was 'buail orthu' (hit them – the screws). At 2.00pm the Block PO made an unprecedented move and sent for the Block OC to see him in his office. The PO informed the OC that he had been instructed to wash everyone in the Block, that he would carry out his orders, no one would be harmed and he foresaw no problems. The OC asked him why, if that was the case, five men had been so brutalised that morning? The PO said they had resisted; if we wanted to give passive resistance, such as sitting down and refusing to walk, then they would be willing to carry us out gently. But, he said, if we so much as breathed heavily on one of his officers, we could rest assured that we would be slaughtered – that morning was only a slight indication of what we could expect.

It was obvious that the men that morning had been selected as a warning of things to come and sending for the Block OC, Joe Barnes, was a response to the screws translating and reporting the messages being shouted from Block to Block. The next few days were hell, especially for the Block OC. We had great respect for him and knew he faced an impossible decision: to give the order to resist and have everyone badly beaten, or to refuse the order, which would let the screws claim that we bowed down to them in the face of threats – and so leave us open for it in the future.

PEADAR WHELAN . . .

Because of the way the screws had us terrorised in H3, the order was seen as suicide for us. We believed that anyone who hit a screw would get kicked to death. The pressure was just everywhere around the wing. We'd been shouting about this all night to the other Block and, when all the shouting was finished, Hugh Rooney called us to the door for the Paidrín. I remember putting everything into it that night, looking for something: help, comfort, security, courage, I don't know. But it was an indication of how serious I took religion then. I believed God would help me get through the crisis, protect me enough to get over whatever beatings I might get. Ironically, I never prayed to God to get us political status; I just hoped He'd help me get through the tight spots.

JOE MCQUILLAN . . .

Normally after the nightly bedtime story, which ended around 12, everyone would doze off. That night the whole wing lay awake. The OC had been trying to reach a decision all day and hadn't done so yet. About 1.00am the order was sent down the pipes: 'buail orthu'. We were shattered. Some Blanket Blocks could recall seachtain dona's (bad weeks). H3 had suffered this constantly for months on end and so we knew the PO was not making idle threats. I couldn't sleep that night; I don't think anyone did. Early the next morning a countermanding order was sent around: we were to sit on our beds and not resist. The relief was as if a cloud lifted off the wing revealing the sun.

Starting around 6 December, the screws began to cut our hair. They came to a cell and ordered the prisoner out for a haircut. He immediately sat down. They dragged each man in turn to a chair in the middle of the wing. The first half a dozen or so had their heads and beards shaved. Then, as time went on, three or four screws circled each man; one would have the shears, one the scissors, one the thinning scissors, one the manual scissors. Men were left with various combinations of bald spots and tufts, half moustaches and beards.

On 8 December, it being a holy day, we got to mass. It was the first time we had seen each other since the cutting and in most cases the first time we had seen each other without the long hair and beards. As each person came into the canteen, those already there would guess who it was. It was amazing how many we failed to recognise. But the mass that day had a serious note. The Block OC, Barnesy, was going to mass to stand down because he couldn't issue the order to fight the screws. We had been shaved but not yet washed. Barnesy was also going to try to convince the man who was to take over not to issue the order. The OC of the other wing, Cleaky Clarke, to whom Barnesy was going to hand over was, unknown to us, going to the mass to convince Barnesy not to issue the order. Boy, were we a happy bunch, and our staff remained the same. Only one person spoke out against the decision: Blute.

The following day, the washes started. There was no resistance. We could hear screams and slapping, yet the first person to reach C wing shouted back that they were not touched. After a half dozen others, I was pulled out for a wash. When I reached the wash house, I noticed dozens of screws and several MOs. I was pulled up right at the side of the bath and was asked to step in. I refused and was pushed into about six inches of lukewarm water. I was asked to wash myself and again refused. Then one of the screws poured shampoo over my head and, as I shut my eyes, several others scrubbed me with deck scrubbers. My first reaction was to put my hands over my privates. As the scrubbing stopped, a bucket of water was thrown over me. It was ice cold; I thought my heart would burst. Now I knew where the screams came from. I was lifted out of the bath and brought towards two MOs. A screw at either side of me held my arms out while the MO fetched a large paste brush which he dipped into a bucket of white paint-like substance and slapped all over me: under my arms, chest, around my privates; then, turning me around, he ran the brush between my buttocks and over my back and legs. I was given a new towel and pushed around to the clean cell. Here I discovered a new mattress and clean blankets. Magic. My old mattress had been down to about two by five feet. I had a brilliant night's sleep that night: fresh smelling skin and hair, lying on clean bedding, the worry of the last few days over me. We later heard that the forced-washing was a policy designed to demoralise us. It had the opposite effect. The next day the cells were as dirty as ever.

BIK McFARLANE . . .

It wasn't long before we in H4 had to face the ordeal. What heightened the tension was the fact that we would physically resist. During the week leading up to the forced-wash, men became quite nervous and jittery; some developed stomach disorders such as diarrhoea. There was a real fear that someone, perhaps many of us, would be very seriously injured. Jibes from the screws were countered with defiant retorts, but there was no remedy to the nervous apprehension which enveloped the Block.

PETER CUNNINGHAM . . .

The screws started with our wing in H4. The volume of noise and activity that morning told me that there was an unusually large number of screws on the wing. The sound of footsteps, the rattling of their keys mingled with stifled talk and menacing laughter added to my apprehension. Although there were more than 40 of us on the wing, the circumstances of our confinement meant that each cell and the men in it were on their own: prisons within a prison. The screws, only too well aware of this, applied themselves accordingly.

There was a lull of sorts in the screws' activity, followed by the sound of a cell door's bolt being thrown and the voices of two of our comrades shouting out to us. We stood powerless in our cells, cold and hungry as we'd been given nothing to eat, listening to their voices and screams being drowned out by the thuds of the screws' boots and batons. There was yelling and shouting as they dragged Dinker and Midge along the landing, kicking and punching them until they reached the other screws, who were waiting to further beat and degrade them by shaving their heads and washing their bodies with scrubbing brushes. The screws continued in this vein, moving from cell to cell, working their savage way up one side of the wing and with each assault my apprehension intensified. My cellmate, Rab Collins, and I paced up and down the cell, exchanging looks, sharing thoughts and telling each other the obvious. The bewilderment, rage, fear, hatred, powerlessness and vulnerability that consumed us was to know no respite until unexpectedly they stopped at our cell for their dinner.

The screws had left 10 of us – five cells – to stew. Myself and Rab cursed them for stopping and leaving us to suffer this break in their offensive. The sound of a trolley ended our cursing as we strained our ears to hear what was happening; cell doors were being opened and closed without any beatings. The screws opened our door and gravely passed us a bowl of rice each. Although my stomach had been doing somersaults throughout the morning's savagery, I still managed to empty that bowl of rice and savour its soothing effect, even if only momentarily.

No sooner had I finished the rice than a familiar deep voice boomed out our names, 'Frankie, Johnny, Peadar, Rab, John Anthony, up to your windows. C'mon ahead lads'. Within seconds, all 10 of us were up at the windows. We stood talking about the morning's events, wishing they'd continued so it would be over and done with, until Doc Mór (Big Doc – Kieran Doherty) cut in: 'It's a week to Christmas lads; how about a few Christmas carols?' And that is exactly what we did, with Doc leading the way with 'Silent Night', which was very unusual for him because he hadn't sung before. It took our minds off events until we heard the screws coming back onto the wing.

As we stood at the windows giving each other words of encouragement and support, Doc, talking to no one in particular, but to each one of us, said, 'Don't worry about it; we've probably got worse hidings outside; just get into them lads.' At that instant a cell door's bolt was thrown – it was Doc's and Gerry's cell. Our cell was supposed to be next and there were cells on either side of Doc's cell. Obviously they feared him; the element of surprise would catch him and Gerry unawares and lessen the risks for themselves. They resumed the sequence: charging in on us shouting and yelling, kicking and punching and eventually dragging us up to chairs, where they shaved our heads and slapped us, Nazi-style, across the face, ordering us to sit still.

I remember sitting on that chair, naked, with 20 or more screws standing and walking around me, grabbing at my hair, smirking into my face, and I was thinking, 'I hope the grub's half decent'. Everything taking place was registering but in a trance-like way, even when I was lifted by the arms and legs and carried into the washroom to be dropped into a bath of water and washed with a scrubbing brush. It was scary, but even scarier when Rab reflected, as we sat discussing it that night, 'You realise that most of the screws are probably indifferent to what they are doing to us'.

SEAN LENNON . . .

We in H5 got wind of the forced washes and, after discussion, it was decided that we would resist it with force. Everyone was told to get ready for it and as soon as the screws came to the cell to take us out for a forced bath, we were to fight them the whole way, even when they succeeded in getting us into the bath. We all realised what this meant, but saw no other way out. When the decision was shouted around the wings and to the other Blocks that night, it was stated that, if any man felt that he wasn't up to it, he could leave the protest the following morning. Everyone stood their ground.

I was in the cell with Bobby Sands at this time and we decided on the way we would attack the screws if they came to take us out. We knew we would get beaten very badly and accepted it. We decided that during the hours that the screws were on the wing – 7.30am to 12.30pm, 2.00pm to 4.30pm, and 5.30pm to 8.30pm – we would stay alert and have only the towel around our waist and the blanket around our shoulders. This would allow us to keep warm as we waited and, when they came, make it easy to get the blanket from around us, giving us more freedom of movement. When we heard them at the door, we'd get our backs to the wall facing them as they came rushing in and take it from there. The other men were doing the same thing.

The atmosphere during the hours the screws were on the wing was frightening. We could feel the tension even though we were locked in a cell – there was an eerie silence and not a word could be heard from the other cells. I walked the floor most of the time; I couldn't settle waiting for them coming. Not that I was eager to fight them, but I would have been relieved to have it over and done with. Little food was eaten – our nerves wouldn't allow it. Once the screws left the wing, we could feel the tension lift from our shoulders and men came to life again and began talking out the doors and windows. We were getting the scéal back from H3 where they had started the forced baths, and it wasn't nice. The forced washes happened in H3 and H4, but stopped at H4, for some unknown reason. They never came to H5, although the waiting was as bad as the actual beatings; it was mental torture.

Bik McFarlane . . .

Despite the ferocity of the forced washes, men emerged with spirits steeled by the experience. Firstly there was immense relief at having endured such an onslaught without being slaughtered entirely. Plenty of scrapes, scratches, bruises and abrasions, but no broken bones or cracked skulls, in H4 at any rate. There was something akin to a sense of achievement in the air as men chanted victory slogans and sang rousing Republican songs. We laughed and yelled, even slagging each other's ridiculous sheared heads – tufts of hair sticking out and bare patches where scissors sliced too close. We related our own experiences and I took particular delight in claiming a small victory when, with one screw standing on my bare feet and four others holding me in arm and head locks, the electric shears seized and broke as soon as they were pushed into my beard. A tally was taken of how many screws each of us managed to wallop before being battered into the ground. There was great satisfaction that we had stood firm and fought against impossible odds. It was our victory. Morale was high in those last couple of weeks of 1978.

Joe McQuillan . . .

On Christmas Day we came back from mass full of great expectations; we had noticed trays of cakes, trifles and other assorted goodies sitting in the cell known as 'the hobbies'.

A member of the Board of Visitors made an appearance calling into several cells. She was an elderly woman, Ms Blackburn, and would leave copies of small religious magazines in the cells that she visited. And always she had sweets in her handbag but couldn't give us them because 'the warders are watching'. Christmas Day was no exception; the screws stood with the cell doors open watching every move. No sooner had she left the wing than the screws returned to the cell she had been in. They accused the two blokes, Eric Wright and Peadar Kane, of having cigarettes and set about searching them and the cell. They found nothing, as they hadn't existed in the first place. The screws, Jimmy Crocodile and the Cruimh (the

Maggot), beat the two blokes and then pulled them up the wing into cell 26 for a mirror search. This also proved fruitless. Not content with this, the screws sent for the MO. When he arrived, they told him that they wanted him to carry out an internal search of the men's back passages. We heard the MO arguing, 'For Christ's sake, it's Christmas'. The argument was hot and heavy with the screws calling the MO a 'Fenian-lover', and telling him that they would see him 'in the club later'. Eric and Peadar were thrown back into their cells with another kicking. Merry Christmas.

The dinner came. It was a dismal failure, almost the same as any other meal: very little, stone cold; the only difference was that there was a meagre piece of turkey. Tea was the traditional salad. It was depressing. Several of the blokes in the wing now facing us called over to their mates and asked what they thought of the great meal. We thought that the banter was good craic; food was always a great topic of discussion, each person taking delight in elaborating. We had a good laugh at the blokes in B wing telling us about the creamed spuds, roast spuds, brussel sprouts, ham and stuffing. Their tea: Branston pickle, sweet mince pies, lemon meringue, trifles, Christmas cake and fruit. For our part the blokes bemoaned that it was a let down after all the expectations. B wing asked what they were on about; it was a great meal; they were not winding us up. To prove the point several of them came to the windows and stuck their arms out, showing the cakes and so on.

The OC decided that he would go against the orders of not speaking to the screws and would ask them where our food had gone. The screws denied that it had existed. The OC stated that if B wing got it then it would have been there for us as well, and what about the stuff we had seen in the hobbies? 'It fell on the floor,' was the reply. At supper time the screws came around with the Christmas cake – they must have sliced each piece into four as the portion was no thicker than one's finger.

For weeks before Christmas several of the men had been organising a Christmas concert. Not being able to come together and not wanting to shout back and forth alerting everyone about the arrangements beforehand, they had worked out a system for getting the parts to those doing the acting. When the screws had left the Block and as soon as the rosary was finished, the agenda was revealed: quizzes, a pantomime and a singsong. The pantomime started off the night's entertainment.

The minute it began, a radio blared out all over the wing drowning out the voices. Some minutes later the screw on night guard, The Buachaill Bo/The Ballymena Cowboy, went to the OC's cell and asked if we would hold back the slopping out for a few hours – if we would, he would put the radio on and let us listen to it for the night. The OC asked for a consensus; most of the wing hadn't heard a radio in over a year and so agreed that the concert could hold for another night. The screw went away, turned on the radio, turned off the radio, turned it on, went up and down the stations, then off once more. Twenty minutes later it still wasn't on. No radio. We should have known. So the concert was put back on. Each time one of the blokes went to say his lines, the radio blared. When we settled down to listen to it, it went off. The screw was hell-bent on making sure we had no entertainment.

Like several screws, the one that night was 'not the worst'. That meant that if he was on duty with another screw who 'wasn't the worst' and if you asked for toilet roll, he would give you a lot of paper. If he was on with a 'not so good screw', he would give you three squares, 'one up, one down, and one across'. If he was on with a bad screw, you got nothing and so tore a wack off the foam mattress. He would also be in the thick of the kickings. Tonight he was drunk and enjoying himself; no doubt he would have great fun in the screws' mess recounting his exploits the following day. On Boxing Day the screws came into the cells to remove the Christmas cards. After the shout went out from the first cell, the rest of the wing tore up their cards rather than give the screws the pleasure of removing them.

A weekly high point was the Sunday tea: not because the meal was any different from the rest of the week – it wasn't – but it held a treat in the form of an apple, the one piece of fruit we got each week. It was savoured with relish, the pips and even the stem being consumed with great delight. Alas, for the past three weeks we had eagerly awaited their arrival only to be disappointed.

Then one morning a search team came into the Block. This was unusual, as the wing screws normally did all the searching and no wing shift was due. The orderlies were called out of the wings and locked in their cell. (The large cell used as a classroom had been converted into a dorm to house eight orderlies, most of whom were Loyalists). The search team came into our wing but went into the canteen. The back wall of the canteen had been used as a store for such items as the tin lockers and beds removed from the cells before they could be destroyed. After a short while the search team left and the orderlies unlocked.

They came into the wing and we could hear them banging the lockers about and then a row developed, each accusing the other of being a 'tout' and saying what they would do when they got the one who squealed on them. No one owned up to it. Then the voice of one of the screws could be heard saying, 'Are you looking for the home brew? Barney Bubble-eye (one of the orderlies) told the PO about it this morning'. The orderlies, with full knowledge of the wing screws, had been using our apples to make drink for themselves. We expected the rest of the orderlies to do something to

Barney Bubble-eye that night in the dorm. All their talk about what they would and wouldn't do to him proved to be hot air, in case he had them charged. They had proved that not only would they be willing to carry out any action against us in order to gain extra remission and ingratiate themselves with the screws, but they were also willing to cut each other's throats in the process.

At the same time it was sickening listening to screws treating orderlies like dogsbodies, even worse listening to the orderlies grovelling in return. '1060, where are you? Come in here and polish my boots'. 'Yes sir, no problem sir. Is that a good enough shine for you sir? Could you lift your foot, sir, so I can get at the heel, sir?' Looking out the side of the door we could see 1060, a 30 year-old Loyalist, Defender of the Crown, down on his knees polishing the boots of a screw (a 20 year-old screw who also claimed to be a Defender of the Crown) while they were still on his feet.

That topic was always one the screws took great delight in rubbing into the so-called Loyalist orderlies. If the orderlies were the Defenders of the Crown then how come the Crown had turfed them into jail? The aim of the screws was not to prove to the orderlies the error of their ways but more to prove that they were more loyal than the orderlies. 1060 was heard to argue in 1978, at the start of the no-wash protest that, if his commanders decided the Loyalists would protest against being branded as criminals, then he would be 'away in the morning'. A week later the Loyalists embarked on a Blanket protest. 1060 suddenly developed a bad case of wax in the ears and found it difficult to hear his call. 1060's wax problem came back the following year when the UFF/UDA announced they would shoot Loyalist prisoners engaged as orderlies in the Blanket Blocks. The god called 'remission' conquered their hearts.

There was a steady turnover of orderlies in the wing, not because of any moral stand taken by them, but because the role they performed earned them early release. At the start of the protest two brothers from Ballymena who worked in our Block took great delight in using the high pressure hose to wash down the yard. It enabled them to direct it at open windows and more than occasionally to smash the windows. They enjoyed it even more when all the windows were smashed by us. They could then turn the hose on us all, drenching the cells. Once the hose was turned on in the yard, a shout would go out from one of the lads and if we were lucky, it gave us seconds to grab the mattress and roll it around the blankets and then hold it either side of the window frame to stop it being soaked.

The abuse from these two brothers equalled anything that the screws gave out and so it was decided in the wing that something would have to be done. The following day, while they hosed the catwalk side (as this is only five or six feet wide, it meant they were closer to the cells), one of the blokes hit one of the brothers on the face with his excrement, and told him that it was the least he could expect if they continued to mess us around. Minutes later the screws stormed the cell and, while several screws held the bloke, the orderly beat him senseless. A week after this, one of the blokes in the wing on the yard side managed to get some elastic bands and made a catapult using a wire out of the window as a staple. It hit the orderly on the bridge of the nose, missing his eye by millimetres. Neither the orderlies nor the screws saw where it came from. Several cells were searched but nothing was found. The brothers left the Block.

THOMAS LOUGHLIN . . .

A screw called Fat Geordie had the habit of putting the hose into the cells (through the window) and soaking them. Whenever he did this everyone rushed to close the windows. One day, when Fat Geordie was doing the rounds, the lads got word and the windows were shut. However, Bobby Sands decided not to do this; he stood at the window while Fat Geordie continually soaked him and his cell. Everyone reckoned that Bobby had cracked up but that evening, when the governor came round to do the CCs, he was greeted by an avalanche of water when Bobby's door was opened. He went into the cell and found Bobby lying there shivering. He immediately called for a stretcher and Bobby was taken to the hospital. It was some time before Geordie used the hose again.

BIK MCFARLANE . . .

At the end of 1978 we could take comfort from a number of developments: 1) Concerted onslaughts by the administration served only to strengthen our resolve; 2) The bond of comradeship which sustained us through increased resistance greatly frustrated the torturers of the POA whose morale plummeted; 3) The response to the barbarity of the screws by our comrades outside at times left them reeling, particularly with the execution of the second-in-command of Long Kesh, Governor Myles, who was the chief perpetrator of the regime in the Blanket Blocks.

However, we had also come to the sober realisation that our no-wash protest had peaked, and while we had gained valuable propaganda and international attention, we had failed to achieve concrete results in bringing a successful resolution any closer.

5

Craic and Camaraderie

1976-1979

Deprived of the usual diversions of TV, radio, books etc and locked up for 24 hours a day, the Blanketmen provided their own entertainment. That 'craic' was to be had in such circumstances was a measure of the bonds of comradeship forged on the protest. To the outsider Blanket humour would have seemed very black, even cynical, as literally nothing and no-one was sacred. For the prisoners, however, the peculiar brand of humour was an antidote to the harsh surroundings and a means of drawing all within the circle of shared experience.

Much resourcefulness and effort was displayed in the organisation of entertainment and educational activity for the whole wing – from concerts and quizzes to debates and ranganna Gaeilge (Irish classes). Equal resourcefulness was evident in smuggling tobacco, the bia beatha (food of life) for so many.

Felim O'Hagan . . .

'When this is all over, we'll remember only the good bits.' That's what we used to tell each other during the Blanket and I suppose in a way it's true. Wherever two or more ex-Blanketmen are gathered together, there you will hear of The Day I Touched For Three Ounces On A Visit, or The Night of the All-Block Christmas Singsong, or whatever yarns happen to be the favourite on each Block. And there's a strange thing: there are tales of certain events of almost mythical status which appear to have taken place in all the Blanket Blocks. It could be a collective mind at work but, me, I reckon the men who were in H3 and H5 are just liars.

In fact I started off in H3 but spent only a couple of months there; our wing was moved to H4 (along with a wing from H5) to open it as a third Blanket Block. I came on in April 1978 along with five others. At that time there were still beds in the cells but four days after I arrived it was decided we should break the glass in the spy hole of the cell door. We smashed it with the bed-ends on the Saturday night — next morning the screws came in and that was the last we saw of the beds. Three blankets, a mattress, piss-pot, towel, cup, Bible, water gallon — these were to be my companions for the next three and a half years. Oh yes. And a cellmate.

Cellmates were a mixed breed. Quiet, noisy, funny, dour, rakers, head-the-balls, sensible heads, starvos, picky-eaters (a real treasure), all-day-trainers, cabbages — whatever the type, we had to put up with each other 24 hours a day, seven days a week. I had only one row with any of my four cellmates in all that time, a verbal flare up that was over as quickly as it had begun, the result of tiredness, a sore throat, and a large measure of arrogance on my part.

The cell was our whole world, a concrete cube of a womb outside of which all was hostile. Wing shifts, going to mass or the doctor were times of nakedness, psychologically as well as physically. And to the visits — that half hour each month of furtive contact bounded by mirror searches. Each time, my mother would feel my hand at the start of the visit and tell me how cold I was, her eyes anxiously on my face, asking if everything was all right. I'd reassure her and pull my hands away, not because I was annoyed or embarrassed but lest the screws think we were passing anything. As it happens we were, or rather we had, as the beart of tobacco was always the first business on the agenda — most times it was safely away before we even sat down.

Craic and camaraderie there was; they provide the golden memories of the Blanket. It takes a bit of an effort to recall the long days filled with boredom. There was plenty of brutality in the H-Blocks but no doubt everyone who has ever seen the inside of a prison will agree that it's the sheer boredom that sometimes gets to you. We had singsongs, quizzes, ranganna and discussions, but sometimes you are left on a grey afternoon in November, the dinner is over and there's still hours left to go to the tea and you're fed up watching the wagtails in the yard and you've run your favourite memories through your head for the thousandth time — and it's just plain boring.

But imagination is a wonderful thing. Put a blanket lengthways on the floor, wrap another one around you, five steps, turn, five steps, turn and you were off to a wild headland in Donegal, or a cosy fire at home, or the last female company you knew outside, or with your comrades in the haven of a safe house. Or dreams of a huge feed. Food used to be my last thought at night and my first in the morning — I would pray for a full bowl of cornflakes brimming with real milk but I never did get it. One period in 1979 in particular I remember; a new screw took over as class officer in the wing and he starved us. Within a couple of weeks all we could see at mass were ribs sticking out everywhere.

JOE McQUILLAN . . .

The craic in the wings could be first class at times. Many a night was spent lying back in bed listening to the singsongs or the one-man concerts. Some of the men had excellent voices and did credit to Simon and Garfunkel, the Eagles or Harry Nilsson. Occasionally two such men would be doubled up together; then the duets would be unbelievable. Others were brutal, and that's putting it mildly, but at least they had the courage to sing which is more than I had.

A lot of the songs sung were close to the originals. Different blokes would know bits and pieces and put them together like jigsaw puzzles. Kevin McCracken was notorious for putting in pieces that 'sounded right'. Others just stuck in what they thought sounded good. The words of the songs would then be shouted out to anyone who asked for them.

TOM HOLLAND . . .

The general idea of having singsongs was sound, but when you take into consideration that each prisoner had only a limited knowledge of songs, and even at this a lot of the lads wouldn't hesitate to chance their arm with the words, the enthusiasm soon wore off. A more specific problem was the singers (a term used very broadly) who loved singing but who, unfortunately for us, couldn't sing a note — Martin Hurson was such a person.

When Martin sang a song he would shout in to me in the next cell and say, 'Well, what did you think of that, Dutch?' Not so jokingly I would reply, 'Martin, I've heard the words before but I can't recognise that tune.' No harm to him but he was woeful. During the singsongs, as the MC went around the wing, everyone would have their fingers crossed that Martin would, when called, recite a poem instead of attempting a song.

One night in April 1978 we were in B wing, H3, and as usual a singsong was in progress. It was around 11.00 pm and the lights of our cells were out, as they had been since March 13th, the day we embarked on the no-wash protest. Martin was called for a song, and simultaneously the wing moaned.

But the moans soon turned to cheers when Martin very modestly announced, 'I only know one song and I've been at this door singing it now for the past five months. I'm singing no more till I learn a new one'. A sigh of relief spread around the wing — absolutely brilliant, Hurson-boy. However, the MC of the night was not to be deterred; he would have none of it. 'Martin,' he calmly retorted, 'you were given the words of a new song on Sunday at mass'. 'Yes,' Martin replied, as if he was waiting for that very response, 'but I haven't learned it off yet and it's far too dark with these lights off to read it from the toilet paper in front of me.' Good oul Martin, don't back down, mate, we're all behind you. At that a screw's footsteps were heard on the landing. 'Bear in the air,' someone shouted. The screw walked straight down the wing to Martin's cell and turned his cell lights on from the outside, then unconcernedly walked away. Within seconds the words of 'Sean South' were ringing around the wing, and as Martin Hurson continued his dreadful singing career the curses were piled on the screw — he had a lot to answer for.

Peter Cunningham . . .

Morale in the wing was sky-high after we embarked on the no-wash protest and, the wing being full of teenagers, it was also very noisy with stacks of craic. Singsongs were brilliant due to the variety of singers and songs. Some were good but most of us were woeful, although it was the woeful singers who gave the most craic as their 'singing' would be accompanied by the barking and howling of the rest of the wing. Those few who had a bit of talent — John Downey, Curley McQuaid and John Pierce — would be respected and listened to and usually kept to the end to entertain the rest of us with their repertoire of songs.

My cellmate, Rab, was called to the door for 'a song of your own choice', which for a long time was 'Vincent' by Don McClean, the only number he knew. He'd been waiting his turn, clearing the vocal chords and running over the lines. He pretended he wasn't interested, so the lads coaxed him to the door where he cleared his throat again, took another drink of water and started to sing. No sooner had he got the first few words out, 'Starry, starry night . . .', than the lads started to accompany him with well-timed raspberries, shouts of 'who's making that noise?', 'stick the mattress in it', with the rest of the wing in stitches as amid it all Rab kept on singing. No matter how bad the singer he always got applauded — banging and yelling — at the end.

Another form of craic was the Ugliest Man in the Wing and Bore of the Wing competitions. Word would come up the pipe, 'give your points to so and so' and he would end up the Ugliest Man in the Wing or the Bore of the

Wing, and sometimes both. Occasionally it would backfire on the instigator and he would find himself as the Ugliest Man or the Bore of the Wing.

Kevin Campbell . . .

Many a thing was done to while away the nights, from singsongs to storytelling. All the lads would pull their mattresses to the door and settle there for the night. The country men would tell yarns about the countryside and ghost stories, which always got a laugh from the lads. We would hear how other countries won freedom, places like Cuba, China or Vietnam. These usually generated lots of questions and men took real interest. Many a debate took place after one of these stories and would last for ages.

Joe McQuillan . . .

The quizzes were another interesting form of entertainment but not designed to broaden one's mind with knowledge, useful or otherwise. They were run on the basis that the referee's decision was final, the referee normally being the one who was asking the questions in the first place. 'Right, for two points, who was the main highlight at the Woodstock festival?' Team A: 'Was it Jimi Hendrix?' Quizmaster: 'Wrong, it was Bob Dylan'. A few weeks later: 'Who was the main highlight at the Woodstock festival?' Team A: 'Ah-ha, we remember that one; it was Bob Dylan'. Quizmaster: 'Nope, you're wrong. It was Jimi Hendrix'. That question always came up; it was always the wrong answer no matter what, and always good for a row.

One night the left side of the wing challenged the right side, so it would be a fiercely fought competition. Our side were two points in the lead, one question per team left, two points per question. Seosamh Arrachtach (Joe Monster, so called because when he asked for his name — Joe McNulty — in Irish someone give him that and he used it not realising what it meant) was the last to ask a question for his side: 'Who was the French Prime Minister in 1976?' Gerard in his best Belfast accent answered, 'Jis-guard Day-stan.' 'Wrong,' says the Monster, 'It was Giscard D'Estaing.' 'That's what I said!' argued Gerard. 'You said something but it wasn't that', said the Monster. Rules being rules, the referee's decision was final, and the wing being the wing everyone engaged in half an hour of shouting, bawling and abuse giving. It was now Gerard's turn to ask the final question to the far team and give them the chance to equalise. Gerard asked Joe Monster: 'What was the screen name of the main male character in the series Roots?' Immediately the walls began to thump, a rule being that the answer shouted out the door by anyone other than the person being asked the question would mean the loss of the points, but the answer could be passed on down the pipes. Cell 25 rapped the wall to cell 24, 'It was Chicken George; pass it on'. Cell 24 rapped 23 and so on down the line until, finally, cell 15 rapped cell 14, Joe Monster's cell. During this time our side had been giving Gerard dog's abuse for asking such a stupidly easy question. Everyone had heard the right answer being passed along 10 cells and now the Monster got up to the door to equalise. Joe cleared his throat bringing silence to the wing, 'Gerard, would the answer be Chicken Charley?' The roars of abuse from his team drowned the laughter from ours.

Several weeks later Joe Monster did the same thing again. 'Who sang Build Me Up Buttercup?' Ten cells later Joe proudly answered, 'The Brown Faces'.

During the summer of 1978 we had noticed an increase in the number of rats to be seen in the yard and also an increase in their daring. One particular rat became very popular, although most of us started off hating rats with a passion. Due to a Michael Jackson song and a film released about a rat, we named him 'Ben the Bowler-hat'. Food would be thrown out into the middle of the yard to attract him. In the beginning he would scurry along the far wall, listening, watching before he would move on. Running into the middle of the yard, he would check the food, run back to the safety of the wall and then repeat this several times before finally grabbing a piece of the food and retreating. Within a fortnight the well-fed rat would waddle along the wall, make its way straight into the middle of the yard to the food despite the sound of people shouting to each other to get up to the window. Grabbing the full rounds of bread he would hop like a kangaroo out of sight, the night's attraction over.

The broken beds, tables and so on that had been removed from the cells in March 1978 had been dumped in the yard and now the screws decided to take them away. A screw and two orderlies went out to the yard to sort it out. They worked out of most men's view but a scream from one of them brought everyone to their windows. Ben, as fat as a balloon with his easy lifestyle, was running along the far wall pursued by one of the orderlies who was the same shape, fat and obscene, closely followed by his two companions. Ben reached the bottom of the yard but for some reason didn't go out the hole to freedom. He turned and ran back towards his pursuers. It was like a sketch out of a comedy as the screws and the orderlies turned and ran in the opposite direction. Ben having noticed them also turned and ran in the original direction. The orderlies stopped and once again chased after Ben. But Ben was now running a lot slower. One of the orderlies reached him and kicked him several feet along the ground, where he lay motionless. We called the orderlies all the murderers of the day. One of them who wore glasses, Tommy from Derry, bent over Ben to pick him up. Ben moved and startled Tommy. His fat mate, Jonesy, was in the process of bending over to see Ben and so the back of Tommy's head came into contact with his face. This knocked Tommy's glasses off, smashing them on the ground. Good old Ben. Our hoots of laughter enraged the orderlies who took to chasing after Ben. This time the glassless Tommy kicked Ben about 10 feet into the air. Ben the Bowler-hat was no more.

JOHN PICKERING . . .

Often after mealtimes on the Blanket you would hear the dull rattle of plastic as cups were swung from window to window. This was how the inedible food was passed on to the wing 'seagulls', those who ate everything yet remained hungry. The cup would be packed with rice, potatoes, peas and whatever else was going. But the most commonly disliked piece of food was the dreaded yellow cake, or 'nuclear waste' as we called it. This was supposed to be a 'treat' for supper; it seemed more like an ominous threat however. Although everyone claimed to hate it, they still ate it.

One evening during the winter of 1978, our wing decided to have a game of bingo. The prizes were nine slices of yellow cake for the winner of the full house, and four slices for the single line. A towel was sent down the line to collect the cake and then passed to a middle cell for safekeeping and easy distribution. My cellmate, Ciaran Dawson, and I were to organise the game. We drew all the cards on the wall, then shouted out to each man his numbers, only one card each was permitted. Ciaran then drew a board on the floor so he could place a small piece of paper on each number as it was called out; all very fair and legit.

Then before we started, a towel was sent up the line to our cell. Inside the towel was a small and hastily written note, it went like this. 'A chara Pickles, cad é mar atá tú? Had a brilliant visit today but feel exhausted now after all the excitement. Anyway, looking forward to the Bingo tonight — I'm starving, maybe you would like a wee beart up later on? But first let's see if I win some yellow cake! Do chara, Doc mór'. Well, I didn't need an interpreter for that — what some men would do for a piece of tasteless yellow cake. We returned the towel and after a brief discussion a decision was reached. Dawser reasoned that a frame like Big Doc's would require more fuel than the average sized Blanketman and besides, the nervous energy used on his visit today would have left the poor man exhausted. We decided Doc's health came first and foremost.

At six thirty all eyes were down, the silence only interrupted by occasional whoops of delight as someone ticked off their number. After about ten minutes there was a mad scream down the wing, 'Bingo! Yahoo! Bingo!' Johnny Mór was in hysterics; he'd won the single line. As he ranted and raved voices around us started to grumble 'Fix! Fix!' claiming we'd let Johnny win because he was an Andersonstown man. Others began to join in the commotion, relishing the excited reaction of Johnny to the accusations. Johnny was panicking in case he didn't get his cake.

Meanwhile, Dawser and myself were quickly discussing what to do about Doc; the lads would surely not believe or forgive two Andytown men winning in succession. There was nothing else for it; Doc's health was paramount, and certainly more important than the men's wrath.

The game restarted and continued quietly as everyone settled down again. With a copy of all the cards we could monitor the state of play, so we decided to quickly give Doc all his numbers — bar one — just to let him sweat it out for a while and add some real bite to his hunger. All the while we were sweating ourselves in case a mistake had been made and someone else would shout Bingo. After a few tense minutes, we decided that was enough and braced ourselves for flak (though not before some bright spark shouted 'I betcha Frankie McDonnell or Big Doc wins the full house').

'All the fives, fifty five!', I roared. 'Check! Check!!' Doc's voice echoed around the wing, immediately followed by a thunderous clamour as the wing erupted. 'Fix! Fucking fix!' they screamed. The mixers were out in full force stirring it; they had a field day, and on it went for ages.

Later that night we received a towel down from Big Doc. Inside were a few skins, a beart and a small note; 'A chara Pickles, phew! If you're not at mass on Sunday, don't worry, the lads will understand. I do, because I'm not going myself. HA!! Could you imagine the racket they'd be making if we'd been playing for snout! Anyway, the lads seemed to have enjoyed the crack (almost as much as I enjoyed the yellow cake). Enclosed you'll find some snout and a few skins. Have a smoke. Oiche mhaith, do chara mór. PS Do you fancy another game tomorrow night, mo chara!'

JOE MCQUILLAN . . .

I awoke with a start. I had heard a yell; my cellmate was already awake. More shouts, screams then a loud thump followed by silence. It was about 12.30am and I had dozed off during the bedtime story, 'The Exorcist'. I had been turned away from the film on the outside, too young, but had read the book on remand and wondered why all the fuss. Before the bloke rose to tell it, Gal Gallacher had called up the wing to the OC, Brian McCool, 'Here Brian, will you order him not to tell that story'. 'What's that, Gal, you're not serious are you?' 'I am, Brian,' replied Gal, 'I saw it on the outside and couldn't sleep for nights after it'. All the macho heads were now calling Gal a cry baby, afraid of his shadow, making squeaky voices at him and demanding that the story start right away. Gal made another attempt, 'All right, but as I'm on my own tonight, how about leaving it until my cellmate returns?' (His cellmate had been taken to the boards earlier that day.) He wasted his breath expecting any sympathy, as the era of 'consciousness' was still a few years off yet. So my cellmate and I thought that it was Gal in the horrors who had wakened us.

The following day the night's events unfolded. Seany Toner and Seamy Delaney were doubled up. Seamy was a devout Catholic and Seany an ardent atheist. While Seamy stood at the door listening to the 'Exorcist', Seany moved around the cell; he didn't believe in God so why should he believe in the devil. While the story was being told, he took a string out of one of his blankets and tied the end of it around the handle of his piss pot. He led the string up the side of his bed hiding it from view. At the end of the book Seamy sat down on his mattress, saw that Seany was sleeping, and began his nightly prayers. Seany, watching him out of a slightly open eye, tugged on the string, and the pot moved slightly. Seamy froze, and looked around the cell for the sound. But he saw nothing and returned to his prayers. Several minutes later Seany pulled the string again and this time Seamy caught the movement. Seamy hissed Seany's name but got no response. The pot moved further towards him. Seamy shook Seany, 'Right Seany, stop the messing about'. Seany asked him what he was talking about and at the same time tugged the string, then sat right up and said, 'Jesus, did you see that? Are you trying to mess me around?' The pot moved again and Seany shouted to Seamy to throw his rosary beds at it — not the sort of thing that Seamy expects from an atheist, so he began to panic. Grabbing the beads he ran towards the pot and kicked it into the air. Seany felt the string in his hands go taut and gave it a tug. The pot stopped dead and dropped straight to the ground. That was enough for Seamy; he went into hysterics. Seany, being an ardent fan of the cinema, slapped Seamy in an attempt to calm him down. This he repeated five or six times before he finally succeeded.

One bloke in the far wing, Hector, had been shot in the leg while being arrested; as a result one leg was shorter than the other. At the time the hospital wanted to amputate the leg because of the mess it was in, but Hector refused. During one bad move the running affected his leg and it started to twitch and spasm. The prison doctor said it was in a dangerous state and should come off. Once more he refused and after months of arguing, the prison issued him with a walking stick. At mass one Sunday a priest from the Philippines came in. He told us of the brutal regime under Marcos: the torture, disappearances, the execution of students. He was a very down-to-earth man. After the homily at the 'Lord hear us', instead of going off on his own and the rest of us responding, he invited anyone who wanted to make a contribution. While he explained what he wanted, the bloke sitting behind Hector removed his stick and passed it to the back of the canteen. Martin stood up, 'For our wives and children, Lord hear us'. 'Lord graciously hear us.' Sean followed, 'For our parents, families and friends.' Next Hector got up, 'For the bastard who stole my walking stick.' There was stunned silence until the priest, seeing the funny side, laughed, making way for the rest of us. No one was excommunicated and the walking stick was returned in double quick time, never to be removed again.

A lot of the screws who messed around during the moves would be timid on their own. One such screw we had named 'Vinegar-face'. In response to this, Teapot and Hector scraped the words 'Vinegar-face has no balls' onto their cell door. That afternoon when Vinegar-face came around with the tea, he noticed the writing and said, 'Whoever wrote that has no balls; they wouldn't sign it.' That night when he came around with the supper the notice had been amended, 'Vinegar-face has no balls, signed Teapot and Hector.' Teapot and Hector stood at the door and said to him, 'Who has no balls?' He just closed the door and walked away.

Sean Lennon . . .

Just a few weeks before the no-wash protest began Bobby Sands was moved from the far wing into the cell with me. I got to know Bobby while on remand. My first impressions of him were of a very energetic and outward going person who seemed to know what he wanted. He was very sociable and easy to get on with. If he wasn't organising protests while on remand he was playing football, doing quizzes or something else to help keep morale up. He was the target of the screws, who saw him as one of the main movers in the jail. However, he was moved in along with me and I was with him until we were moved up to the isolation wing in H6. I got to know him as well as I know most of my relations.

When you live with a person 24 hours of every day in an area 9 feet by 7 feet then there isn't too much you don't know about him. I remember the very first political discussion I had with him; it was to do with the Easter Rising and when all was said and done, we agreed to disagree. He was right in what he was arguing and it was my lack of awareness of class politics at the time that made me argue from a pure nationalistic point of view. In later years I saw clearly what he was saying and now feel the same way as he did all those years ago. That discussion went on for most of the day and we only stopped to get the grub in, then back to it hot and heavy.

When we weren't debating we were doing quizzes between ourselves. He'd ask me questions and I'd do likewise and we would award each other points for the right answers. He was also teaching me the Gaeilge and it was his persuasion that made me carry on with it. He was a compulsive writer and at every chance he had the pen out drawing up articles and doing poems and songs. He was also a brave decent singer and wasn't a bit shy when it came to his turn for a song. As a matter of fact he'd sit in the cell clearing his throat for an hour before being called and then when he got to the door it was a fight to get him down. But the lads enjoyed the singing.

Another thing which we started to do at night was tell books we had read over the years. The person would get the story strung together and when the screws put the cell lights out, which was usually around 11pm, he would go to the door and begin the book. I found this very enjoyable and it was very popular with all the men and lasted for the duration of the protest. Bobby proved himself to be a worthwhile scéalaí.

One of the yarns made famous was the time Bobby told us the book 'Trinity' (by Leon Uris) out the door. It was while we were in H6 and it took him about four weeks to put it together — it was worth it at the end of the day. Bobby was a perfectionist and to ensure he got it right he asked the lads in the conforming wing which was facing us to help him in his research. He shouted across the yard to them at night with certain questions and if they didn't have the answers he asked them to find out the following day from the lads they worked with in the workshops. This went on until he was ready and it took him three to four weeks to cover it — that was spending two to three hours nightly at the door.

In H6 I was in the cell with Larry Marley, who was a compulsive smoker; as the snout came in he just smoked one after the other until it was done. On one particularly cold winter's night when the snow was lying on the ground there wasn't a bit of snout in the place and Larry and all the smokers were doing a wee bit of heavy wack. But as we sat on the mattresses in the cell talking, a big plastic bag suddenly came through the cell window, or rather through the gap that once was a pane of glass. The bag landed between us and in it we found to our delight not only snout, but a bag of sweets. Well, I can't express the look of happiness on Larry's face at that. 'A gift from heaven,' says I, but we knew where it came from and we thanked the source when the chance came. Once the word went around, the wing came to life and the lines were organised to get the snout across to the other side of the wing so the lads there could join in the celebration. I didn't smoke at this time, so myself and the other non-smokers got tucked into the sweets. Wee things like this may seem insignificant, but when our very food couldn't be taken for granted, such things assumed great importance. The morale in the wing was 100% (plus VAT!) that night.

DAVY GLENNON . . .

When I had to go out to the MO's room for treatment, I would grab whatever cigarette butts were around, making sure I wasn't caught by the screws. This was common practice among us. One particular day I was between the grilles at the bottom of the wing with Hush Hush (Kieran Fleming), both of us waiting to see the MO. It was a bad day for smokers; everyone in the wing was out of tobacco, so a good-sized butt was all the more valuable. I was telling Hush Hush that I was going nuts for a smoke when I spotted the screw sitting at the table between the grilles with an ashtray packed full of enormous butts. I said to Hush Hush, knowing I had no chance of getting at them, that I'd be a happy man with those butts. He said to me, 'Do you want them?' (Silly question.) Then he said to the screw, very authoritatively, 'Give that ashtray over,' which the screw did. Hush Hush opened my hand and emptied the ash tray into it before giving it back to the screw empty. The screw and I looked at each other; I think we were both amazed at Hush Hush's brass neck. But I wasn't worried because I had my smoke and some spare for the other lads.

EOGHAN MACCORMAIC . . .

There was a big Scottish screw working in the wing for a while and he was what we called a 'red', which meant that he didn't know the ropes. He was a smoker, and someone asked him for a smoke one day and he said he would think about it. I suppose it was before he realised that he was supposed to hate us. Now at this time on the outside speculation was rife that the Brits were about to concede to our demands and that the return of status was more or less imminent. I'm sure the screw had heard as much himself, and within the Block we were keeping up a pretty confident appearance of victory.

A few days later the screw was shutting Joe McDonnell's door after the slop out and Joe asked him for a smoke. 'If I give you one will you pay me back when you get your status?' asked the screw in all seriousness. It was like 'Remember me when you come into your Kingdom.' Quick as a flash Joe replied that he certainly would. 'Well,' said the screw, 'I'd like to give you a cigarette but I can't. You see, I've started using roll-ups,' and he took a pouch of tobacco from his pocket. 'This wouldn't be of any use to you,' he said, opening the loose tobacco.

Before he had the words out, Joe had his hand buried in the pouch and he lifted out a handful of tobacco, hardly believing his luck at the screw's stupidity. 'But you've no papers to roll it in,' said the screw. 'We'll manage,' said Joe. Of course the screw wouldn't have known at that time that we were using toilet paper for the hand-rolling tobacco.

The screw shut the door and walked away shaking his head, knowing he had been conned but not quite knowing how. But he wasn't finished. A few minutes later he returned and asked Joe how he was going to light the cigarette. Joe said nothing but pointed his finger at the cell light. 'Why didn't I think of that,' said the screw really impressed and, satisfied, he walked away. That night Joe couldn't stop laughing at the stroke, and the whole wing of course shared the spoils of his battle.

6

Brutality and Resistance

January 1979 – September 1980

In the next year the prisoners had to tap deep reserves of resistance as the screws continued their offensive. 1979 began with the removal to H6 of around 30 prisoners, among them were those the prison administration regarded as the leadership of the protest. While the regime in H5 was eased somewhat, conditions in H3 and H4 worsened and brutality there reached new heights.

In September the isolation wing in H6 was closed down and the men in it dispersed throughout the other Blanket Blocks. Talk of a hunger strike to bring the protest to a head was common, but the leadership of the Republican Movement made clear its opposition to such a course. In October a National H-Block/Armagh Committee was formed to co-ordinate publicity and protests outside. After much discussion the prisoners in January 1980 issued their Five Demands, a redefinition and explanation of what they meant by political status, and it was around these demands that support was sought nationally and internationally.

In March Cardinal Tomás Ó Fiaich began talks about the prison crisis with the British Secretary of State Humphrey Atkins. These were to drag on for six months before ending inconclusively, just prior to the visit to Ireland of Pope John Paul in September 1980. Despite significant pressure the British remained intransigent, offering only the most minor of concessions to fob off bodies like the Catholic Church. Having tried every avenue to achieve an honourable settlement, the prisoners were left with only one option: hunger strike.

BIK MCFARLANE . . .

January 1979 concentrated our minds on two unrelated aspects: the sub-zero temperatures of an unusually bitter, freezing winter which had to be faced in windowless cells and with screws heaping snow through the bars in shovelfuls, and the sinister removal of 32 of us to H6 where we expected to be subjected to a concentrated onslaught. Our camp leadership was among our number and if the Brits could break any of us, then it could possibly lead to a drop in morale among the Blanketmen.

FELIM O'HAGAN . . .

The weather at the turn of the year was atrocious: bitterly cold, too cold sometimes to stand yarning at the windows even with three blankets wrapped around you. We were often forced to lie along the heating pipes in the cell, hugging them in an effort to get some warmth into our bodies.

JOE MCQUILLAN . . .

I never liked to pace the floor at the best of times; as the floor was at freezing point, there was less chance now, though some of the hardier men would still pace it for up to 12 hours a day. Pouring the urine out the door and having to bale out in the middle of the night became a painful exercise; the ice-cold liquid turned our hands purple. When it snowed the screws came round in the middle of the night with shovels and threw masses of it into the cells on top of us. Despite the snow landing right beside the heating pipes, it would still be there the following morning. Wing shifts were all the harsher as we were left for up to 12 hours with only a thin towel. To make matters worse the winter was a bad one, with the night of January 13/14 1979 having the lowest temperature ever recorded (the weather station at Magherally, near Banbridge, recorded minus 17.5°C). It was also this night that the screws said the heating system broke down, but we were more inclined to believe it was deliberately turned off. It is amazing that no one froze to death.

During the summer we had fed maggots to the birds. Now one particular wagtail became more and more adventurous, coming first to our window and then daring to come into the cells to forage in the corners for morsels of food. It had only one foot and a stump where the other should have been. Being original, the wing decided to call him 'Hoppy'. We agreed that he should be sworn in as an honorary Volunteer which would allow him to enter any cell without being harassed. It was a cheering sight to watch him dart around the cell with his one leg, hopping only feet from one's head.

Felim O'Hagan . . .

One day in January the screws opened our door unexpectedly and my cellmate, Paddy Quinn, and I immediately tensed, preparing ourselves for a cell-search and the customary beating it entailed. However, the screws ordered Paddy to get his stuff together – not a big job as he only had a bible and rosary beads – and said he was moving. Paddy asked where he was going, the screw replied curtly 'H9'. Now, I knew there were only eight H-Blocks and suspected the screw was messing; but still, there was a doubt planted in my mind. Had they built another H-Block? If so, was it even in the camp itself? Could they be taking Paddy somewhere else, Magilligan perhaps? As we somewhat apprehensively said 'slán', I was left to puzzle about what was going on.

A half dozen or so other men from H4 were also moved that same day and, after a few days, the full picture emerged. Around 30 men had been taken out of the three Blanket Blocks and placed in one wing in H6. (There was no such place as H9, I discovered). H3, H4 and H5 are all in the same phase; H6 is in a different phase, separated by an internal wall, and is about as far away from them as it's possible to be within the camp. Those moved included Brendan Hughes (the Blocks O/C), Bobby Sands and many whom the prison administration would have considered 'leaders', or at least those with greater experience of jail. It was obvious that they were being isolated. We didn't know then what exactly the screws were up to, and what it would mean for us in H3, H4 and H5, We were soon to find out.

Sean Lennon . . .

Each of the three Blanket Blocks lost around 10 men. When we arrived in H6 the PO told us that the towels would be taken away and we'd have to wear the trousers when on the landing; we would also have to go out to the circle to see the governor (the usual procedure was that he came to us). We held a meeting that night. We all realised what they were up to; if they could get us to wear the trousers outside the cell and go to the circle to see the governor, then with their view of us as the 'leadership' of the protest, this would be a major breakthrough for them. We also accepted that if we did comply with these new restrictions, they'd implement them in the other Blocks within days. So we decided that we would refuse to wear the trousers and also refuse to move out of the cell naked. We would only leave the cells if we were allowed to wear either a blanket or a towel. When the screws came to get us to go to the governor or any other place, we refused. They came in and trailed us to wherever they wanted us. They also used violence against us, but we stood firm.

BIK MCFARLANE . . .

After the initial couple of weeks of constant brutality and harassment our situation levelled off to a bizarre, uneasy sort of peace. The wing shifts were more frequent but, apart from the actual struggling to resist the mirror search, no one was physically attacked in H6. Brutality took the form of food rationed to a bare minimum and frequently stolen, water being jetted through door slits, constant moves and the more frequent humiliation of the mirror searches.

We quickly settled into our routine: pacing the cell the customary and inhibitive five steps up and down during the morning and afternoon; ranganna Gaeilge during the quiet of the dinner period; debates, discussions and entertainment in the late evening. The little lines, drawing tobacco-rolls across the corridor between cells, religiously made their early evening journeys – religiously in more than one way, as silent prayers were mouthed against potential mishaps en route. Lighted wicks were slipped through joints in the wall along the heating pipes and every evening those who indulged savoured the aroma of Old Holborn, or in dire times of tobacco famine, dried tea-leaves augmented by the shredded dried stalk of an apple. We survived admirably in a limbo-like environment. The excess of brutality which we had all experienced the previous year now largely passed us by, only to be unleashed with fury upon our comrades in the other Blanket Blocks, in particular H3 and H4. There was a frenzied savagery on the loose on those Blocks throughout 1979.

PETER CUNNINGHAM . . .

The moves of the OCs and perceived leaders to H6 was an obvious attempt to undermine us. It failed and in a sense turned in our favour as it strengthened us. The screws, although given to bouts of physical abuse, hadn't systematically gone overboard with their beatings and pettiness. But as soon as those lads were taken from our Block, H4, to H6 they just upped everything. The mirror search was well and truly established by now and became the source of most of the screws beatings which had steadily increased in viciousness. One of the screws' offensives became known as 'gan tuáille'.

'Gan tuaille' means 'without a towel' and that was what they tried to make us do – walk about naked. When moving from wing to wing or from cell to cell for a search we would normally wear towels. We refused to move about naked and when they came for a cell search, which was a pretext for trying to implement their ruling, we would sit down on the floor after they had pulled the towel off. They would kick and punch, drag and trail us along the landing up to cell 26 where they forced us over the mirror. They carried on this way every day for a week, giving each cell a 'search' every other day with one or two of the lads picked for special attention: cell-searched every day.

Their next offensive came in the form of 'wall-facing'. This applied during wing moves and was enthusiastically enforced. When we came to the grilles between wings, a screw would tell us to face a wall and when we refused, he would push – or sometimes slam – our faces into it. Leo Green, the Block OC, asked the PO why this wall-facing was being implemented. He was told it was because they didn't want us to know the geography of the place – at least someone found matters humorous.

LEO GREEN . . .

At times, beatings were simply a manifestation of the screws' hatred of all we stood for. At other times, they were systematic, obviously organised and measured in degree and, therefore, clearly acting as an instrument of NIO prison policy.

My own experience of brutality at its most intense occurred in the last two weeks of April 1979, one of which is indelibly etched in the minds of POWs who were in H4 at the time as the 'Seachtain dona' (bad week). By then, incidents of ill-treatment and attacks on prisoners in H4 were almost a daily occurrence. During these particular weeks the situation boiled over and seemed for a few days to have gone irretrievably out of control, and likely to result in the serious injury of many prisoners.

In mid-April two screws were executed, one by the IRA in Tyrone and the other, a woman, by the INLA in Armagh. We had long become accustomed to the screws exacting revenge on us in the wake of such attacks on the outside. Usually the jail administration had simply turned a blind eye. On this occasion they appeared to have given it a stamp of approval. For a few days they ensured a tense uneasy calm in the Block. They then withdrew the Block PO and SO, the two senior screws charged with running the Block. Jail management handed over control of the Block to ordinary screws for the next two weeks. For the first of these the screws ran rampant. In a period of 10 days something like 150 incidents occurred in which men were assaulted.

PETER CUNNINGHAM . . .

For a few days the screws did cell searches; some beatings were handed out, but not everyone was beaten. Then after mass on Sunday things went into overdrive. Each of us was beaten after being forced over the mirror. That afternoon and every morning and afternoon for a week after it cell searches were carried out and each of us was beaten while we stood over the mirror refusing to squat.

There was no let-up as they hit the cells in the mornings and afternoons, a cell every second day. Again one or two were picked for 'special attention' and these men were hammered every day. By the Wednesday or Thursday we knew when it was our turn to be beaten. If we were in any doubt, the screw, 'after consulting my black book' as he put it, let us know which cells he would be 'visiting'. There were instances of one particular screw coming around the cells and asking some of the lads why they were giving him 'dirty looks' during the beatings. They came to our cell, and asked Rab Collins, my cellmate, to stop giving dirty looks and had the neck to ask him to promise that when he would be in the big cell tomorrow not to give dirty looks. As soon as they left our cell, we just looked at each other and said, 'these characters are going to kill somebody'.

On Thursday the worst thing possible happened when one of the lads left the protest. This was what they wanted and it just whetted their appetite. They increased their brutality, concentrating on the cellmate of the man who had left and one or two others. Tea was poured over men's heads, apples smashed into their faces and heads along with the usual kicking and punching. At 8.30 every night, when the screws left, the relief that washed over our wing was beyond description. To hear talking, laughter and words of encouragement and support coming from behind cell doors as we joked with each other was the sweetest, most heartening and most welcome part of the day, but more so on this particular night.

The following day, two new men from the Crum came on to our wing and were immediately subjected to beatings and verbal abuse with the promise of more when the class officer returned. Saturday morning came and the two men left the protest but not before being put into the class office facing the big cell from where they were able to hear and see the rest of the wing being beaten as they stood over the mirror refusing to squat. That afternoon another of the lads left the protest and one screw in particular went haywire, no doubt encouraged by results so far. All pretence of cell searches and mirror searches was cast aside. In his quest for further results he went from cell to cell with the backing and assistance of the other screws and on certain occasions the orderlies, punching and kicking, ranting and raving. He threw meals at some men and in those cells with just one man he would increase his brutality in the vain hope of breaking others. The atmosphere in our wing was unbelievable and made even worse when the same screw walked or ran up and down the wing kicking at cell doors shouting and yelling, 'I'm the king of the wing! I'm the OC!' The following day, Sunday, saw an end to that particular phase.

LEO GREEN . . .

On Sundays when we all came together for mass in the canteen it was usually like the Tower of Babel. That Sunday after the seachtain dona it was more like the Tower of Pisa – none of us very sure just how much longer we could hang on. I remember well the faces that day. I took some reassurance from seeing that others were as shaken as myself by what was happening. There were no smiles, no longer any cause for or pretence of optimism. The scéal maith (good news), the American dockers, the other optimistic rumours were all by then an age away.

April 1979 was the culmination of a politically chastening process which had been underway for the previous six months. The harassment and ill-treatment we had endured had shown us our own naivety. The light at the end of the tunnel we had heard about so often in messages of support seemed altogether extinguished. Our protest as it stood showed little sign of bringing about the conclusion we sought. We were in a corner and becoming increasingly aware of it.

PETER CUNNINGHAM . . .

Throughout 1979 the screws continued to beat, degrade and humiliate us constantly. They cut our food and tampered with it; they regulated the pipes, colder or warmer depending on the time of the year; they sometimes stopped visits; and they even attempted to sow ill-feeling among us by giving in one plate full with food and the other almost empty.

CIARAN McGILLICUDDY . . .

I only thought of leaving the Blanket once. I had been in my cell for about five months on my own and I was feeling really down. I had a great fear of the beatings – I was really afraid. The night before the screws had beaten a number of men. They were doing cell searches and each time they came down the wing, I'd pray they'd pass my door. I was standing in the corner of my cell shaking with fear. They didn't come to my cell that night. The next day I went over whether I should go or not. I kept saying to myself, 'Sure you're only a kid; these are all men and some of them are going'. I walked up to the bell button and, as I reached for it, my granny came into my mind. I had asked her the day I came into the Block to help me. Once I thought of her, I turned away from the bell and took whatever they did to me.

In July 1979, while I was at mass, one of the lads gave me a pen and a few skins to write on. I hid them up my backside and went back to the wing. When I got there the screws were doing the mirror search. When they got me bent over the mirror one of them said he could see something. They took me out to the MO who said the same. They asked me to give them whatever it was but I refused. They sent for a van to take me to the boards. They had also seen something on Pius McNaught. On the way down to the boards we got talking and we agreed that if they were going to take the stuff out we may as well give it to them as they'd get it anyway.

When we got to the boards they stood us at the top of both wings and called Pius first. Off he went. The cell he went to was only about 15 feet away. I heard a lot of moaning and a bit of a beating and the next thing about eight screws came out, each with a big smile. One was carrying what looked like a pair of pliers and in them he had a little parcel which was covered in blood. I nearly died. I couldn't understand it as we had agreed to give them our parcels. I assumed he had changed his mind.

They took me down to another cell in the other wing. When I got to the cell I went right to the back wall and turned to see a crowd of screws standing around me. They asked me for the parcel but I had made up my mind that since Pius wouldn't give it, I wouldn't, so I refused. Three screws were standing at the door and the other five were in the cell. The MO was at the door. When I refused they told me to turn and face the wall. I said 'No', so one of them grabbed me by the hair and turned me round. Two more grabbed my arms up my back. My arms were straight out from my body with my hands bent back towards my elbows. This made me bend over and with one screw pulling my hair; my head was nearly between my knees. This was beside the small stool in the cell which was about two and a half feet off the floor. They put my shoulders onto this. The screw who had my hair let go as my head was now caught and forced down onto the stool. Then two more screws came and lifted my legs into the air. This left me upside down with my head between my legs, four screws holding me with the screw who had been holding my hair free to do his work. I could hardly breathe and I thought I was going to pass out. They were all laughing out loud and then he came with the pliers. I remember him putting them into me and he nipped me two or three times. If I cried out, the screws holding me would push me to keep me quiet. They got the pen and paper and they all kept laughing at me.

When they left and the door closed, I sat down on the small stool. Once I knew they weren't coming back, I cried. I had no clothes on. It was 12.00pm when I went to the boards and the next thing I remember was the door opening for my tea which was at 4.00pm and I was still sitting on the stool with no clothes on. I remember feeling dirty, I wanted to ask for a bath. Everything was going through my mind and I wondered if I could take any more of this. The only thing I thought to myself was that they couldn't hurt me any more than this.

On the way back to the Block I asked Pius why he had refused to give them his parcel. He said that he didn't; he had given it to them like we agreed. I said I heard the beating and he said that was just them giving out a bit of stick.

I know for me the above has, since that day, been a very emotional topic to talk about even though it happened over ten years ago now. It gives me great pain whenever I talk or think about it.

KEVIN CAMPBELL . . .

Things started to change in H5 with the introduction of a new Block PO. This brought an end to the real brutal regime which had existed up until then; although beatings still went on, they were not on the same scale. We were now getting sugar on our porridge and jam twice a week. To the outsider this may seem really nothing, but to us it was like getting £100. We had nothing, so anything over and above this was just heaven. At first we couldn't understand this change in tactics. In the other Blocks nothing had changed. They were known as 'The Nightmare Blocks'. After discussing the new tactics, we in H5 concluded that it was the Brits using their old tactic of divide and conquer; they were trying to create an atmosphere where the Blanketmen in the other two Blocks would start asking questions such as, 'What are the men in H5 doing to receive such treatment?' and effectively cause a split. But this failed and we saw through the change in direction. Even though they changed the food slightly, the physical conditions didn't change at all; we were still living in maggot-infested cells with filth and squalor around us.

SÉANNA WALSH . . .

While we were in H6, Fermanagh/South Tyrone MP Frank Maguire came in to see us. The lads on the wing were feeling a bit glum − the 'pony express' had failed to get through with the 'bia beatha' (the food of life: tobacco); Rab McCallum from Ardoyne had been caught coming back from a visit with a half ounce of tobacco in his mouth; it was confiscated and Rab was put on report till the boards were ready to process him for smuggling contraband. The lads weren't expecting another shipment until the next week and they hadn't a butt between them; everybody was feeling sorry for himself. Into the middle of this breezed Frank.

We heard a bit of activity at the bottom of the wing. Jonesy (a Welsh former British soldier was on the wing as class officer) could be heard saying, 'Look at what we have to put up with here; believe it or not he had this in his mouth and he was trying to smuggle it into the prison'. 'Well, maybe if they were allowed tobacco they wouldn't try to smuggle it,' was the reply. Right away the lads knew this visitor was no ordinary NIO yes man and so the shouting started. 'Cé hé sin?' (Who's that?') 'Níl a fhios agam' (I don't know). As the lads at the bottom end of the wing crawled on their bellies to get a look out of the right hand corner of the doors, he came up and asked to get in to see a couple of the lads. He was directed to Bobby and the Dark who weren't long in letting the rest of us know who he was. They gave him a bit of an earbashing but he was pleasant and understanding enough of our situation, having been a Republican prisoner himself in the fifties or thereabouts. It was shortly after the general election, and what really had him buzzing was that Austin Currie had run against him and had been disowned by even his own SDLP colleagues who saw Currie, rightly, as a spoiler rather than a meaningful contender. In the end the people of Fermanagh and Tyrone rallied around Maguire and he was returned with an increased majority, leaving Currie with a miserable few thousand. After half an hour or so of craic he headed on to visit the rest of the lads in the other Blocks and as he's safe from the wrath of the prison regime now, it would do no harm to recall how the lads were puffing well for the following few nights, courtesy of the member for Fermanagh/South Tyrone.

JOE McQUILLAN . . .

Just as we had survived the cold winter without windows the administration, not wanting us to enjoy the coming summer, tried out their new invention: a new window, more of a cage that fitted over the outside of the window frame. It had two sides, an outward sloping roof but no bottom. It sat about a foot out from the wall so any attempt to burn it would only fall on the ground. The bottom of the front was frosted perspex. The top few feet were made of clear perspex. If we wanted to see out we had to stand on the pipes; this gave a view of the sky. On the inside of the cells they put up a metal wire grille; the wire was about 5mm thick with holes in it barely big enough to get your finger tips into.

SEAN LENNON . . .

While we were in H6 the screws put a non-political Protestant prisoner into our wing. They probably expected us to persecute him as they and the Loyalists had done. He was called Billy M and he came from East Belfast. He had bought stuff from the prison tuck shop for his daughter's birthday and requested from the governor permission to bring it down on the visit with him to give it to his daughter, rather than have her get it from a stranger. His request was refused so Billy protested about the pettiness and was sent to the boards where he went on protest. He was moved back on to the conforming wings, but after a while he was back on the boards where he continued his protest. While we were in H6 there were about a dozen Loyalists on the Blanket in the wing across the yard from us, a wing which also held conforming prisoners. The screws put Billy onto that wing but the Loyalists put him off, so he ended up in our wing. We had a meeting among ourselves and decided that we were not going to continue with the messing about of Billy, so we allowed him to stay, much to the dismay of the screws. He was there for a few months, then he was moved.

JOE MCQUILLAN . . .

We got a new orderly, Tommy M from Derry. He came into jail on a Republican charge for killing a soldier. After his trial he decided not only to change his religion – he had 'seen the light' – but to get out of jail early, so he became a Blanket orderly. He seemed to take delight in abusing his former comrades and the people he had grown up with. He had been working in the other Blocks and the first we knew he had moved to H3 was a voice shouting at one of the 'decent' screws, 'What are you giving those bastards so much grub for? Are you a Fenian lover?' At first we thought it was a screw, then when the doors opened we saw Tommy. He was now siding with the screws and the British government in an attempt to criminalise us. Some religious minister wrote a song about him proclaiming how great a conversion he had made, how he denounced violence and followed the way of the Lord. If only he could have seen the fine fellow at work.

BIK MCFARLANE . . .

With the growing awareness that the Brits now had the measure of us as far as the no-wash protest was concerned, we looked of necessity to our ultimate protest action. Our situation was impossible to resolve successfully without recourse to hunger strike. We could not, nor would not submit to criminalisation of ourselves and, by extension, of the liberation struggle. We discussed the hunger strike option and raised it with the leadership of the Republican Movement. It was felt that an excellent opportunity was on the horizon with the forthcoming papal visit to Ireland – a hunger strike, reaching a crisis period around September, when the Pope would be here, would be sure to cause a furore and provoke responses from political and religious circles.

There was uncertainty as to exactly when a crisis period on hunger strike would occur, but a figure of around 30-35 days somehow took root. There was even a suggestion that we only gear ourselves for a 30-day hunger strike and then suspend action approaching the believed crisis, offering the

Brits some space to manoeuvre and simultaneously indicating a degree of flexibility on our part. This tactic was considered and possibly forwarded to the leadership, but a number of us felt that this was a highly dangerous manoeuvre. It could send the wrong signal to the Brits (and to our own support base) that we weren't prepared to carry a hunger strike to its ultimate conclusion. Therefore any follow-up hunger strike action was bound to be met confidently by the Brits with an increased risk of deaths. Those who had reservations expressed them to the camp staff and urged the OC only to consider hunger strike action if it were to be complete and uninterrupted – not a tactical 'partial' hunger strike. Very few amongst the 30 or so in H6 at the time were aware of these particular tactics being discussed. The camp staff 'think-tank' consisted of only three or four men with very limited input from the OCs of other Blocks. Both myself and my cellmate (Joe Barnes) were somewhat on the periphery at that stage, although occasionally we were asked for our opinions.

Such was our thinking during that summer. Overtures were made to us by Cardinal Ó Fiaich dissuading us from hunger strike action, in order not to place John Paul II in an embarrassing position. With it came the promise to pursue the British administration relentlessly to seek an honourable settlement for all concerned. The Republican Movement leadership made it crystal clear that they were very much opposed to the hunger strike. They further pointed out that mobilising support at that stage on the issue would be extremely difficult – at least to the degree necessary to reflect the gravity of the situation. We should hold firm and explore other avenues. But no other avenues existed which carried any significant weight of pressure. So we were faced with quite a dilemma. How could we hold firm against the clamour of our own ranks who were being systematically brutalised on a daily basis, when we could offer no light at the end of the tunnel?

His Holiness came and went, as did we from H6, dispersed through the other three Blanket Blocks. Eight of us went to H3 and I found myself doubled up with my mate Jake Jackson.

A 'reception committee' battered each of us over the mirror. There was a foreboding atmosphere hanging over H3 and I could feel the tension as I walked onto the wing to be greeted only by a strange, subdued silence. The screws displayed a higher than previously experienced degree of animosity and were at pains to point out that our 'holiday camp days' in H6 were at an end. They assured us we would from then on know what a 'real protest' held in store – an obvious reference to the barbarity they had meted out to our comrades over the previous 18 months.

The following days were to reveal the full horror of life in H3 as men related nightmarish experiences of barbarous treatment. I listened helplessly as men were repeatedly beaten during mirror searches after their visits. Men were doggedly resisting here, refusing to be broken, but morale was anything but high. It was a depressing place indeed.

LEONARD FERRIN . . .

One of the worst wing moves I can recall happened in direct response to the dispersal of the isolation wing from H6 in September 1979. The men who arrived in H3 were mostly dispatched to the opposite side of the Block from us (D wing). They included The Dark, Bobby Sands, Tom McElwee and Bik McFarlane. It had seemed at this period that the screws had all but given up the severe beatings, which had been regular occurrences during wing moves in H3. They had adopted the more subtle tactics of humiliation by forcing us to endure mirror searches. But plans were afoot to ascertain who held power – the prisoners or the screws in H3.

In B wing we learnt the following day that we were to move across the Block to C wing which lay empty. Before the move got underway the stand-in PO, who was a liberal type, was relieved of duties and moved elsewhere in the camp. It was then we realised that a 'show' had been organised by the powers-that-be and we were to be the unfortunate battered cast. Each man from cell 3 to cell 25 was beaten mercilessly from B wing to C wing. Such tactics reinforced our resolve to win. It seemed to trigger off a collective message that we weren't going to allow them to grind us down. I'm sure our torturers knew that we remained unbroken, as 48 Blanketmen sang them out of the wing that day with a chorus of 'Provos March On' ringing in their ears.

SEAN LENNON . . .

The stories began about the treatment being handed out to the lads in H3. Although we were getting all the scéal from all the Blocks regularly about the goings-on and the beatings, it wasn't the same as hearing it at first hand from the men themselves. The biggest bone of contention was the mirror search. Although at times it was rough enough, after a while the practice in H6 and H5 became a case of pushing and shoving. They pushed us over the mirror, we tried to push ourselves back off it and the odd slap came from time to time. Not so in H3 and H4. The men there were being beaten very badly every time they were put over the mirror and morale wasn't the best.

After the Dark and those from whom he sought counsel analysed the situation in the cold light of day, the logic of the year before, when the Block OC hadn't given the order to fight the screws when they came to take them out for forced baths, was recalled. So a decision was made from a purely tactical point of view that, instead of refusing to go over the mirror, we would go over it without protest, thus taking from them another excuse for beating us. Some may say that this went on for years with no change but once the 'Leadership' were moved in they decided it was time for change. Well, that wasn't the case and, had the OC comprehended fully the extent of the beatings over this issue while he was in another Block, he would have made the same decision. The reality was we were all scattered around the camp and we saw everything from the perspective of the Block we were in at any particular time. The decision was made and there was great relief in the Block when the men were told.

All sorts of questions were being put to myself and Joe, the lads thinking we were privy to heavy scéal. When we couldn't answer their questions they wouldn't believe us, thinking we were holding out on them. It was true we didn't know much more than them. No matter, the Dark began to clarify a lot of things for them.

LEONARD FERRIN . . .

During 1979 Tom McElwee was moved to a wing in H3 which held the Dark and Bobby Sands. He was an appellant at the time and therefore entitled to receive five 15 minute appeal visits per week, which made him a vital link in the jail communications - so much so that Bob used to panic whenever they received wing moves or cell searches for fear of Tom lashing out at the screws. Like the rest of the lads, Bobby knew that Big Tom was fearless in facing up to the tyrant screw. He would constantly stress the importance of him avoiding trouble and being sent to the boards, because the staff could ill-afford to lose his services as a courier and link man. Tom usually replied that unless it were 'dire circumstances' he wouldn't strike out, though these assurances never did much good for Bob's nervous system.

Then one day all hell broke loose. Tom had been out on a visit and was returning to his wing in H3. He had in his possession a comm for the camp OC from outside and as he approached his wing he sneezed. The comm fell to the floor beside the feet of the grille screw (The Albanach) who stooped to capture it when – bang! – he hit the back wall. Two other screws were witnessing the whole happenings from C wing. One of them, known appropriately by the Blanketmen as Beal Mór (Big Mouth), attempted to rush Big Tom, while the more sensible chap looked in the opposite direction. As Beal Mór tried to wrestle the retrieved comm from Tom, he was dispatched in the same way as the unfortunate grilleman. Tom casually proceeded down the wing to inform the lads that, even though he would undoubtedly be going to the boards for leaving the screws in a heap, he wanted them to know that the comm was secure and even found time to jovially seek absolution from Bob by claiming that his predicament fell within that 'dire circumstances' clause he talked about.

The other incident took place a year later, in 1980, as Tom left the canteen after mass. It was quite normal procedure in those days that the men would be searched before and after the Sunday mass. It usually consisted of each man having his only form of clothing – prison trousers – frisked and his mouth and hair searched. These checks were often used by the bigots to express their abhorrence of Catholicism. On this particular day a number of the lads mentioned that, along with the verbal abuse from the search team, they had received a rough search from a screw known as Beola Móra (Big Lips). He was a large grey-haired man well in excess of six feet tall, but very short in self-esteem and gullible to his colleagues' manipulation. Beola Móra had been involved in a number of assaults on Republicans prior to this incident and had the reputation of a showman who attempted – at the prisoners' expense – to win the favour of the 'pack'.

Mass finished and the lads started to filter back to their cells in pairs (controlled movement enforced by the administration). As Tom and his cellmate left the canteen and approached the search, they could see that out of the horde of screws mingling at the check, Beola Móra was one of the two searchers. Would Beola Móra try to impress the onlookers? He pulled at Tom's beard while checking his mouth, then gave his trousers a frisk. As Tom parted his feet to allow for the inside of his trouser legs to be rubbed down, Beola Móra brought his hand up in a rapid movement so as to strike Tom's testicles. This was the final straw. Tom threw an almighty punch that sent Beola Móra's false teeth in all directions. Tom was subsequently taken to the boards. It was but one of the hundreds of cases throughout the years where Republican prisoners have been logged into jail administrators' manuals for breaching 'Prison Rules'. History and their consciences shall judge them.

Thomas Loughlin . . .

Getting scéal was always difficult when there were no visits. One morning Big Jonesy, an orderly, was cleaning up the piss at the top of the landing. He called one of the lads up to the door and said that at least 18 Brits had been killed on the border and Mountbatten was also killed. Before he could be asked for details, he rushed away. The lad who got the scéal couldn't make the connection between the Brits and Mountbatten, 'What could he be doing on the border with them?', he wondered. He reckoned it must have been the Indian border, as 'Lord Louis' had something to do with India, 'and didn't Jonsey say something about a boat?' That's it then, 18 Brits and

Mountbatten were killed in a boating accident in India. That's how the story went until we heard the real way of it and when we did the panic set in. We thought the screws would kill us. They didn't, but showed us newspaper headlines which screamed 'Bastards'. Now that was amusing.

CIARAN McGILLICUDDY . . .

The new 'hen-box' windows cut the flow of air and prevented the sun from coming into the cells. They also made it difficult to pass gear to the cell next door. So the lads came up with an idea. One man got some string from his blanket, tied a small bit of mattress to the end, dipped it in water and dropped it out the window through the wire grille. The man next door tied a small kite or parachute made of paper to the end of another piece of string and dropped it out of his window. After a while the wind had blown the parachute and both strings were tangled up.

In the winter of 1979 they put plastic chairs into our cells. The order came to break them and do our best to break the window boxes. It was a great feeling as we broke our way through the wire and then the boxes. Later the screws came into the cells to take what was left. We started to break up the chairs after the 8.30pm lock-up to give us time to do our work before the screws came around. About eight screws ran into the cell; two grabbed us, put us against the wall or pinned us down while the rest took every bit of chair and other bits and pieces from the window out of the cell. I think everyone in H4 got a beating but it didn't matter as everyone's morale was sky high. We started a singsong with H5 and it went on till the early hours. We had beaten them and their windows.

Two lads who broke their chairs looked at the wire on the window and said there's no way they could break through that. So they sat down and had a good laugh at all the lads trying to break through the wire. They later said they nearly died when they heard the window boxes getting smashed. They ended up the only ones in the Blanket Blocks with the windows still in. Boy, did they take some stick.

THOMAS LOUGHLIN . . .

One evening after 5.30pm Fr Toner came into the wing; this was not unusual as he often dropped in to see us. That night he went into the cell of Spotto Devine and Eunan Brolly. Nothing appeared to be amiss as it was near Christmas time, a period when the screws tended to lay off the beatings even though most of them were drunk. So, most of the lads felt a bit secure and not too unhappy. Fr Toner visited one or two other cells then left the wing. I don't suppose anyone noticed. However, about five minutes later we heard a cell door opening and the screws shouting 'cell search'. This was always a sign of trouble, thus everyone was on his guard. As expected, the screws started beating the two lads demanding to know what the priest had given them. After about 10 minutes they went into another cell and did the same thing. My cellmate and I were that nervous that we emptied the piss pots out the window and decided, once the screws opened the door, we would batter them. If you're going to get beaten in that situation you may as well fight back, particularly as the screws were drunk.

Before we knew it, the machine for cleaning up the piss was switched on, which meant we couldn't hear a thing. This lasted for nearly two hours and during that period all of us were at the ready, waiting for the door to open; it was really a frightening situation.

What added to it was the sudden knocking on the pipe and the word being passed on that the screws were taking the lads into cell 26 and kicking them senseless. Everyone was praying for lock-up to get the screws off the wing. When the machine was switched off just before 8.30 the wing was like a morgue. The OC got up to the door and asked what happened, who was beaten. Tom McVeigh got up to the door and said the screws had him in cell 26 for about two hours interrogating him and beating him about. Apparently, one of the screws used to be an RUC man who worked in Andersonstown. He claimed that one day the IRA opened fire on him and he said he recognised Tom as the gunman. So he tried to get him to admit this. 'Well,' one of the lads shouted, 'did you sign for it?' Everyone laughed; the atmosphere was one of 'Thank God it was him and not me'.

JOE MCQUILLAN . . .

Two screws, Noddy and the Buachaill Bó, came to give the grub around the cells. They started a whole issue over the dams at the bottom of the doors (made from food to stop the urine flowing back into the cells). These dams had been in use for almost a year. As one of the blokes bent down to lift the food, a screw grabbed his hand and ran it along the dam of rotting food. The bloke, Sean Campbell, shook the goo off his hand and some of it spattered on the Buachaill Bó. He rushed into the cell with his baton drawn and Sean, to avoid the baton blow, struck out and punched him, sending him flying out of the cell where he bounced off the wall facing the open door. The other screw slammed the door. Several minutes later it reopened. The screw who had accompanied the Buachaill Bó asked Sean to come out of his cell. Sean refused. The screw told Sean that he had nothing to worry about as he had witnessed the lot and Sean was not at fault. After several minutes of reassurance from this screw that nothing would happen, that he only wanted to cool things down and so on, Sean agreed and went out of the cell. As he reached the landing the cell door was closed behind him, locking his cellmate in.

Several screws then ran up the wing with their batons out and beat Sean to the ground. He was trailed out to the circle and into the MO's room. From 12.30 until 2 o'clock every screw in the Block took it in turns to hold him against the wall while the rest punched him, kicked him and squeezed his testicles. For the first 20 minutes the screams were loud and bloodcurdling; the next hour brought long low moans full of agony. We thought they were going to kill him. Our wing was like a tomb. Not a sound from anyone, not even the clatter of rosary beads. At 2 o'clock the screws threw Sean's blanket back into his cell and his cellmate, Tomboy Loudon, said it was covered in blood.

A lot of men were approaching breaking point and wondered how much more they could take. Some newly sentenced men would come onto the protest Blocks, get up to the doors, make mad 'tiocfaidh ár lá' speeches, and leave the next morning saying they would 'see us in the Cages'. Mostly we ignored these people. When men who had been on the protest two, three, or four years left we could understand their feelings.

I remember one bloke, Jimmy R, who had been on the protest three years, telling the screws that he wanted to leave. When this happened the bloke would be taken straight out of the Block to the work Blocks. In this case the screws told the bloke that he would have to wash, shave and have his hair cut in this Block. All year the screws worked hard to demoralise and break men, yet when they succeeded they still weren't content. After several minutes we could hear the screws calling him a variety of names, shouting to one another, 'Is the bath ready for this tramp? What's the matter with you leaving? Have you no balls? Can you not stick it?' After his bath and haircut and shave he was brought into cell 26 to be given the prison uniform. From there we could hear thumps and shouts and abuse. A couple of minutes later we heard the screw say, 'Fuck him, if that's what he wants put him back into the shit'. Jimmy came back down the wing and shouted to us all that he was staying. You could hear that he was choking the tears back. 'I'm sorry, lads, for thinking about leaving. I don't know what's getting into me, but I can't go, I can't leave.' I felt as if I was on top of the world.

CIARAN McGILLICUDDY . . .

1979 had been a very bad year for beatings. On New Year's Night an SO was going round the cells asking everyone if they were alright. He had a few drinks taken and no one talked to him – how could we be alright living in such conditions? When he got to our door he asked my cellmate, Liam

Berkery, how he was. He didn't get an answer so in he came and hit Liam on the face. He asked him again and again how he was but he still didn't get an answer. This went on for a few minutes and then he started talking to the wall like a madman. He turned to me and asked me how I was. By this time I was really afraid but there was no way I would have answered him after what he had done to Liam. So it was my turn for a few slaps around the head. By this time he was starting to get mad because he was getting nowhere. He turned to Liam and once more asked him how he was. With this he hit Liam a punch in the face. I remember Liam's head rocking back and the blood splashing over the back wall. It was like the slow motion action on TV. At this the SO started to worry about what he had just done so he told Liam that he had fallen and hit his head on the pipe and that was how he had bust his nose. He beat him again so he would agree. He turned to me. As soon as I saw him looking at me, my arms were around my head. I didn't want my nose busted but he tried his best to get at me. He kept going from Liam to me shouting, 'He hit his head on the pipe!' There were three screws around the door.

He turned to me, grabbed me by the hair and pulled me into the wing. He ran me up the wing. I didn't know what lay ahead. He ran me into the canteen and pushed me forward, making me fall onto the floor. I jumped up. He just kept shouting, 'He hit his head on the pipe, didn't he?' He pushed me over to a table and pulled my hair back so I was bending backwards. It was so hard it brought my feet up onto the table. I rolled into a ball and he kept hitting me, more on the back as I had covered up. I could see his face and it put the fear of God into me because I could see that he had lost control of himself. I could also see fear in the faces of the other screws as they didn't know what would happen next. I was pulled off the table onto the floor and kicked. After about a minute a screw, who was in another wing across from us, came running into the canteen to pull him off me. The SO was like a drunk man being held back from a fight in the pub. He was shouting at me that he'd kill me. I was sent back to the cell.

The next day Fr Toner was in our cell and saw the blood on the wall. Liam had a black eye and was bruised all over. Fr Toner made a protest to a governor. We put our names down to see a doctor so he could do a body sheet. It wasn't until ten days after the beating that we got to see a doctor, nine days after we had asked to see him.

We took a case against the prison governor. A man from the NIO came to ask questions about what had happened. We refused to go out because it was the NIO who ran the H-Blocks and paid the screws extra money for the job they were doing. There was no way he would have found against the screws. When we refused to see him we were dragged from our cell by the feet along the wing into the circle and then asked if we had a complaint to make about a beating.

PETER CUNNINGHAM . . .

It was shortly after the new year, 1980, that we heard that a hunger strike was imminent. Cardinal Ó Fiaich's talks with Atkins confirmed it for us and although we didn't expect anything to come out of the talks, there was always the possibility, however slight, that maybe...

During 1980 things eased off; the beatings were less frequent and our food was increased. There was also an unusual turnover of screws working in the wing. Throughout the year men, for various reasons, were leaving the protest and few if any, were coming onto it.

FELIM O'HAGAN . . .

By the beginning of 1980 I had settled myself in for a very long haul. My cellmate, John Nellis, and I used to talk about how it was a matter of battening down the hatches and serving out the rest of our sentences in Blanket conditions. A stoicism had set in and at that time I really believed we were there for the foreseeable future. I didn't feel that bad about it; I was doing life and I wasn't going anywhere for a long time whatever the conditions. In hindsight it was a selfish attitude as it ignored the reality of those who had remission to lose. But worse, it was a passive attitude; I had yet to learn the lesson that nothing happens unless you struggle to make it happen. Passive resistance is fine but it doesn't win wars, and the struggle in prison was as much part of the war as actions outside.

As 1980 wore on the talk of hunger strike became more common. It had always been an option but by the summer it was obvious that it was a certainty.

BIK McFARLANE . . .

October 1979 had seen the formation of the National Anti-H-Block/Armagh Committee to concentrate specifically on highlighting the situation in the Blocks and Armagh jail and rallying support for our protest action. Prominent activists such as Bernadette McAliskey, Fr Pearse O'Duill and John Turnly[1] threw themselves fully into the campaign alongside members of the

1. John Turnly, an Irish Independence Party councillor for Larne, was shot dead by loyalists in Carnlough, Co. Antrim, on June 6th 1980. A Larne UDA man, Robert McConnell, and two others were later convicted of the murder. At his trial in March 1982 McConnell stated that he had been trained by the SAS and that they had directed him to target H-Block/Armagh activists. This claim is amply borne out by the subsequent attacks on prominent activists: Miriam Daly was murdered on June 26th 1980 in Belfast; Ronnie Bunting and Noel Lyttle were murdered on October 15th 1980 also in Belfast; Bernadette McAliskey and her husband Michael were critically wounded in an attack at their home near Coalisland, Co. Tyrone, on January 16th 1981.

Republican Movement and the POWs' families. Then in January 1980, after careful consideration and debate, our five demands were published: 1) right to our own clothes; 2) no prison work; 3) free association with other POWs; 4) a visit, parcel and letters per week; 5) return of remission lost due to protest action on the Blanket. Supporters could campaign around a very specific programme. The five demands, we felt, also gave the Brits plenty of room to manoeuvre since no emotive terminology was attached.

SEAN LENNON . . .

Up to then our demand was straightforward: return to political status and the Cages. As we debated, two lines of thought emerged; one being that the demands remain as they are and if people don't want to support them, so be it. The other was more pragmatic, in the sense that it called for a re-definition of the words 'political status'. In the eyes of some this term was in itself a block and there were lots of people and groups who would not stand under a banner demanding political status. For that reason, it was a problem and if we were looking to gain as broad a platform as possible, this had to be looked at. It created a debate within the Blocks. When all was said and done the term 'political status' was redefined and manifested itself in the five demands which were broadcast world-wide and broke down a lot of the barriers which had been there.

BIK McFARLANE . . .

It mattered little what term was applied to our status – we were POWs, naked or clothed, and we did not need to convince anyone of that fact, the Brits included. The five demands were the key to unlocking the deadlock, but the stakes were too high for the Brits to turn the key without considerable pressure being applied to them. The removal of political status in March 1976 was designed to criminalise POWs and, coupled with a military and propaganda drive outside, it was hoped to inflict a deadly blow to the people's struggle for freedom. The conveyor belt of Castlereagh, Diplock and H-Blocks would ensure heavy casualties for the Republican Movement, rendering activists isolated and largely ineffective, save for a few small pockets of resistance which could, the Brits felt, be contained. Therefore, submitting to criminality was not simply an internal jail issue. The battle against it was an important factor in the overall struggle for self-determination. In essence, we had to be victorious in a battle the Brits could ill-afford to lose.

SEAN LENNON . . .

In January 1980 the first National H-Block march took place in West Belfast. The well-supported march was of course banned by the RUC from going to Long Kesh and the route was blocked by thousands of RUC and soldiers. Things began to take on a new pace and there was an air of optimism within the Blocks, and all sorts of rumours began to do the rounds. A rumour could be started out of nothing and after a few circuits it became fact and names from outside were actually put to it.

With the pressure mounting, the Brits came out with some minor concessions: an extra visit per month, a letter per week and they would allow us to exercise in training gear. We rejected these ridiculous concessions. There wasn't a Blanketman who would have accepted those things – we had come through 4 years of protest and were coming to the peak and no way was the victory we wanted going to be stolen from us by the Brits trying to buy us with such concessions. We had drawn up our demands as the grounds to bring the protest to an end and the Brits' concessions did not come near those demands.

We were genuinely trying to find a solution to the protest because we knew, had the Brits not moved, we would be forced to go down the road of hunger strike, a road all too familiar to Republicans. So the H-Block Committee, in conjunction with us, tried to find the solution and raise the people's awareness of the crisis within the jail. They also internationalised it. For our part we organised ourselves into a very effective propaganda machine and smuggled comms calling for help and support began to leave here in hundreds and reach into all corners of the world. This forced the Brits to set up a special propaganda machine in the USA to try and counteract the truths coming from the H-Blocks, but they failed. We were bringing the H-Blocks to the attention of the world. The British 'Dirty Tricks Department' got to work and leading H-Block activists were murdered in their homes; this was seen as a blatant attempt to scare people from getting involved in the H-Block campaign. But this didn't deter the people and they continued to organise and demonstrate on the streets of the North and the South. They were also organising delegations to go to England and abroad to gather support for our five demands, and were very successful. The Brits were now under pressure, and the pressure was again coming on within the Blocks for a hunger strike. The time was right in the minds of the Blanketmen.

Because of the pressure being brought to bear on the Brits, they entered into talks with Cardinal Ó Fiaich and the Bishop of Derry to try and find a solution. These talks went on for the best part of the summer of 1980. After a few months we realised that they were not going to produce anything.

Many in the Blocks wanted to release a statement that the talks were going nowhere and the Brits were not interested in seeking an end to the protest; all they wanted was an outright victory over the Blanketmen and the Nationalist people.

I was very much in agreement with this trend of thought at the time. I saw the talks as a means for the Brits to stall for time and then crush us when it suited. Had they wanted to resolve the situation in the Blocks they would have done so when they entered into talks with the churchmen. The IRA had stopped its campaign against the screws and we were ready to respond to any situation that would bring an end to the protest and all the sufferings, not only in here, but on the streets where our people were being beaten as they marched in our support. We, at a moment's notice, could have responded to any positive signs from the Brits and we continually said this, but the Brits just weren't interested in a solution. We were left with no other course of action but hunger strike. The Brits had closed all avenues to solutions; we were left frustrated and the pressure could not be held back any longer. The protest had to escalate if we were to get anywhere, so the stage was set firmly for hunger strike.

Bik McFarlane . . .

Summer came and there was still no sign of any positive results from Cardinal Ó Fiaich's months of talks with Atkins and Co at the NIO, although we had never been optimistic of any real developments along that avenue. From experience, the Brits have never moved significantly under the pressure of quiet diplomacy. So, we again addressed the awful option of hunger strike. There was intense and passionate debate on the dire consequences of employing such a tactic, not only for those embarking on hunger strike, but for the Republican Movement and our people outside should we fail. We were effectively moving ourselves into the front line of the struggle, not by a burning desire to fill that position, but by an unfolding set of circumstances, four years developing, which had cleared all obstacles from the path of head-on confrontation with Thatcher's government. The inevitable had finally arrived.

7

The First Hunger Strike

September 1980 – December 1980

From the earliest days of the Blanket protest the prisoners had known that a hunger strike might well be necessary to win their demands. For over four years they had sought other means and now, faced with the indefinite continuation of the protest with little prospect of success, they embarked on a course which they believed would bring the final showdown. Numbers on the protest were now around 500, boosted when the hunger strike was announced by the arrival of some who had previously been in the conforming Blocks.

For the Republican staff in the H-Blocks it was a time to lay plans and to arrange practical details for the efficient running of the hunger strike – reliable communication with outside had to be set up, volunteers assessed and a precise strategy decided upon. For every Blanketman it was a time to look with pitiless honesty at himself, and to decide if he could endure that slow, awful death of starvation.

On 27 October seven men began the hunger strike. Support within the Nationalist community for the prisoners' demands was widespread, with marches and demonstrations daily throughout the North and in the 26 Counties. On 1 December three women in Armagh prison joined the hunger strike, and they were followed two weeks later by another 30 men. Behind the scenes, efforts at mediation apparently bore fruit, and on 18 December the fast was ended following assurances that a resolution was imminent. The episode finished in despair and confusion, however, when the prisoners realised that a settlement was still not in sight.

LEO GREEN . . .

My own view of hunger strike alternated somewhat during my time on the Blanket. Initially I had believed that the Blanket protest by its own steam would bring about a restoration of status, and the merits of a hunger strike were therefore academic. By mid-1980 such illusions were long gone. The intensity of all that had occurred in the intervening period by way of attempts to break us had convinced me some would die on hunger strike before it swung the pendulum our way and forced the Brits to concede. I felt uncomfortable at the thought of anyone paying such a price and uneasy that we were edging towards what could well be a last ditch stand. But a hunger strike was inevitable. The mood in the Blocks was for it. The spark of optimism which had been rekindled by Cardinal Ó Fiaich's engagement of Humphrey Atkins in dialogue on the situation had waned due to the stalling tactics of the Brits, and been completely killed off by their arrogant total dismissal of the Cardinal's suggestions. Many had for long dug deep within themselves in search of reserves to help them endure the protest. The well for some was slowly drying up. The choice was stark: sit and hope a solution would fall into our lap or go for one final intensification of the fight for political recognition. In effect, no choice at all.

BIK MCFARLANE . . .

In the months leading through summer to the autumn a small group of us in H3 (the Dark, Bobby Sands, Tommy McKearney, Ricky O'Rawe, Jake Jackson and myself) engaged in heavy debate as to our intended course of action. Who would be selected, what our approach to negotiations and mediators would be, improving lines of communication with the leadership of the Republican Movement, searching for avenues which would circumvent any potential isolation of those on hunger strike and examining the horrific prospect of potential fatalities. Feedback was sought from our comrades in the other protesting Blocks and a shortlist of names drafted for consideration. There was no shortage of volunteers.

LEO GREEN . . .

One Sunday in early September I was given a comm at mass which someone had acquired on a visit. It was from the Blocks' staff. I read it there and then. I read it two or three times. The message was sombre and clinical. A hunger strike would begin in October. I was to inform everyone in the Block, ensure all were aware it would be to the death if need be and ask for volunteers to go on it. I was to select 10 from those who volunteered, put their names in an order from which they would be drawn if required at any stage for the hunger strike, and send the list off to the Blocks OC, Brendan Hughes. From the lists submitted to the OC, seven men would be selected to go on the hunger strike initially and the remaining names would form a list for future additions to the number on hunger strike or replacements for anyone who died. Everyone was informed that Sunday. The atmosphere in the Block immediately assumed an urgency and expectancy it had long lacked.

FELIM O'HAGAN . . .

When the formal proposals were put to us for discussion by the staff it was a time of personal confusion, honesty, contradiction and a touch of self-loathing. I was not in favour of the hunger strike. I did not put my name forward. I ask myself now, as I did then, what is the exact connection between those two facts. Sitting here 10 years later, my belly full, smoking a roll-up, the radio on – those mundane fruits of the sacrifice of ten lives – I still wonder, and I cannot be sure how true is my memory of those times. I was not in favour of the hunger strike for the very pragmatic reason that I did not think that it would get us our demands, and the price of failure could be the defeat of the overall struggle. At the same time I hadn't a clue about an alternative way forward – and sitting passively on the Blanket for another four years was hardly likely to shift the Brits.

If I didn't favour a hunger strike then it was quite rational of me not to put forward my name. But is it that simple? I did not volunteer because I was afraid – afraid of taking the responsibility of failure upon my shoulders, afraid of letting people down – but most of all I was afraid of dying, and especially of that long slow death. The realisation of that fear was not a comfortable feeling. I was involved in a struggle in which people died; I justified the deaths of many of them and here I was baulking at the thought of putting on the line my own life for a cause which intellectually I could justify to my complete satisfaction. I knew only a couple of the 10 hunger strikers personally and I've often wondered what extra quality gave them the strength to go the whole way. I still don't have the answer.

Once the decision was made and the first hunger strike began, it was a time of reasonable optimism. For a year or so beforehand we had engaged in a sustained propaganda drive and with the help of the RAC (Relatives' Action Committee) and the Republican Movement, we had mobilised large sections of the nationalist population. Each visit brought news of the increasing support and there was an air of expectancy in the Blocks.

LEO GREEN . . .

Ideas as to how best we could heighten support for the hunger strike were tossed about among ourselves and then passed to outside. A renewed letter writing campaign began, thereafter churning out hundreds of letters, written on toilet paper or cigarette papers, to all and sundry and calling for their support for the five demands. Volunteers came forward for the hunger strike. Word came again from the camp staff to impress upon all who had volunteered to consider fully the implications of hunger strike, the strong likelihood of death and the traumatic effect on their immediate families. A few men withdrew their names. I was left with 20 odd names of men in H4 willing to take part. Reducing them to 10 and arranging them in order was an uncomfortable task. I believed some of these men might well die. I sent the list of 10 to the Dark.

He replied immediately, seeking clarification on the inclusion of my name, given the views I had sometime previously expressed to him opposing hunger strike. It was an obvious contradiction and he needed to be sure that those going on hunger strike would be committed to it. My reservation about hunger strike had evaporated with the decision by the Blocks Staff to go ahead with it. I confirmed my desire to join the hunger strike and assured the Dark of my committment to it.

Away from the renewed sense of purpose which had gripped the Block, I gave considerable time to thoughts of my family, most particularly my parents, and the possible impact my going on hunger strike would have on them. They would be supportive, I knew that. They had always been so. My concern was their health. Both my parents were old and had already suffered the death of my brother, assassinated by Loyalists a few years previously. My going on hunger strike could finish them off, I thought.

I had foregone family visits for my first two years on the protest. I began taking them in April 1980. Whether it was the long gap since I had seen them or the increased time I had spent thinking about them, I am not sure, but when I resumed visits I certainly felt closer to them than I had ever been.

In September I wrote to my brother asking him to inform all the family that I might well be going on hunger strike. I asked him to explain to them my reasons for volunteering for it, and the likely consequences, but in as optimistic a way as possible. I outlined also the pressure I felt they would come under to intervene and how I thought they should respond to it.

BIK McFARLANE . . .

Those in the leadership of the Republican Movement were meanwhile stating their opposition to the hunger strike and an ongoing series of exchanges ensued between them and ourselves. In the midst of all this we were stunned by the announcement that one of our comrades, and a long-time prominent Republican activist, Martin Meehan, had embarked on a hunger strike against his conviction on the word of a paid perjuror. A shock wave reverberated around the Blocks and through the Republican Movement outside. The dangers of this independent action were all too obvious and frantic attempts were made by us to persuade him to end his hunger strike, but without success. The Brits were now in a position to monitor the physical effects of a prolonged hunger strike on the individual, but also to assess the support-rallying potential of the Republican Movement as they took to the streets to highlight Martin's case. Further representations were made to him from a variety of sources, including the IRA's Army Council, but it was not until his 66th day that he terminated his hunger strike.

In the meantime our preparations went ahead. Originally it had been envisaged that 10 men would embark on hunger strike, and, when the figure had been streamlined to seven (six IRA and one INLA) and spread geographically, there was considerable annoyance displayed by Bobby Sands at his name being removed. He had expected to be to the fore in this action and he was gravely disappointed. But in reality we could only include one representative from Belfast to ensure all other regions were covered.

I too was withdrawn, but primarily because the nature of my charges would have had a negative effect in a propaganda drive to gather support for our cause (I had been convicted for an attack on a UVF bar in which five people lost their lives). I did feel very much aggrieved because I had been heavily involved in the debate on shaping our protest strategy and had become a strong advocate of adopting the course of hunger strike. I had also become very close to Bobby and Tommy McKearney during that year, and as we had envisaged ourselves playing a central role in a hunger strike, we had come to draw on the strengths of each other, building confidence and trust and mutual reinforcement to face the coming ordeal.

We occupied three different cells, but only one separated me from Bobby, and Tommy was next door on my other side. Small notes scribbled on toilet paper were regularly shunted along the pipes between our cells. There were frequent conversations at the windows, the box-like structure attached to the outside affording a degree of amplification for our voices. And despite the severity of our existence we never lost that flare for humour. On reflection, perhaps that was one of the essential ingredients for survival. We shared our thoughts and feelings, and I even became an official critic for Bobby's poetry, probably because he trusted me to be forthright with my opinion. I only abused my position on one occasion to retaliate after he informed me he had thrown one of my superb articles into the corner with the rest of the rubbish. An excellent tribute he composed about our women comrades in Armagh jail received such a murderous shredding that he took to the window in a passionate defence and explanation of his poem. When we could no longer contain our stifled laughter, he immediately twigged that he had been the victim of a prank. The torrent of abuse which flew in my direction in the aftermath was anything but poetic, yet scoring such a victory was music to my ears.

We launched into a letter writing campaign which outstripped all our previous endeavours. Anyone who could possibly exert the most minute influence was targeted, both nationally and internationally. We used up a phenomenal amount of cigarette paper and sheets of toilet paper with 'Property of HM Government' clearly stamped on them, imploring individuals, groups, political parties, trade unions and churches to press the British Government for an honourable settlement.

On 10 October the announcement came from Sinn Féin that a hunger strike would commence on 27 October. The Brits attempted to wrong-foot us by publicly announcing that they were scrapping prison uniforms in favour of civilian-type clothing for all prisoners. But this cynical ploy was exposed when it was revealed that prison-issue clothing had simply acquired a new title, 'civilian-type', as opposed to uniform. So, the Brits made little or no impact with this. Even apart from their manoeuvre on clothing, they would still have to address the important issues of work, visits, association and return of lost remission if they were serious about finding a solution.

Leo Green . . .

At the start of October the names of the seven who would begin the hunger strike arrived from the camp Staff. The seven were from different parts of the Six Counties, an obvious attempt to maximise support. My name was among them. I wrote to my family confirming that I would be on it. A week or so later I received the news I had feared. My father had taken a stroke and was seriously ill. After a further anxious few days I heard that his condition had stabilised. He remained partially paralysed and thereafter confined to a wheelchair until his eventual death in 1983.

My last visit before the hunger strike was particularly emotional, the atmosphere of the visit made all the more difficult by the attentive stare of the screw watching the visit box. We were getting two visits a month then. Unsure of what lay ahead, I thought this might be the last chance of seeing my mother. As things turned out, a few weeks into the hunger strike we were given weekly visits. My mother arrived on most of them, always with reassuring reports of growing support for the hunger strike. Throughout the hunger strike my family were an enormous source of strength. Prior to 27

October I had anticipated that visits would become more and more difficult, emotionally, the longer the hunger strike went on. As the days went by, however, I looked forward increasingly to seeing my family.

Hunger strike, despite its seemingly eternal association with Republican prisoners, was something I knew very little about. My one previous experience of it had been participating in a 48 hour token hunger strike in support of one that was at an advanced stage in Portlaoise prison. I wondered about how it affected the body as it progressed. I thought about Michael Gaughan and Frank Stagg dying on hunger strike in jail in England and wondered had they lingered at death's door for hours, days, or even weeks. I was by no means preoccupied with death, but merely wanted to know what to expect. Larry Marley, always quick to cheer people up and instil confidence, assured me laughingly that he knew someone in the Cages who had been on hunger strike for 30 days and could still do 50 press-ups! I didn't believe him. In any case, I thought, I couldn't do 50 press-ups at the best of times never mind while on hunger strike. Larry was prone to a little exaggeration, but I found out years later he had been telling the truth.

In those last two weeks before the stailc there was a lot of encouragement from those around me, men I had shared and endured the two previous years with. There were sobering moments as well, though not all intentional. Gerry McDonnell (Blute) was in the cell next to me then. He was loudest out the doors at asserting the certain success the hunger strike would bring. At the pipes as well, when we discussed the way things would go he was all assurance and encouragement. Yet when it began and reports of enormous support were coming in thick and fast, Blute summoned me to the pipes one evening and calmly asked me to write up a comm to be read out to all my friends in the wing if I died. He assured me he would keep it safe. Only Blute had the neck to ask this, I mused. Reluctantly and somewhat 'sobered', I complied.

Bik McFarlane . . .

With the Dark leading the hunger strike, the burden of command passed on to Bobby, and with it an unenviable responsibility. I assumed the position of PRO, my first major task being the drafting of our statement announcing the hunger strike. It was an arduous task, chiefly because I was extremely concerned at conveying the politically correct message, and secondly because the Dark sent it back to me on three occasions to be amended. I was beginning to doubt if I'd ever complete it, but was relieved that the fourth attempt got the green light.

STATEMENT AT START OF FIRST HUNGER STRIKE

We, the Republican Prisoners of War in the H-Blocks, Long Kesh, demand as a right, political recognition and that we be accorded the status of political prisoners. We claim this right as captured combatants in the continuing struggle for national liberation and self-determination.

We refute most strongly the tag of 'criminal' with which the British have attempted to label us and our struggle, and we point to a divisive partitionist institution of the six counties as the sole criminal aspect of the present struggle.

All of us were arrested under repressive laws, interrogated and often tortured in RUC barracks and processed through special non-jury courts where we were sentenced to lengthy terms of imprisonment. After this, men were put in the H-Blocks and were expected to bow the knee before the British administration and wear their criminal uniform. Attempts to criminalise us were designed to depoliticise the Irish national struggle.

We don't have to recite again the widespread, almost total forms of punishment, degradation and deprivation we have been subject to. All have failed to break our resistance.

For the past four years, we have endured brutality in deplorable conditions – we have been stripped naked and robbed of our individuality, yet we refuse to be broken. Further repression only serves to strengthen our resolve and that of our female comrades enduring the same hardship in Armagh jail.

During this period many individuals, religious figures, political organisations and sections of the media have condemned the way in which we have been treated. Yet, despite appeals for a resolution of the H-Block protest, the British government has remained intransigent and displayed vindictive arrogance in dealing with the problem. They refuse to treat this issue in a realistic manner, which is just another reflection of their attitude to the entire Irish question.

Bearing in mind the serious implications of our final step, not only for us but for our people, we wish to make it clear that every channel has now been exhausted and not wishing to break faith with those from whom we have inherited our principles, we now commit ourselves to a hunger strike.

We call on the Irish people to lend us their support for our just demands and we are confident that this support will be very much in evidence in the coming days.

We call on all solidarity and support groups to intensify their efforts and we also look forward with full confidence to the support of our exiled countrymen in America and Australia and throughout the world.

We declare that political status is ours of right and we declare that from Monday 27 October, 1980 a hunger strike by a number of men representing H-Blocks 3, 4 and 5 will commence.

Our widely recognised resistance has carried us through four years of immense suffering and it shall carry us through to the bitter climax of death, if necessary.

Leo Green (IRA), Lurgan; Brendan 'The Dark' Hughes (IRA), Belfast; Raymond McCartney (IRA), Derry; Tom McFeely (IRA), Co. Derry; Tommy McKearney (IRA), Tyrone, Sean McKenna (IRA), Newry; John Nixon (INLA), Armagh.

SEAN LENNON . . .

The day before the hunger strike began there was a massive protest on the Falls Road as a show of support for us and it was a good start (if it can be said that there is a good start to such a sad event).

It is hard to describe men's feelings that day; we all knew it was the biggest step in the protest and the last one. There were men who didn't agree with it but gave it their full backing because it was going ahead anyway. It was either this or end the protest and we were not prepared to do that. My own feelings at the decision were ones of great sadness and I expected men to die because the Brits wouldn't give in easily. In our eyes – and the Brits' – there was more to this than just jail conditions. It was another policy of theirs to try and defeat the Republican struggle. If they were successful in their criminalisation strategy it would go a long way to defeating our struggle. So it was a head-on confrontation between us and them and they weren't going to give up easily; nor were we, because we also realised the dangers involved if we were defeated.

LEO GREEN . . .

Sunday, 26 October was a mass with a difference. It had been anticipated that the hunger strikers would all be moved to the hospital immediately it began. This then was a day for handshakes all round, brief expressions of encouragement, everyone carefully selecting their words, anxious not to betray a trace of the gravity of the situation which seemed about to unfold. It was a day of charged emotions, those people I knew best having most difficulty in verbalising their feelings. For once I was glad to get mass over, out of the canteen and back to my cell.

At 4.00 that afternoon the tea came round. This would be my last meal. The screws knew who would be on the hunger strike, so I wondered what they'd be thinking serving up this tea. The door opened. In came the usual

Sunday tea: cold pie and a handful of peas. As if in answer to my thoughts one of the screws spoke his own, 'Make the best of it', he sneered, 'it's your very very last'. The door was slammed. I looked at my cellmate, Jim Valente, and both of us laughed. I had wondered about their thoughts but cared none for them.

The following morning the hunger strike began. From then until it ended the screws would dutifully place plates brimming with food in my cell at each meal time. For those first days they would come right into the cell and set the food beside where I lay.

On the first day of the hunger strike I was visited by an assistant governor, known particularly for his arrogance. This day he surpassed himself. He announced with obvious enjoyment that hunger strike slowly wastes away the body; the fat and muscle tissue are first to go, then the vital organs are eaten up till eventually a point of no return is reached and you lapse into a coma and die. 'You realise that you are going to die?' he enquired smilingly. I ignored him and he left. Over the next few weeks I heard this same spleen from other governors.

Bik McFarlane . . .

On the eve of the 27th we held a concert on the wing, and listened to moving speeches from the Dark and Tommy. Morale had climbed to new heights because we were now entering the final phase. Soon it would all be over, though at what cost we couldn't say. Some of us felt that we would surely lose a number of those who would take that dreaded step the next morning, so that evening had a sombre strain running through the light-hearted atmosphere. Nonetheless, it felt good to be 'on the road home'.

On the morning of the 27th we were greeted with the news that Seán Glas (John Chillingworth) was returning from the non-protesting Blocks with a host of comrades who for various reasons could not sustain the no-wash protest. Sean had been sent from our wing some weeks previously to agitate within the conforming Blocks and had done an admirable job. I don't believe that the administration were ever under any illusion as to Sean's motives for his move into the conforming Blocks. They could do little else but to allow him to masquerade as a 'model prisoner'. So, when we heard that he was 'leading the troops back,' an enormous cheer went up.

Leo Green . . .

In a physical sense the first 10 days were the most uncomfortable of all. I experienced severe headaches and back pain. After that initial period the pain subsided and then disappeared altogether.

We were kept in the Blanket wings for 12 days or so and then all of us moved into a wing together, a hospital wing previously set aside in case of an outbreak of disease due to the conditions those on the protest were enduring. Walking down towards my new cell, I looked at the cell cards of the top six cells. I knew only two of these other men on hunger strike personally, Tommy McKearney and Raymond McCartney. This hospital wing was inappropriately named, I thought. This might now be death row. We were not totally isolated however. The other wings in H3 were Blanket wings, and we would see the men in them at mass.

That first mass in H3 was an introduction to the others on hunger strike and an opportunity also to meet again many I had not seen since remand. Each of those few Sundays in H3 someone from the other wings was tasked to gather from us information about our physical condition: our weight, blood pressure or details of any physical pain or discomfort we might be experiencing. These details were necessary, we knew, for outside. It was important that those who were working tirelessly on our behalf to build and sustain support were kept abreast of our condition. As well as that, there was an obvious concern in the Block about how we were. It became, nevertheless, a major irritation to have to constantly give such details, compounded most probably by everyone's lack of knowledge of what to expect our state of health to be. The more we reassured those saddled with the uncomfortable task of gleaning the required details from us that we were not ill in any real sense, the more they seemed to believe we were playing down our condition. 'You must have pains,' I remember one of the men saying to me.

BIK MCFARLANE . . .

We watched the days roll slowly by, taking all relevant medical details of the Dark and Tommy – weight, pulse, blood pressure and temperature. Advice was sought about how much water should be taken and what signs to look for – headaches, dizziness, stomach pains, etc. But our task wasn't to last very long because the Administration decided to move all the hunger strikers to a sterile wing (A wing H3). We managed to keep contact by having someone shout across from B wing and at mass on Sunday morning we were all together. It was my first meeting with Raymond McCartney and John Nixon; I already knew Leo Green, Sean McKenna and Tom McFeely.

We usually discussed their condition and how the situation was developing outside with rallies, meetings and international pickets, etc. But I felt a little awkward trying to find the right things to discuss. Maybe they would feel that I lacked confidence in them if I continuously harped on about the thousands protesting and marching on streets and lanes from Belfast to

Boston and all over Europe. I didn't wish to appear as if I had to constantly reassure them that things were going well.

SEAN LENNON . . .

I will never forget as long as I live the sight of the hunger strikers that first Sunday at mass. They looked like very old men; stooped over, whiter than white and the bones in their bodies were sticking out. One man in particular, Tom McFeely, really frightened me when I saw him. He just looked like a skeleton with skin pulled over him. I had tears in my eyes and my heart ached for them. We were all speaking to them, but not really saying anything. What could we say to someone who could possibly be dead in a few weeks? Because of the shock, it took me a while before I could go over and have a word with them. I had read about the effects of hunger strike and listened to older Republicans telling me about the damage it did to them during the campaigns of the past. But you need to actually see a person on hunger strike to really comprehend what it's all about. It is frightening. When I went back to the cell after mass I couldn't get them out of my mind. They had a real profound affect on me, one that will stay with me forever.

To help break down the hunger strikers' isolation, we organised singsongs out the doors at night for them. It helped to keep their spirits up and break the isolation. Anyone who has been in isolation will understand the great benefits of this; to know in your own mind that you aren't alone is sound but it always helps to strengthen you when you can hear friendly voices, no matter how far away they are. We did this for a few hours every night and it also gave us a great feeling of pride and strengthened our resolve to struggle on, no matter what. Here we were in a wing on the Blanket singing to seven of our comrades who were on hunger strike and maybe would not be among us again. It was very real but at the same time unreal.

THOMAS LOUGHLIN . . .

There was no real trouble from the screws during this period, but they did give some verbal abuse, such as, 'This time next week there will only be 43 for dinner'. In H3 Srón Dearg was his usual self. One day he was bringing round the tea and giving plenty of verbal when he came to Hugh Rooney's cell. He told Hugh that he should think well of the food he was getting, because 'your comrades on hunger strike would be glad of it.' Hugh pulled him into the cell and battered him; the other screws pulled him out and oddly enough no action was taken against Hugh.

LEO GREEN . . .

Weight loss apart, my physical condition changed little while I was in H3. Two things which unsettled me stick in my mind, though. Firstly I became aware of a smell from my body. Initially, because of the circumstances, I thought it might be my imagination playing tricks. I was reticent about mentioning it to the other hunger strikers, but I did and was relieved to discover that some of them too sensed a smell from their own bodies. It was the smell of the body wasting itself, the smell you sometimes sense when paying respect to the dead. Either I became used to it or it went away completely, but after a few days it left my mind and I never thought of it again.

The other experience I recall was more unsettling. For three days, sometime around the 20-day mark, I craved food. To fight it, I occupied my mind with memories of past events in my life. But whatever I recalled, my mind found some avenue to return my thoughts to food. If I thought about going to the All-Ireland Final, for example, my concentration shifted away from the details of the match towards a vivid recollection of where and what I had eaten that day. I consciously switched off from such recollections by reading a couple of books. I read *Oliver Twist* and Hardy's *Tess of the D'Urbervilles*. I read slowly and gave free rein to my imagination. Other than for those three days, food rarely again entered my head for the remainder of the hunger strike.

In the first week of the hunger strike we heard all sorts of reports about huge support for it. Our perspective may have been a little distorted by the fact that it was the only thing we heard news about. After the first few weeks, however, we were permitted newspapers, a radio and we had access to the television news in the evening when we had a period of association. Support had levelled out then. We were not perturbed about this. We had expected the Brits to play a game of brinkmanship with us. We knew also that the hunger strike would be at its most potent the nearer we got to death. It would be a long wait, longer still because the sleep requirement diminished, either naturally or in response to the four-hourly visit by medical screws to rub cream on protruding bones to prevent bedsores.

Shortly after moving to H3 the screws who were on the wing were replaced by MOs. The MOs had all very obviously been well briefed on how to deal with us. Their approach was an amicable one. The hostility, however, between ourselves and screws which had built up over the years of protest was too well cemented for this new approach to cut any ice with us, if such was the intention. The distance between ourselves and them remained. Their job may have been to administer medical attention but they were screws nevertheless.

Dr Ross was the senior Doctor in the jail then and for the next four or five years. In the years leading up to hunger strike the doctors in the jail had shown little interest in the health of prisoners on protest. One doctor, nick-named 'Mengele', had watched unmoved while prisoners were kicked and punched and dragged from their cells for him to examine their scalps for head lice. This exercise was carried out as an attempt to legitimise the force-washing in advance. Ross was charged by the administration with monitoring closely our condition. His approach was non-antagonistic and he left it to other doctors he brought in to examine us to comment on the damage hunger strike would do to our bodies if it didn't kill us.

On one occasion he brought in a specialist from the City Hospital in Belfast. Previously Ross had tried to persuade us to see a psychiatrist but we had refused. When this specialist arrived I wondered if he might be a psychiatrist or was he even a doctor of any description. He actually convinced me that he might not be. He placed one end of his stethoscope above my heart and with the other ends in his ears, instead of listening, proceeded to lecture me on the futility of dying on hunger strike. He claimed to have travelled the world and to have witnessed countless deaths in wars, in accidents and from illness. 'It's not worth it,' he said. 'Once you die only your family cares and they too soon forget about you.' I left him in the middle of his ramblings on the futility of death. I have since discovered he was indeed a doctor, but whatever his brief that particular day, it was certainly not medical attention. Ross, as it turned out, killed himself several years later. His attendance at the deaths of 10 Republican hunger strikers had undoubtedly left its mark.

After 37 days we were moved from H3 to the prison hospital and accommodated in separate cells there. We were still permitted an association period daily and continued therefore to see each other at evening time. Sean McKenna's condition had been worse than the rest of us from an early stage in the hunger strike. By this time, although still able to walk, he was in little mood for conversation. Sean rarely took association. We had little to talk about in any case. We were aware of NIO attempts to suss our position via Fr Faul and two Nationalist councillors from Dungannon. This meant nothing of significance, we realised. On one occasion an NIO man came to see us along with the jail governor. He was not interested in dialogue as such and confined himself to arrogant assertions about the uselessness of hunger strike and ambiguous statements about how 'imaginative' the jail regime could be were both the hunger strike and the Blanket protest to end.

BIK MCFARLANE . . .

Regular contact was maintained with the leadership of the Republican Movement and a number of us had begun using our visits solely for this type of contact. We tried to keep a steady flow of information to the hunger strikers. We were concerned when they were transferred to the prison hospital because firstly, we believed it signalled the beginning of the crisis stage on hunger strike and secondly, our contact was reduced substantially. We now had to rely on information coming via visits, lawyers and prison chaplains. The British meanwhile were continuing to project their 'not an inch' stance, but pressure was mounting steadily on them to introduce a prison regime which would end the impasse. Of course, as always, pressure was heaped upon us to call an end to the hunger strike in order to allow space for the British to manoeuvre and to permit interested groups such as the Church to apply pressure for an honourable settlement. But it was a waiting game and all we could do was to be sure of ourselves and determined to seize victory.

Bobby had a small crystal radio set which he had smuggled in and each evening he would give us a complete newscast of local and international events. Generally we were abreast of developments and able to gauge reaction as the hunger strike drew to its critical stage. There was also contact with a Redemptorist priest, Fr Brendan Meagher, who was to act as mediator between ourselves and the Brits. Bobby had a number of visits with him and on one occasion he celebrated mass in H3. We felt that we were on top of the situation and had a clear indication that one of the main demands, the right to wear our own clothes, would not in any way present an obstacle in negotiating a settlement.

At the beginning of December three of our women comrades in Armagh jail joined the hunger strike (Mairéad Farrell, Mary Doyle and Mairéad Nugent). There had been much debate at the outset concerning their desire to play their full part on the protest – their commitment to hunger strike action was total. But a number of factors needed consideration, which eventually mitigated against their inclusion on 27 October. They already wore their own clothes as a right and possible Brit moves to improve the regime at Armagh may have gone some way to meeting the remainder of the demands. It was also believed, though from what medical standpoint I have no idea, that one or all of our women comrades would reach a critical stage on hunger strike before our comrades in the Blocks, and the Republican Movement of 1980 quite frankly could not have lived with the prospect of women volunteers dying on hunger strike before we had reached the crisis period in the Blocks. While it was a joint protest throughout and regular contact maintained, nevertheless the main focus of attention centred on the H-Blocks, and therefore any decisive action had of necessity to lead from there. The women joining the hunger strike a number of weeks after 27 October meant it was likely that some of the hunger strikers in the Blocks would have died before our comrades in Armagh reached a crisis stage, and with the women becoming critical in the aftermath of deaths here, more intense pressure would surely build.

Séanna Walsh . . .

When the women went on hunger strike on December 1980 the lads were shattered, even those who were expecting to replace possible dead comrades. I remember talking to one of them at mass, Jim Devine, and we covered the whole picture. I asked him if, as I suspected, he was doing heavy wack. Didn't he believe that we were in with a good chance of victory? He said he believed victory was certain but he felt guilty because the women had now embarked on it and they would die first.

Thomas Loughlin . . .

On 8 December the wing was in total silence when all of a sudden someone shouted out, 'Jesus Christ!' It was the man with the wing radio. The next thing pipes were being rapped with loud whispers of 'Did you get that news?' All up the one side of the wing were utterances of 'Jesus, you're joking.' One of the lads on the other side of the wing couldn't bear it any longer, so he got up to the door and asked what had happened. 'John Lennon's been shot,' came the reply. 'Well, fuck you and John Lennon; you put the fear of God into us'. They thought one of the hunger strikers had died.

Leo Green . . .

Around 45 days or so the scéal picked up. A leading SDLP man informed the family of one of the others on hunger strike that he could 'deliver' the five demands if we would direct him to. He implied that he had been in contact with either the NIO or other Brit sources. Other sources close to the Movement on the outside relayed the same optimistic news. These reports had come from people close to the Haughey government. Haughey, they maintained, had received assurances from the Brits that they would resolve the situation and that no one need die on hunger strike.

Sean Lennon . . .

During the hunger strike I don't think there was a time when I believed the Brits were going to break. I hoped for it every minute of the day, but that's all it was; 'live in hope, may you die in despair!' Every day was an uphill struggle.

I thought about how I would react to the death of one of the lads. I saw lots of my friends and comrades die during this struggle and every time it happened my heart was sore. But never before had I seen a comrade die in such a violent manner as what death by hunger strike must surely be. I continually told myself to be strong and prepared for the worst that was to come. It was something that stayed in my mind. During yarns with the lads out the door or at the pipes we never spoke about their deaths coming, although it was always to the fore of our minds. It was a sort of unspoken rule not to talk about it openly.

BIK MCFARLANE . . .

As we approached the middle of December and ever mindful that the Brits would take us to the very brink before attempting to get us to settle short of our demands, we escalated by adding 30 men to the hunger strike. It grabbed the headlines and demonstrated to the Brits that unless a negotiated settlement was arrived at, we had considerable numbers willing to continue with hunger strike action if our comrades died.

THOMAS LOUGHLIN . . .

When the other lads joined the hunger strike it caused many to question the reality of the situation; why do we need more men on the hunger strike? Are we in a crisis and going to lose? At this period very few thought anyone would die and even this 'crisis' failed to change that perception. However, those who did believe it had a strange way of letting it be known; 'Take your last look at Chamois (Ray McCartney)' one of the lads had said in the early days of the hunger strike. One other line of thought was that a civil war would begin if any of the lads died. No one sought to allay these fears and countless hours were spent discussing the outcome.

LEO GREEN . . .

In those last few days of the hunger strike everyone's condition began to deteriorate much more rapidly than before. My hearing began to give trouble whereas the eyesight of the others was badly affected. Our speech became a little slurred and walking was faltered. Sean McKenna, in particular, was by now critically ill and Tommy McKearney not far behind.

On the morning of 18 December, we were visited by a priest who had been involved in mediation. He had been in touch with the Haughey government, the Brits and the Republican Movement simultaneously. He assured us that a solution was there and that he would be back later that evening confirming it. As evening approached, preparations were made to transfer Sean McKenna to an outside hospital. He was lapsing in and out of a coma. We decided at around six o'clock, on the basis of the assurances we had earlier that day received, to end the hunger strike. A few more hours would be needed for what lay behind these assurances to be clarified, but in a few hours Sean McKenna would be dead.

Thomas Loughlin ...

On 18 December, just after dinner time Bobby Sands left the Block to go to the hospital. As he walked down the front yard one of the lads shouted to him, asking what the crack was. Bobby gave the thumbs up and said that it was only a matter of time, days if not hours. Thus everyone in the wing was really optimistic. That night sometime after nine o'clock we heard a lot of screws coming into the wing, so everyone got up to the doors trying to see out. It was Bobby and he appeared to be in a jovial mood. It was at that point we knew the hunger strike was probably over. But was it victory? It was the most tense period any of us had ever experienced.

Hugh Rooney was the OC and Bobby went into his cell. He was there for a few minutes and during that time everyone just looked at one another. When he left Hugh got up to the door and began speaking in Gaeilge. His first words were 'bad news', then he went on to say that we had not won anything but all was not lost. The outstanding memory for me was the reaction of my cellmate. He didn't know one word of Gaeilge so had no idea what was going on. Rather than ask for a running commentary he waited until all the news was over. When he saw me sliding down the wall he soon got the message; he turned and got into bed. When I went to tell him, he said, 'Did we win?' 'No,' said I, 'but ...' 'Are any of the lads dead?' he asked. 'No,' I replied. 'Then there's nothing else to hear,' he answered.

Séanna Walsh ...

I was in the cell with Paul Brennan (one of the 1983 escapees). He was one of the men who had joined the hunger strike in the final stages. At that stage Paul had been on hunger strike for a few days and he may have had a problem with his liver because he had turned a yellow colour. When Bobby came to my cell he was accompanied by Fr Murphy and a lot of screws. I threw my arms around him when he walked through the door but then I saw that all was not well with him. We whispered into each other's ears about the night's events and then briefly about families. He was shattered and he just told me that the lads had ended the hunger strike on the basis of a 30 page document.

He had been told before the hunger strike ended that he would be going to negotiate with the Brits that night, but the Dark seemed to think that was opening enough. He didn't realise that the Brits, not having anything signed and sealed either outside the jail or inside through Bobby or the Dark, would feel under no obligation to concede anything once the pressure was off. The Brits had simply agreed to negotiate, to implement some formula to end both the hunger strike and the Blanket protest. Sean McKenna actually died in the prison hospital. When the word was given to try and save him, he wasn't breathing any longer. (Editors' note: Sean McKenna was later revived in hospital.)

When he was leaving, Bobby asked me who to see in the other two wings; I told him the names of the various OCs and I also told him to call in and see Francie Hughes because there was a chance that he would refuse to end his hunger strike even though everyone else would end theirs. With a shake of the hands and tears in his eyes, he left. As the door closed behind him, Paul asked me: 'Well?' I told him the lads had ended the hunger strike and that although there were negotiations going on, we hadn't won the five demands. He dropped down on to his hunkers on his mattress in the corner beside the pipes and with his head on his chest he began to sob.

The lads began to shout; 'Cad é an dóigh? Cérbh é sin?' (What's happening? Who was that?) 'B'é sin Roibeard, a chairde. Tá an stailc críochnaithe. Thosaigh an seachtar ag ithe arís anocht' (That was Bobby, friends. The strike's finished. The seven started eating again tonight). 'Bhuel, an raibh an bua againn?' (Well, did we win?) 'Tá Roibeard ag caint leo go fóill. Ní bhfuaireamar ar gcúig éileamh ach nílimid buailte go fóill.' (Bobby is still talking to them. We didn't get our demands but we aren't beaten yet.) After an initial buzz of rapping on pipes and hurried conversations out the windows, a thick cloud of depression settled on the wing. After a few hours Paul went over to his dinner that was lying at the door and began picking through it for bits and pieces that weren't completely unappetising.

LEO GREEN . . .

While the hunger strike was ending the priest who had visited us earlier that day was on his way to Aldergrove airport to meet with a representative from the British Foreign Office and collect a document which, it was anticipated, would represent the solution he had been assured was there. He arrived back in the camp at midnight with a copy of the document. Typical of the Brits, the language in places was ambiguous. The deciding factor would be the spirit in which it had been drawn up. This would soon be tested. Relief that the hunger strike had ended without the loss of life soon turned to despair. The Brits, it became clear, had no genuine desire for a solution. Their sole concern had been to end the hunger strike and they had employed cynical brinkmanship to achieve it. Fifty three days of hunger strike and we were no further on. Whilst we were not immediately aware of it, the very minute the hunger strike had ended that same process which had rendered it inevitable had seized control. Almost immediately a second hunger strike loomed on the horizon.

8

Confusion, Frustration, Determination

December 1980 – March 1981

A s 1981 dawned morale among the prisoners was low – to many it seemed that they had played their final card, yet the winning of their demands was as far away as ever. Bobby Sands, who had taken over as the Blocks OC at the start of the first hunger strike, was involved in negotiations with the prison administration on the basis of the 18 December document presented to the hunger strikers. For a time it appeared as though movement was possible, but soon it became obvious that the British demanded nothing less than absolute surrender.

Confusion among the prisoners and their supporters was dispelled as determination grew, for the British had badly miscalculated if they thought that the fight against criminalisation was about to be abandoned. Less than two months after the hunger strike ended, the prisoners announced that another would begin.

Those 'concerned' groups and individuals who had clamoured for an end to the first hunger strike in order that a settlement could be reached in calmer circumstances, fell strangely silent when it came to pressing the British to compromise. The lesson was not lost on the prisoners: the winning of their demands rested solely on their own strength and on the support of their own people.

Bik McFarlane ...

My initial reaction was one of total disbelief – I simply couldn't take this in. We had the breaking of the Brits and I felt confident that we would have secured a successful resolution. The lever with which to prise a guaranteed settlement from them now seemed to have slipped from our grasp. Bobby told me to collect my thoughts while he wrote a quick note to Brownie (a pen-name used by Gerry Adams). But before he finished, he was again called to the hospital – it must have been approaching 10.00pm. There was deadly silence in the wing as his cell door was opened – bolts thudding back after normal lock-up times always carried a distinct and ominous ring. I had a sudden feeling that it would be a bitter irony indeed if Bobby's second visit to the hospital was to meet with Fr Meagher (whom we had codenamed 'The Angel') to discuss terms for a settlement, but now obviously too late to favour our desires. And I clearly recall shouting out my door to Bobby that I didn't want him returning to tell me that such was the nature of this visit.

It was the Angel alright, equipped with a document which had been presented to him by the Brits a few hours earlier. When Bobby came back to the wing again, he outlined the Brit document, but the feeling was that various interpretations could be applied to it. If the Brits wished, now that the intense pressure had eased, they could choose to apply a negative interpretation.

Thomas Loughlin ...

Later that night of 18 December, around midnight, Bobby came back from the hospital once again. The lads asked him the crack; he said that things had taken a turn for the better. We all became very optimistic. That was the last our wing saw or heard of him until Sunday, four days later. In H3 there were only two occupied wings: Bobby's was in D wing, ours was in B wing, so communication was difficult. The next day, however, Spotto Devine had a visit. When he came back, he gave us some great news. First of all, there was a notice up in the Sinn Féin centre informing families of what they could send in to us: meat, cigarettes, etc. It later emerged that this was the parcel that the Cages men were allowed. Secondly, there was to be a victory march on the Falls Road that Sunday. So the message was clear; we had won. Thus our wing was on a massive high until that Sunday when we went to Mass and saw the faces of the other wing: that's when the penny dropped.

Laurence McKeown ...

The cell door opened early. It wasn't yet time for breakfast. A tall, broad-shouldered man in a suit took one step inside and said, 'This is a copy of the statement made by the Secretary of State yesterday in the House of Commons'. He dropped a leaflet onto the bottom of my bed, or rather onto the rectangle of sponge that served as a mattress. The screw with him turned to us before closing the door and said, 'If yous can wash shortly, we'll get yous moved over to a clean wing and see about getting you some furniture.' The words on the tip of my tongue were, 'Fuck you and your clean wing and your furniture', but they were left unsaid.

This was the first morning of what I would consider my worst period of imprisonment. The previous night, just after the screws had left the wing to go home, there was a bit of commotion, a rattling of keys. Then all of a sudden my cell door opened and Bobby Sands stepped in. He was out of breath and appeared excited or agitated. He was looking for Pat Beag – Pat McGeown – who was OC of H6, but the screws had brought him to me by mistake. He said, 'It's over; the stailc's críochnaithe. It's OK, the boys are OK'. We asked him what the crack was, but he just repeated, 'It's over' and asked which cell Pat was in. He left then, and spent a few minutes with Pat. He appeared exhausted, as no doubt he was with all the responsibilities he had throughout the period of (what was later to be known as the first) hunger strike and with the number of Blocks he was visiting that night to carry the news about the end of the fast.

I was in the cell with Mackers (Anthony McIntyre) at the time. I had been moved in with him three days previously when he and I and 28 others in the camp joined the hunger strike. We just looked at each other for a minute and then passed the scéal down the pipes about the end of the stailc. There was some cheering from a few of the lads and a lot of questions. Shortly after this, when Bobby had left, Pat Beag got up to repeat what we had heard. He said Bobby would be in contact with the hunger strikers again that night and would arrange to meet with all the Block OCs the next day to keep them up to date. The scéal was shouted over to the other wings.

There was much discussion out the window the rest of the night. Speculation was rife as to how exactly the stailc had ended, who had been involved and what would occur the following day. Because a lot of these points were still unanswered, there was a reluctance to become too excited. Years of protest had made us cynical about the Brits and the manoeuvres they would make. This feeling was strengthened by radio reports that night saying simply that Republicans had called off the hunger strike. Suspicions began to grow and were confirmed by our early morning visitor. However, we also realised the Brits would not want to publicly concede defeat, so we reckoned that possibly what was being played out was an exercise in media manipulation.

Later that morning Pat was called to go to H3. With his departure, the speculation again began in earnest. The administration was facilitating the meeting of Block OCs so we guessed something definite must be thrashed out. We had been aware of how Bobby had been allowed up to see the hunger strikers any time he wanted – just request a van and it was there – and all the NIO statements about not recognising prisoners' self-appointed leaders was just so much nonsense because he regularly met and spoke with governors about the situation. So we were expecting some definite news.

Séanna Walsh . . .

Before breakfast the door of my cell was opened and I was told to get some clothes on. I walked over to where the class officer was standing and I asked him was I going to the hospital for a meeting. He told me no, that I was going over to H3. He said, 'Fair play to yous; you've got everything but the name. Sure yous have earned it.' I went out and got into a van, even though we were only going from H5 to H3, about 250 yards. It was still dark. The escort in the back of the van said he was glad to see it would all be over by Christmas. I grunted, not knowing whether to agree or disagree. When I went into H3, I was brought into Bobby's wing and put into cell 26 which was empty except for some lockers with all the clothes in them and a few tables on which were religious magazines. Bobby came bouncing in with his towel on and closed the door over. He had a 30 page document in his hand and his mood was ebullient. He told me that there was absolutely nothing concrete in the document but it was so wide open he could drive a bus through it. Bobby said that the document was wide enough for interpretation – that if he had got the Brits around the table to negotiate on the basis of the document, he said he could have 'taken the trousers off them'. If he negotiated now that it was ended he just didn't know how much leeway he would be able to claw back. He said that the Brits were divided, as far as he could make out – some seemed to be advocating movement and concessions, while others appeared to be interested only in making us eat dirt. He told me he had been at a meeting the night before, after he left our Block. Bobby's observations about the division in the Brits' camp came from outside, I believe, and it was something he was to touch on again and again over the next two to three months. The whole top strata of governors and chiefs in the prison plus most of the NIO prison section seemed to believe we were well and truly hammered, that they could do what they wanted with us. We were, they believed, mortally weakened and had no cards to play.

Laurence McKeown . . .

When Pat returned from H3, he told us that all the Block OCs had been brought to H3 to see Bobby. Bobby told them about a document the Brits had presented to the hunger strikers the previous evening and, upon examination of this, it was considered to fulfil the five demands we had put forward. The document was to be further discussed and details thrashed out, but on the basis of what was on offer and as Sean McKenna was in a critical state by that time, the hunger strike was called off. Bobby had been called to the hospital and informed of this. He then went round the Blocks informing the lads as we already knew from his own visit to us. Later that night he was called back to the hospital for a talk with the hunger strikers. It was then that the first doubts about the Brits' sincerity began to emerge. In a brief chat Bobby had with a government official there was no talk about specifics and generally a reluctance to enter into dialogue. Not all this came out, though, in Pat's talk at the door. Some of it I was piecing together in my own thoughts and confirmation of it only came at a later date.

I can understand that at the time Pat didn't want to raise any fears which might after all be unfounded, but he was having difficulty explaining to the lads why we were still without our clothes and still spreading shite on the walls. One bloke, totally convinced and overjoyed at our victory, shouted up to him, 'Here Pat, what do you reckon with that dickhead who came round this morning!' This was intended as a very humorous remark about what appeared to him to be a ridiculous exercise. It drew a less than exhuberant response. A man returning from visits told of a victory march organised for West Belfast that Saturday night. We weren't so sure.

Pat attended meetings over the next couple of days. With the feedback from each one, the position became clearer – if you read between the lines. Some who were doing that reading began to put these questions direct to Pat. He didn't have answers to them. In fact, he was in an impossible position of agreeing with the inference in the questions but having to give answers which portrayed a more positive picture. Dialogue was ongoing, he said, between Bobby and the No. 1 governor and NIO officials. In fact, the No. 1 governor, Hilditch, who had been abroad on holiday, had flown home early to take control of any negotiations. Suggestions were made to allow us to have pyjamas or football rig-outs so that we could immediately move to clean accommodation. This was refused by Hilditch.

At this stage, given what I saw happening in the Blocks, coupled with what we were hearing on the radio, I began to view the situation as very bleak. This opinion was strengthened when the administration no longer permitted meetings between Bobby and the Block OCs. Some of the screws has also begun to voice their opinion that 'Yous got nothing'. This in particular made us feel very demoralised. Our struggle through the Blanket and no-wash protest culminating in the hunger strike was, on an everyday practical level, more waged against them than Thatcher or the British government or the NIO. The screw in the wing was the enemy and the hunger strike which was to defeat him had not achieved its purpose.

All the hopes which had been built for an end to the protest and victory for our demands were now dashed. It wasn't a case of just 53 days (the duration of the hunger strike) that we had waited and hoped for victory. It was four years of protest, four years of being confined to a cell, no books, no exercise, no TV, magazines, washing facilities, clothes, adequate food and all the other smaller but no less important aspects of life we take for granted. The hunger strike was to end all that. All our hopes had been pinned on it. There would not only be the victory in terms of a change in our material living conditions but also an important psychological victory over the screws; that hadn't happened. At least that's how I felt about it.

Some of our lads, strangely enough, still thought that things were OK and that soon the whole situation would be resolved. I felt a rage at what the Brits had done. I realised also that they had played a very shrewd game. By presenting those on hunger strike with a document which catered for a resolution to all our demands and agreeing to thrash out the details later that evening they had left those on the hunger strike with the moral dilemma of what to do with a comrade who could die at any moment. Their decision, the understandable and predictable one to make, was to call off the stailc and thus ensure Sean McKenna didn't die. With the public announcement that the stailc had ended the Brits no longer felt under the same pressure and reneged on the document. They now put forward their interpretation of it, which effectively meant granting us nothing.

Séanna Walsh . . .

The Saturday after the first hunger strike finished I was in a cell with Paul Brennan; next door was Jackie McMullan and Willie (Deek) Johnston. Jackie was carrying 'Mrs Dale' at this time. He listened to a programme on Saturday night on which Bernadette McAliskey was in a studio with a few others, and she was presenting the Republican position. She said that while we hadn't won our five demands, we'd get our own clothes over the next few days, which would allow us to come out of the cells and eat our Christmas dinner together in the canteen. And she wished us luck in the long draw-out days of the negotiations that were to follow. This gave rise to a general buzz throughout our wing and when I was over talking to Bobby a day or two later, I was called into the PO's office on my way back into H5 and PO Sam H asked me, 'Well, do you want me to get these canteens ready? Yous will be getting your own clothes in for Christmas, won't you?'

SEAN LENNON . . .

From the first hunger strike ended until that Sunday felt like months. We were hearing a lot of rumours. The following day men returned from the visits with all sorts of scéal. Gerry Adams had been on TV and he had a document outlining the conditions under which we could end the protest and it was a favourable one. It had been given to us by the Brits. Adams was saying they had backtracked. Another lad reported there had been a victory march for us on the Falls Road. These type of rumours fuelled speculation within the Blocks that an agreement had been reached. We were still waiting for formal word; Bobby was busy trying to see what was there, if anything, and sorting things out with our people outside and meeting with the administration. It took a couple of days before we found the true situation. I was totally shattered and very angry, but not in the least surprised with the Brits. Weren't they renowned for such things?

Immediately we began to ask what would be our next move. What would we do? Men were advocating the immediate restart of another hunger strike. Others were asking for time to reflect and see in what direction we would or could go. Let the dust settle. The first main objective was to clear up the confusion, not only within the Blocks, but more so among our own supporters outside. While this was all being done, Bobby was talking to the administration and trying to find a solution.

SÉANNA WALSH . . .

That Sunday Fr Faul said mass in H5. His sermon was about how 'perfidious Albion' could never be trusted; that once Patrick Sarsfield had surrendered after the Siege of Limerick, the ink wasn't even given time to dry before the British double-crossed the Irish and ignored all the statutes of the treaty; that you could never ever take the British at their word; their word meant nothing.

CIARAN MCGILLICUDDY . . .

My first visit after the first hunger strike was with my mother and father. On the way to the visits I noticed a marked difference in the screws; they didn't know what was going on and they feared for their future, so they weren't their aggressive selves. There were many other Blanketmen in the visits and their visitors all seemed to be in great spirits. But each Blanketman had an empty look in his eyes. When my mother and father came in, they gave me a big hug and waved to the other lads telling them how great the Blanketmen were. I was shattered. Halfway through my visit I saw another Blanketman greeting his family. My mother and father waved to him and his visitor stuck a big cigar into his mouth. He looked at me and I could see he was almost crying. His eyes seemed to be calling out for someone to save him. I felt empty when talking to my family. They wanted to know what clothes I'd need, whether I'd be out sooner. They were on cloud nine and I was at rock bottom. We had to present a good face because, although we knew the Brits had backed off, we knew Bobby was doing his best to bring the protest to an end and give the Brits and ourselves room to breathe. I left the visit feeling very low.

Bobby was coming from Block to Block, to the hospital and from talks with the administration. One time he was in our Block talking to our Block OC, Larry Marley. It must have been the first time we saw him in for a meeting and word was passed along the pipes not to be cheering him on his way in and out. Most men were feeling pretty low, but the minute Bobby walked into the front yard and we saw him we couldn't hold ourselves back and we cheered like mad. There was the OC of the Blocks walking down the yard and we banged like mad on the wire grilles. It was just a natural reaction. I felt very proud that day because within myself I knew the lads were still strong and were still in there fighting. Later, Bobby was talking to one of our lads and he told him to thank us because, even though he didn't want any cheering, when he heard us he was proud. That made me feel brilliant.

Sean Lennon . . .

I know Bobby's immediate reaction after the hunger strike ended, because he said to us, 'If we don't get any movement from the Brits within a very short period of time, then we will be starting a new hunger strike'. And he announced that he would be leading it. We also had a responsibility to keep the protest intact and ensure it didn't start to come apart. Had this happened we would have been completely beaten because I believed, had men started leaving in any sort of numbers, the whole thing would have collapsed.

We began to talk about where to go from here, always looking on the optimistic side of it, not allowing any discussion to go along the road of going into the system. We deliberately did this because, with the state of play in the Blocks after we heard there was nothing, any such talk could have easily led to men moving away from the protest. A few did go but the vast bulk of men remained. They decided they were not going to be forced into submission by the Brits and that we had gone too far and suffered too much to just pack it in now. We were strong and dedicated to seeing the protest through to a successful conclusion.

SÉANNA WALSH . . .

In the immediate aftermath of the first hunger strike Bobby was adamant that there was no other way but another hunger strike. But after the initial few days, he began to believe that he might be able to salvage enough to allow us to create an acceptable ambience to do our wack. Most important of all was the issue of access to our own clothes, so the idea was hatched whereby, instead of us agreeing to conform for 30 days, after which we would be entitled to our own clothes (this was a device by which the administration tried to make us eat dirt and to allow them to claim outright victory), Bobby was working on a scheme whereby all protest would end on a given date. Due to our physical state after four years of Blanket protest, we would 'go on the sick', but use toilets and washing facilities and be issued with prison pyjamas and bedroom slippers. After 30 days we would get our own clothes (so many each day) and take up orderly duties in the wings, and we'd go on to develop it from there. Bobby really believed at one stage that this would work and thus avoid the tragedy which came to be the inevitable consequence of a second hunger strike.

JAZ MCCANN . . .

As Christmas approached, Fr Toner came in to see us and inform us of an agreement that was reached with the No. 2 governor. We were to be moved into a clean and furnished wing the following day and we were to report sick. Being sick would mean that we would not have to work and we would be issued with pyjamas and dressing gowns, which meant that we would not have to wear the prison clothes. This would mean that the protest would end for the Christmas period and Bobby could use that period to continue with his talks with the governor to find a final solution.

The thought of enjoying our Christmas dinner together and watching TV (the first in four years for some of us) excited us. The craic was good that night as we discussed what we would do over Christmas, what programmes we might see and food we would eat. First thing the following morning, as was normal before a wing shift, the screws collected the cell cards, but, unlike other times, instead of the shift beginning immediately after the cards were collected, there was a delay, and a shout came from the circle telling the screws to 'hold on'. Time passed; there was no movement. The wing waited in silent expectation of a special Christmas, but as time passed these expectations faded, and when the screws came back and replaced the cell cards, we knew something had gone wrong. And so it had. Later we were to hear the rumour that, when the No. 1, Hilditch, got wind of the arrangement, he ordered that it was to be stopped. So we were moved into a clean wing but it was unfurnished. They reneged on the agreement for Christmas and the protest carried on as before. Many of us were disappointed to the point of bitterness but it fired our resolve to beat the bastards.

That incident made it abundantly clear to us that the NIO/prison administration had not the goodwill to find a solution. If they could not find it within themselves to allow a liberal interpretation of their rules for Christmas (which called for no loss of face), it was inconceivable that the will was there to find a long-term solution. They were not interested in solutions; they wanted a victory.

Bik McFarlane . . .

There was a great deal of confusion in the Blocks and a degree of apathy taking root. Quite a number of the men who had returned to protest action in October had made the journey back to the conforming Blocks. (In fact, some had even gone in the first few weeks of the hunger strike.) We needed to get some positive movement in order to end the uncertainty – it was soul-destroying sitting there, unable to do anything constructive. So, after further consultation with the leadership of the Republican Movement, we decided on one more attempt at defusing the situation. Two wings were selected – ours in H3 and one in H5 – to end the no-wash protest and move into clean furnished cells as a first step to ending all protest action.

Jaz McCann . . .

In mid-January Bobby resumed his meetings with the governor and an agreement of sorts was reached between them. The idea was that we would gradually de-escalate the protest to facilitate the conditions wherein the administration could implement change. Two wings – Bobby's and ours – were to be moved into clean and furnished wings. We were not to dirty these wings. The two wings would end their no-wash protest and 10 men from each wing would make themselves available for work. The work had to be of an educational or vocational nature, or wing maintenance. The families of these 20 men would leave clothes in for them.

On the appointed date the de-escalation swung into action. The focus in the wing was on the 10 men. They washed, shaved, had their hair cut and prepared for work. The reception from the governor was not what was expected. He said that he would decide what type of work they would do, and that if they did want to conform to prison rules, they would be moved into the work Blocks. He refused to issue them with their personal clothing until they fully conformed. In other words, 'Surrender!'

They didn't give a damn about implementing changes in the regime. I honestly believe that they thought they had us beaten and wanted to rub our noses in it. Had they, instead of shutting all doors, given us a face-saver, there would have been no hunger strike – although that is not to say that would have been the end of the matter. I'm quite sure that we would have entered their system with the intention of wrecking it. I think Bobby went to great lengths to get that face-saver and that possibly the NIO/prison administration perceived this as weakness on our behalf and decided to put the boot in when – as they may have perceived it – we were down. If this was the case, they were to get a rude awakening. The diplomacy was over. We were to make no more overtures or goodwill gestures. The order came to the wing – smash the place! We did so with a vengeance. It was war!

I felt good that night smashing my cell to pieces. I'm sure all the lads did. It wasn't just the satisfaction of breaking furniture but the message that it would be sending to the Brits. The elation soon turned to apprehension when I heard grilles banging and keys rattling at the top of the wing. The screws were in and ready to wreak their revenge.

Two at a time we were dragged out of the cells, run out of the wing and kicked and thumped as we went. They ran us across the circle and into a wing that was half flooded because it was in the middle of being cleaned. We were locked in cells that had nothing in them at all except pools of water. We expected them to throw us in blankets and mattresses later, but they never did. I was absolutely freezing. I was also tired but I had to keep moving in order to keep some warmth in my body. I spent that whole night jumping up and down and walking backward and forward, trying to avoid the pools of water as I went.

After we had all been moved into the half-flooded wing and the screws left, the adjoining wing shouted over to us to enquire how we were. It could not have been easy for them to listen to the wing shift because there was a lot of shouts, screams, banging and thumping. However, while we had all been beaten, the casualty list was not that bad, apart from the fact that one man took a mild heart-attack (and about 40 others nearly took one). Another man thought that his arm was broken, but it later turned out to be only badly bruised. One of the lads who had only one leg was dragged the whole way from wing to wing and suffered quite a few injuries in the process. But the worst had to be spending the night fighting off the sleep and the cold.

The following morning, for the first time ever, I was glad to hear the screws coming into the wing. And when they brought the breakfast round there was another first – I ate the porridge. I was ravenous. I could have eaten a bucket of the stuff. I actually enjoyed it and it was warm. I could feel my innards thawing out and life returning to parts of my body. About half an hour later they threw us in blankets. I wasted no time wrapping one around myself and slumped into the corner to defrost. It's amazing how happy a bowl of porridge and a blanket can make you.

But it was short-lived. Twenty minutes later I heard the bolts of cell doors being shut and the lads shouting 'wing-shift!' We were allowed to walk this time. We were taken out of the Block, put on a bus and driven to H6. H6 had a welcoming committee for us. The minute I set foot in that Block I could sense it – trouble! One at a time we were taken into the washhouse where the mirror-search awaited us. I wouldn't bend and they booted me up and down the washhouse. It was the worst search I had ever received. They punched and kicked me, stuck fingers in my mouth, pulled my hair and it seemed to go on for ever. I was then locked in a cell with no blankets or mattress. The rest of the wing were also without bedding, and it wasn't until about 4.30pm that they eventually threw blankets and mattresses into us. I could have slept for a week but for the fact that the uncertainty of what could happen next kept me on edge.

Bobby's wing, which had also smashed up, were moved into the wing facing us. They had experienced treatment similar to ours. The night was spent shouting greetings back and forth: 'Tell Harry, Mickey and John that Paddy and Andy were asking' etc. The whole thing pissed me off. I just wanted to sleep but the shouting went on and on. Characteristically, Joe McDonnell was one of the worst culprits. He was not into the nauseating business of shouting greetings across. In fact, if anything, he would twist a greeting: 'Tell Harry, Mickey and John that Paddy and Andy said they were no good . . .' and he wouldn't be a bit shy with his language. Joe loved scéal and he busied himself for the rest of our stay (a week) in H6, extracting all he could from the lads facing him in Bobby's wing. When he heard that Bik was facing him, he began to misbehave somewhat. He wanted to know if Bik was the 'lunatic' who was going to be a priest. Of course this was his way of getting the craic going. There was no intention to insult. No one better than me knows this because, what Bik received for a week, I got day after day for a couple of years.

Laurence McKeown . . .

Thus ended a period of confusion and of hopes raised only to be dashed. We now knew exactly where we stood. When a comm came round explaining the situation, outlining the attempts we had made to resolve the deadlock and detailing the manner in which we had been arrogantly rebuked at every turn, I was delighted that we would be embarking on a second hunger strike. For a while it had seemed as if we would just give up or be forced to concede defeat. I knew that wasn't how the majority of men felt. We had been through too much to accept that we had gained nothing. A large number of those who had returned to the protest for the duration of the hunger strike had already begun to leave, realising that the situation was no different from that several months previous. That didn't concern me so much. I had been glad to see them return as it had bolstered our numbers for a while, but at the end of the day it wasn't numbers on the protest that was going to win our demands, but the resolve to see our struggle through to a successful conclusion.

We knew that hunger strike was the only way out of the impasse. The NIO were not prepared to yield an inch, and all the politicians, churchmen and pseudo-liberals who had been vocal during the hunger strike (asking that we end it in order to allow the British government to negotiate free from pressure) were all suddenly mute. Faced with this intransigence, the feeling was that we should take them on and show them that we were not beaten, nor could we be. Our integrity was at stake. We felt that some of our pride was restored the day that volunteers were once again asked to forward their names for hunger strike. We were back in the fight and hitting back.

Bik McFarlane . . .

We were informed by Hilditch in no uncertain terms that we would be getting absolutely nothing whatsoever in the way of 'jail privileges' until he had every one of us working in full conformity under the criminal regime. There was a pretty fierce confrontation in the governor's office in the circle between Bobby and Hilditch, with Bobby defiantly and unequivocally stating our position in very plain language. We were political prisoners and nothing the British attempted would change that. There would be no conformity, no acceptance of criminalisation. Therein lay the end of negotiations and the end of confusion. From then on there would be no uncertainty. We knew what course we would have to take – only one existed which would rid us of the nightmare existence and hammer criminalisation into oblivion. The cost would certainly be very great and we had to give very serious consideration to the fact that, in committing ourselves to a second hunger strike, we would be committing the Republican Movement to a course of action which had the potential for disaster written all over it. There could be no failure – we would either win or die. In fact, we would have to die in order to win.

Morale, which had taken a battering the previous weeks, again began to rise as we discussed the impending hunger strike action. It was at this stage that I took over the position of OC from Bobby, and Ricky O'Rawe filled the post of PRO. I did not relish my role at all and had even argued with Bobby about his selection of me for the position. In truth I was very much afraid of the immensity of responsibility I was about to assume, and I desperately tried to off-load it onto Séanna Walsh, an extremely dedicated and able man, who was also well-known by the leadership of the Republican

Movement and a very close friend of Bobby's. So I argued very strongly in favour of him assuming command. I even had an unexpected ally in the form of a comm from the Army Council which suggested Séanna for the role. While bolstering my argument, it nevertheless didn't do my confidence much good to know that the Army Council, in communication with Bobby, had indicated that I was not the preferred choice. The reasons weren't stated, but my fertile imagination ran rampant – maybe they thought I was weak; perhaps they didn't want a relatively unknown quantity in that position; was I unpredictable or was I too close to Bobby? It wasn't easy to come to terms with the fact that I would be working with people who didn't particularly desire me in that situation. But Bobby won the arguments, both with myself and the Army Council. He felt confident having me as OC, chiefly because we both understood the gravity of the situation and the possible political ramifications if we failed. We knew what needed to be done and he was convinced that I wouldn't let him down when the crisis finally arrived. The argument was wound up on a particularly distressing note for me when he told me that Séanna was very close to him and he believed that if negotiations came about, with himself in a critical condition, Séanna would not let him die. The obvious inference in that of course was that I would allow him to die if negotiations weren't producing our desired settlement.

We set about examining the best possible strategy and selecting names from among the dozens who had again volunteered for hunger strike. It was decided that only four would commence hunger strike, but that a series of replacement hunger strikers would be used in the event of anyone's death. Furthermore, our strategy would be one whereby each hunger striker began at staggered intervals. This would have the effect of negating any potential group mentality developing as a collection of men neared a crisis point simultaneously. Each would have to endure the ordeal alone. It would also send a signal to the Brits that we were accepting that deaths would be inevitable this time, and that no collective of hunger strikers in the critical stages would be there to call a halt. A proper, negotiated and honourable settlement would see an end to the issue.

FELIM O'HAGAN . . .

If I was against the first hunger strike, I was doubly opposed to this second one – at the time I frankly thought it was madness. However, while I had never met nor even seen Bobby Sands in the flesh, it's obvious that he had a very clear view of what defeat in the Blocks would mean for the overall struggle; he was single-minded in his pursuit of victory or, at least, setting the ground for victory. I didn't know what set Bobby off from others (and I detest the 'sanctification' of any person) but he must have had an extra quality of political perception.

It is amazing now to realise that there was only two and a half months between the end of the first hunger strike and the start of the second. Five years exactly since the special category status had officially been withdrawn and we were prepared for the 'final' showdown in the battle against criminalisation. Not that it felt like a showdown; it was more like an anticlimax. So much effort, emotion and sweat had gone into the first hunger strike that it didn't seem possible to regenerate the momentum. It was apparent this time, and Bobby clearly stated so in his comms, that POWs would die. We revived our propaganda effort, sending comms to any individual or organisation here and abroad whom we thought could conceivably help (and many who we knew would tear them up without a second glance – I recall sending one to Hans Dieter Genscher, the West German Foreign Minster!).

SÉANNA WALSH . . .

Fr Niall Carlin, from Derry, came into H5 to say mass one Sunday as we were just beginning to psyche ourselves up for the battle ahead. He was a member of the charismatic movement and used to preach about speaking in tongues and how God would come down at his prayer meetings and give blind people back their sight, how cripples would throw down their crutches and stand up, how metal pins would drop out of their legs and they could then walk again.

We were at mass with the wing containing Martin Hurson, Raymond McCreesh and Francie Hughes. I had been given a list of the lads who had volunteered once again for a hunger strike and asked to explain exactly what we were talking about with a second hunger strike, that we were not just expecting that the Brits would let prisoners die this time, but we were 100% sure that they would. I was also asked to ascertain the demeanour and likely commitment of certain men. Amongst them were Francie and Raymond. So there I was talking to the lads, in as light a way as possible, making sure that they were under no illusions, spelling out the strategy; how there would be no ground this time, that only the man himself would be able to put himself on hunger strike and that as such, no one would have responsibility for anybody else. It also meant that only British concessions or the hunger striker himself could end his hunger strike, not the IRA authority outside, not the jail OC, not even Bobby.

This is what we were talking about when Fr Carlin began his sermon and started to preach about how the Blanketmen and the hunger strikers had been conned in the first hunger strike by the IRA – that they had been cynically used because both John Hume and the Quakers (who run the visitors' cafeteria in the prison car park) had offered to negotiate on our behalf and that we (the Blanketmen) had refused this offer after 'orders' from the leadership outside. He went on to say how evil it was to continue our protest in the wake of this. At this I stood up and asked him what he was talking about. Myself and one or two others in the Block were aware that negotiations had in fact been underway when the first hunger strike ended, that direct contact had been opened with the British government. I told him that he didn't know what he was talking about, that he wasn't aware of the full facts and that he was in the Block to minister to the prisoners' spiritual needs, not to undermine their morale. You could have heard a pin drop.

He looked down at me with disdain and lifted the crucifix off the altar and above his head. 'If you believe in this you'll know that I speak the truth,' he said. I was purple at this stage and I was shouting at him that he was poking his nose into things he hadn't a clue about and that he was out of order. A few of the lads put their hands on my shoulders and told me not to blow; they thought I was going to attack him, but I just stood and stared at him.

I was worried about the effect this would have on the lads and, as soon as mass was over, I turned to them and apologetically began to explain myself. 'You shouldn't have held back,' said Francie. Raymond, who was one of the most pious people I've ever come across in my life, just looked into my face and said that he had no time for Fr Carlin or for all his fancy talk of charismatic meetings with people speaking in tongues and miracles taking place on a weekly basis. 'I've no time for that faith healer and all this fancy new-fangled business,' he said. He just looked at me again, reading my face, and said, 'The last time, when I volunteered for this hunger strike, I really believed we could win without any lives lost; it won't be like that this time, will it? Like, I'm going to die amn't I?' I couldn't say anything for fear of breaking down; I just nodded my head. 'Well, I'll let you know tonight about still being in the first squad'.

That night after lights out he sent over word, 'Raymond says "lean ar aghaidh"' (go ahead). He had spent the whole day going through it all in his head, and on his knees with his rosary. I knew once he had made up his mind there was no shaking his resolve.

With Francie it was just a case of 'Right, when's the big day? Look, is there any loose talk? What are the 'RA going to do when we start dying?' Such strength and true grit against those sort of odds is really awesome.

A couple of weeks later, after we had announced publicly that Bobby was to commence the hunger strike on 1 March, I ran into Francie as I was going into the visits. I asked him how he was; he grinned and said, 'Brilliant; the sooner we're into it the better. The way I look at it, you can fool some of the people some of the time. There was no other way out'. I asked had he told his family that he was going on hunger strike on 15 March; he grinned again and said, 'Well, I told them I was going on it shortly, but sure they'll know the date when they switch on the radio and hear the news'.

Laurence McKeown . . .

With the announcement of another hunger strike came the cold realisation that this time men would definitely die, and I knew that Bobby would be the first among them, as he said he would be leading the stailc. This time the strategy would be different — men would join it at different periods. When he asked for names, I had put mine forward immediately. I had already gone through all the arguments prior to the first hunger strike as my name had been down for it and, given that one consideration in the selection of men for the first stailc had been geographical spread, it appeared at one stage that I could very possibly be a candidate. I had therefore considered the possibilities very strongly and assessed my own commitment. I felt I could go through with it and felt I wanted to do it. I believed that our form of protest had peaked and it required a hunger strike to bring things to a head. I felt no differently now.

The first hunger strike *had* focused attention on what was happening in the Blocks. It had brought people out onto the streets showing the support there was for our five demands and, as nothing whatsoever had been conceded by the Brits, my own view was that there was no way we could avoid another hunger strike. Feelings in the Blocks were very high. There was a good deal of anger at how the Brits had connived to steal a victory from us. To suggest anything other than to hunger strike would have received little hearing. Besides that, there really were no other avenues open to us — other than to surrender. We had discussed it. Often the debate was heated and lacked objectivity. Some suggested everyone should go on hunger strike immediately, but we knew that whatever we did would need to be worked out very clinically and carefully. When Bobby's comm arrived announcing the second hunger strike it answered all our questions and reflected the feelings we had.

One point in it which I was opposed to was the decision to end the no-wash protest. This was to end on 2 March. Bobby would be starting the fast on 1 March. I thought that this would come across as a weakening of our position and that it would seem as if we were selling out Bobby just as soon as he began his fast. We debated it out the door and I was very emotional in my protest against ending it and the majority view expressed in our wing was similar. This differed from other wings and Blocks who thought it was a good idea, something which I only realised once we did it. It provided a lot of publicity on the day we ended it. It removed a good deal of confusion in the public mind and focused media attention clearly on the five demands. I also later realised that Bobby had been ensuring that, if the second hunger strike still did not bring us victory, we would at least be out of the no-wash situation and could much easier move forward into some other scenario.

That all came in hindsight, however. What won me over to accepting it was that it was Bobby who was saying it and also it was he who was going on hunger strike. There was therefore no argument against it in that sense. I have often looked back on it as a good reminder for when I am assessing situations. It taught me to look outside of my immediate conditions and circumstances and not get emotionally tied to particular tactics or to carry on with a particular course of action for no other reason than that it's the traditional way to do it.

Letter writing now began again in earnest to explain the situation: what had happened at the end of the first hunger strike and why we were now being forced to once more embark upon the stailc. There wasn't much talk in the media about it. Bishop Edward Daly came out with a statement against it. Funny how all the bishops had disappeared when the Brits reneged on their earlier deal. Not a word from them at all. Nothing either from all the other supposedly humanitarian individuals and organisations, all those who had called on us to talk, to enter into dialogue to resolve the stalemate. None of them uttered one word of condemnation at the Brits' treachery or appealed for concessions to be made. We realised we had an uphill battle before us to mobilise support, but we knew it was out there in our local communities and further afield.

During February, those who had been on the first stailc were moved out of the hospital and back into the Blocks. The Dark and Nixy (John Nixon, Armagh) came to our wing and the first chance we got to see them was the next Sunday. Everyone was up round them, asking how they were. Nixy was very lively, the Dark much less so, but then it wasn't in his character to be extrovert. I remember looking across at him from the far side of the canteen and wondering just what thoughts were going through his head. A few months ago he had been OC of the Blocks and about to go on a hunger strike which would end a four year stalemate. Now Bobby who had taken over from him as OC was also about to begin a hunger strike, again to end the stalemate. I knew the Dark would feel responsible for the circumstances we were in, even though he had really no control over events.

SEAN LENNON . . .

We didn't want another hunger strike; we hadn't wanted the first one, but both were forced on us. I was at this stage very angry and frustrated, like all the rest of the lads. The atmosphere in the Blocks was on a knife-edge, men were so disgusted with the Brits. We announced we would be restarting the hunger strike which we had suspended in December. We outlined to the world our reasons for having to embark yet again along this road. We called on everyone to stand behind us.

STATEMENT AT START OF SECOND HUNGER STRIKE:

We, the Republican POWs in the H-Blocks of Long Kesh, and our comrades in Armagh prison, are entitled to and hereby demand political status, and we reject today, as we have consistently rejected every day since September 14th, 1976, when the Blanket protest began, the British government's attempted criminalisation of ourselves and our struggle.

Five years ago this day, the British government declared that anyone arrested and convicted after March 1st, 1976, was to be treated as a criminal and no longer as a political prisoner. Five years later we are still able to declare that that criminalisation policy, which we have resisted and suffered, has failed.

If a British government experienced such a long and persistent resistance to a domestic policy in England, then that policy would almost certainly be changed. But not so in Ireland where its traditional racist attitude blinds its judgement to reason and persuasion.

Only the loud voice of the Irish people and world opinion can bring them to their senses and only a hunger strike, where lives are laid down as proof of the strength of our political convictions, can rally such opinion, and present the British with the problem that, far from criminalising the cause of Ireland, their intransigence is actually bringing popular attention to that cause.

We have asserted that we are political prisoners and everything about our country, our arrests, interrogations, trials and prison conditions show that we are politically motivated and not motivated by selfish reasons or for selfish ends. As further demonstration of our selflessness and the justness of our cause, a number of our comrades, beginning today with Bobby Sands, will hunger strike to the death unless the British government abandons its criminalisation policy and meets our demand for political status.

9

The Second Hunger Strike Begins

1 March 1981 – 5 May 1981

B obby Sands began his hunger strike on 1 March. Two weeks later he was joined by Frank Hughes and, a week after that, by Raymond McCreesh and Patsy O'Hara. The tactics of this hunger strike were to differ significantly from those of the previous one: it was planned to maintain maximum pressure on the British by having a succession of hunger strikers reaching critical stages one after another and replacing them immediately should they die. And those who embarked on hunger strike had no illusions – they knew that death was their probable fate.

In contrast to the previous October, public support proved difficult to harness. While sympathy with the prisoners' demands was still widespread, many were exhausted after the strain of the first hunger strike and disillusioned at its inconclusive ending. The H-Block/Armagh committees in many areas found themselves faced with an uphill struggle.

The inertia disappeared dramatically in April. In the Fermanagh/South Tyrone by-election Bobby Sands won a stunning victory, beating the Unionist candidate by almost 1500 votes. The international spotlight was suddenly focused on the H-Blocks as people wondered at such massive popular support for a person whom the British called a criminal.

Among the prisoners optimism soared. In the South the Dublin government came under pressure to persuade the British to compromise, but Taoiseach Charles Haughey contented himself with token and cynical gestures. For a time it seemed that a resolution without loss of life could be found – but such hopes were soon to be dashed.

LAURENCE MCKEOWN . . .

Just before Bobby went on hunger strike, I got the chance to see him when his wing moved from H3 to H6 for a short period during February. That particular Sunday he was busy talking business and the most we got saying to one another was, 'How are ya?' 'Keeping sound.' 'All the best'. He looked OK: thin, thin definitely, but relaxed. It can sound like a cliché, but he did look like someone who had made a decision about life and was happy with that decision, or had that look that reflected contentment or inner calm.

I also got to meet Francis Hughes for the first and last time. His wing had moved across the Block and we were at mass together. There were a few others there from South Derry whom I already knew well and I was quickly introduced to Francie. He was full of concern because he had just been told that week that he would not begin the hunger strike until two weeks after Bobby, instead of one week as had been originally decided. He worried that people outside, supporters in his local area, might think he was letting them down because he was to begin the stailc a week later than he had already told them. Besides that, he was in the very best of form and looked it too. At the end of mass we simply shook hands and said, 'All the best'.

TOMBOY LOUDON . . .

The week before Bobby was due to start the fast, he got up and told a book – *Jet 2* – which lasted right up to the night before he started the hunger strike. The next day, Sunday 1 March, the stailc began and Bobby almost missed mass that morning as the trousers that the screws threw him in were ripped to pieces. But one of the lads next door swung his into Bobby and didn't go to mass. He got a lot of notes from all the lads wishing him the best of luck. I got a note from Bobby and, as soon as I got back to my cell, I'm not ashamed to say I cried reading it; he said that he knew that he was going to die and he hoped that it would only take his death to achieve our demands and to end the suffering we had all endured. He said it would sadden him if he died and everyone didn't understand fully the reasons why. He also spoke of the suffering his family was going through and hoped that he could give them the strength to see it through. He finished by telling me not to worry about him and that he would always be with me.

SEAN LENNON . . .

I saw Bobby at mass on the morning before he went on hunger strike. Everyone was talking to him and shaking his hand; his reply to them was, 'You are talking to a dead man'. He was under no illusions about the outcome. He was a realist and knew that men would die, but he hoped that by his death we would get our demands and no more men would have to die. He was a leader of men and he led from the front all the time, no matter the price. We were all shattered for him that morning and there wasn't a man-jack in that canteen at mass who didn't show it on his face.

BIK McFARLANE . . .

On Sunday 1 March, following an emotional Saturday night of speeches, songs and farewells, Bobby commenced his hunger strike. The following day we called an end to the no-wash protest – it had run its course and would yield no further propaganda value. And it would provide for an easier transition into a new regime at the end of the hunger strike if clean furnished conditions were already in place. Added to that was the bonus of cutting down greatly on the isolation of hunger strikers who would have been moved out of the wings almost immediately. As it transpired, they remained with us for an average of three weeks before transfer to the prison hospital.

JOE McQUILLAN . . .

On Monday 2 March we were to ask for clean cells, the right to wash, shower, shave and have furniture put into the cells. We were told that we did not want to be engaged in any form of action that would take the highlight away from the stailceoirí. From the far wing, where Bobby was, we could hear several of the orderlies and screws singing funeral dirges. It turned out that they were walking up and down outside Bobby's cell with one of the tin lockers on their shoulders as if it were a coffin. One screw in particular took great delight in talking in the side of Bobby's cell door about food, especially hamburgers – how he fancied one with piles of onions, ketchup running over the sides, describing in great detail the taste and delights. Bobby told the men in the wing who wanted to tear him apart just to ignore him. At meal times they would give Bobby's cellmate, Malachy Carey, a normal small meal and would put one in for Bobby that was steaming hot and piled high with food. They would leave it sitting most of the day, and opening the cell door they would accuse Bobby of having eaten a pea as they had put '130 on the plate and now there are only 129'.

LAURENCE McKEOWN . . .

I was still in H6 when Bobby started his fast on 1 March. It got some coverage in the media, but not a lot. Ending the no-wash protest on 2 March generated much more excitement. Bishop Edward Daly made a statement in support of it and made noises to the Brits about their now conceding some reforms. The tactic of the hunger strike itself was, however, discouraged. Before the day was out I was already convinced of the correctness of the decision to end the no-wash protest, despite my earlier opposition.

First thing that morning, Pat Beag had informed the screws that we intended to wash and would want moved to clean accommodation with furniture. Within a short time we were moved over to D wing which had just been cleaned. The move across went very quickly and very smoothly. There was no mirror search, just a lot of screws looking very glum. I think it suddenly dawned on them that times had changed. We were once again dictating wants and we would now be out of the cells, even if only for short periods. Things would never be the same again.

We got new mattresses and blankets that dinner time; sheets came a few days later. It was some time before we got furniture. The screws had to work much harder now; no longer could they sit with their feet up in their office. We had all to get slopped out. Everyone had to be washed and wanted a haircut immediately. For men like myself who hadn't been force-washed it was at least three years since we had last washed.

Because the screws were fairly flexible and the lads were disciplined in not delaying in the showers, everyone in our wing was able to get a shower that day. I was amongst the last and that was after 8 o'clock that night. A pair of hand shears was available for taking beards off and I had great pleasure in removing the straggling wisps of hair I had hanging from below my chin. I had no moustache and looked like one of the Amish people.

The shower was brilliant, the water warm and the soap lovely. There was no shampoo, but I washed my hair with the 'buttermilk' soap which the prison supplies for washing. Although the soap is still held in low regard, I discovered then that it is probably the best to use. It contains just basic soap, no artificial colouring or scents and, even though water hadn't touched my skin for three years, it didn't feel harsh. I never ever thought that this could be the case until about three days later when I got soap and shampoos sent in by my family. I used 'Imperial Leather' and it felt as if I had washed in acid. My face was burning and sore for at least two days.

When the last one had been showered that night, the screws left the wing and the buzz of conversation was everywhere – at the doors, at the windows, on the pipes or just in the cells to a cellmate. I felt warm and clean in newly-washed blankets. I felt the mattress and the floor dry beneath me. I felt the freshness of my recently washed skin. I felt good.

The next day we had great laughs as we met one another on the wing. Some people were almost unrecognisable. In fact, when we got our hair cut some days later, some people were unrecognisable. We were lucky in that

Joe Clarke, a hairdresser by trade, was in the other wing across the Block from us and he got over to cut our hair as soon as he was finished in his wing. Fortunately he cut my hair before his wing was moved back to H5. When it was asked if anyone in our wing could cut hair, Harry McCavana said he could. Some of the samples of his work were worse than those the screws performed on us at the time of the forced washing and haircuts. Mackers was one of his victims so I saw his handiwork close up. No one really cared, though. Certainly not Harry who reaffirmed out the door that night that he could 'cut hair – I never said I could style it!'

JOE MCQUILLAN . . .

The NIO now removed a lot of the extra money they had been paying the screws for working in the 'dirt'. We heard one screw saying, 'I'm not sticking my fingers up anyone's arse if I'm not getting paid for it'. The NIO had said over the years that the searches were necessary for security reasons, but everyone knew that it was for harassment. If anything, I think the screws despised us for ending the protest, despite years of trying to beat us off it, and now that it was over they still weren't satisfied. If we'd realised years beforehand how much it would hurt them, I'd have been in favour of ending it much sooner!

One small concession the administration gave us was access to a 'library'. In fact, it was a trolley with 50 of the worst books imaginable; so they could say we all had a choice because there were 46 in the wing. Still and all, it made a change from the Bible. I had read it seven times from cover to cover, and certain parts of it I'd read 20 times or more on top of that. Another concession was that they stopped messing around with the light switches. Each cell has two switches inside; the top switch turns on one tube, the bottom switch turns on two tubes and, obviously, the two together turn on three. But on the outside of the cells there are also two switches which give the screws complete control. They would either leave the lights on 24 hours a day for a few weeks or so, or do the reverse. Now at least we had control during the day, and the screws turned them off at 11pm. The pressure off my eyes was welcome. Even the short walk to the washhouse twice daily was a great change. But the screws still refused to allow us out to the yard for exercise unless we put on the prison uniform. The uniform had been changed after the first stailc from the striped shirt and grey suit to 'civilian type' prison issue clothes, so we refused to wear them.

FELIM O'HAGAN . . .

To feel clean for the first time in years and to live in a clean cell seemed the pinnacle of luxury. The change immediately lifted morale, and the fact that we now had limited movement outside our cells both made communication easier and wrested back a little control from the screws – the wing outside the cells was no longer their sole preserve. Yet, while we were revelling in the unaccustomed luxury, our comrades were starving; I'm not saying we forgot about them; far from it, but it was certainly an odd situation.

TOMBOY LOUDON . . .

During the wing shift to a clean wing I was beaten over the mirror. As I crossed the circle to our new wing I was diverted into the PO's office where I was told that my father had died the night before. I was totally shattered when I reached the other wing. Bobby was only two cells away from me and I knew I had to tell him as he knew my father well; the news also shattered him and that night he sent me down a little note expressing his sympathy and concern for me. But I assured him I was fine and not to worry.

In the early days of his fast I would stand at the window and shout to him and the lads in the cell in between us would join in the conversation. We talked about our time in the Cages and some of the funny things that happened, like the time he went to the dentist for a check-up and came back with his three front teeth missing, or about the night the camp was burnt. Because our cells were so close together we were always out washing at the same time and I used to slag him about the haircut he got. The screws in the wing gave him a hard time about the food left in his cell. They had the plate overflowing with food and sat it on a table close to his bed; at first it annoyed him but he overcame that and told the screw who kept doing it to catch himself on and act his age.

THOMAS LOUGHLIN . . .

It's not that often you wake up on the Blanket feeling cheerful, but I did that morning, knowing that the no-wash protest was to end that day. Simple things like washing and shaving – often taken for granted – were now something to look forward to. All of us were full of anticipation that morning, particularly myself, as I had a visit with my wife and looked forward to telling her the good news. The hunger strike had started the day before, yet it was not something which dominated my thoughts because in comparison to the first one its beginning was very low key. It was in that frame of mind that I left the cell that morning to go on my visit.

Bik McFarlane was also going on a visit and we met between the grilles at the end of C and D wings. Going on visits always made us nervous because we were entering 'enemy territory'.

When we went out into the circle, Bobby happened to be coming out of the doctor's room. He had his head cocked to one side and looked very pale, but he always looked like that. Bik knew him better than I did, so he greeted him first in a jovial manner. All I could think of to say was, 'Alright, Bobby?' He didn't respond to us except to nod his head.

On the way down to the visit I mentioned to Bik that Bobby looked very downhearted; not that it was odd in any way – anyone facing such an ordeal would look the same way. But Bik's response surprised me: 'Do you know something, kid? You've just seen the face of someone who knows he's going to die'. 'Come off it,' I replied. 'No one will die'.

I'm not sure whether Bik's words convinced me of that reality at the time but I was struck because I couldn't get Bobby's image out of my mind. 'There was a man,' I thought, 'who knows he is going to die. How does he feel? What is he thinking? Is he afraid?' With these questions I was trying to get inside his head. I wanted to be Bobby Sands for just a second in order to experience his feelings. That frightened me because, even though I could understand his motivation, I couldn't understand where his courage came from. It was the type of courage I didn't have and it made me feel a sense of guilt. For those reasons that chance meeting with Bobby will always be my outstanding experience of the hunger strike.

Bik McFarlane . . .

Once again we launched into a massive letter-writing campaign, trying to exert even more pressure on Thatcher's government to adopt a flexible approach and resolve the crisis. As before, the 'concerned and interested' groups took their usual position of calling upon us to terminate the hunger strike and allow the British space to manoeuvre. The harassment and petty vindictiveness from the screws continued unabated and particular attention was paid to Bobby who was jibed at frequently and whose lights were flicked on and off repeatedly. He was still subjected to cell searches and the degrading mirror searches. It is a measure of the despicable character of some of those whose duty of guarding us degenerated to the depraved depths of torturing dying men.

Bobby was followed on to the hunger strike on 15 March by Frank Hughes and on 22 March by Raymond McCreesh and Patsy O'Hara.

Kevin Campbell . . .

Frank Hughes was in our wing. His attitude to the hunger strike was, 'I fought the Brits outside with guns and bombs and now because I'm in jail doesn't mean it's all over. I will continue to fight them and I will use my body as a weapon because our fight for political status is a part of the war'. The night before he went on hunger strike we had a singsong. Frank took it over after half an hour and did a one-man show with songs and stories. Between him and Martin Hurson they had the wing in stitches with their antics and stories about the country folk.

Eoghan MacCormaic . . .

Frank Hughes was always an impressive-looking figure. He had his own boots to wear because of the injuries to his leg, and at the start he had a crutch in the cell. It wasn't long before the screws took the crutch off him; they claimed it could be used as a weapon, but in reality it was because the men in his wing made great use of it at night to pass smokes or whatever up and down the windows, passing the crutch from hand to hand. Frank used to get the crutch then to use going out on his monthly visit, or for walking to the canteen on Sundays for mass. He could move the best ever you saw with the crutch, but when he was going down the yard he would move slowly to allow the screw to get in front of him a bit (the screws always walked behind the prisoners they were escorting to a visit), then he'd lift up the crutch and hold it like a rifle and give the screws 'a full mag' while all the boys watching at the windows would be laughing and calling out to him.

The screws hated Frank, but at the same time respected him. One English MO told me after Frank died that he was always afraid we would have more Frank Hughes because they would never beat us if we did. He did carry himself well, but he was also a joker and a mixer. Most of all, though I think he will be remembered as a soldier.

Kevin Deehan . . .

Raymond McCreesh then joined the strike and likewise he sang a song – 'County of Armagh' – and gave a small speech in which he said he was honoured to be going on the strike. Frank also sang a song that night but he was much weaker physically. But his spirit was the same. Raymond was then moved from the wing and put into C wing.

Martin Livingstone . . .

Raymond was charged with Paddy Quinn and Dan McGuinness and I was the first to talk to them when they came on remand into A wing yard in the Crum back in 1976. They were very suspicious and reserved as we were trying to suss out who they were and what they were in for. Raymond said nothing at all and Paddy gave brief answers. What struck me about Raymond was he was very well dressed – a suit and fancy boots – and we nicknamed him 'the Squire', as his dress suggested somebody with money. He also was very innocent and fresh faced and smiled a lot, although not saying much, but his manners and respect towards his comrades were always evident. He never got involved much in the sport and mixing about the wing, and he always gave the impression of being painfully shy. I never heard him cursing or saying a bad word about anyone, but in times of conflict and confrontation, he was always ready to get stuck in and to contribute to our various protests and actions, even at the early stage. Raymond was very religious and you could see that he'd been brought up in a very devout Catholic family.

Eoghan MacCormaic . . .

One day Tony O'Hara told me that his brother Patsy was back in the Crum, having been set up by the RUC. To be honest you treated all that as just another bit of scéal in those days; you had enough troubles of your own, you'd be thinking, lying in the cell with the walls covered in shite, etc. But it wasn't too long before Patsy was there with us himself, although when he arrived, he went to a different wing from ours. The wing he went to was known to us as 'the super wing', maybe unfairly, but we thought that in the parochial rivalries that each wing had in relation to the neighbouring wing, the Super Wing had a slight over-estimation of their own importance. They were always too busy for our liking having quizzes, féiseanna, amhránaíocht and so on, while we adopted a more 'who gives a damn' attitude to the whole thing and saw our main purpose in life as getting the next smoke and not squeaky-booting.

Patsy's claim to fame as far as our wing went was that he took the time to write out a massive precis of the book *Firepower in Angola* over a period of weeks on to toilet paper which he gave to Tony in our wing to tell as a book out the door. We had to suffer that book and Tony's grinding monologue for what seemed like weeks on end. Tony had visions of himself as being in the tradition of the seanachaí but his ambitions seemed to be to take the longest time on record to tell a book out the door. For that reason Patsy was universally 'hated' by our wing and no doubt loved by his own for inflicting three weeks of Angola on us.

Harry Murray . . .

When Patsy – known to us as 'Scatter' – came into the Crum on remand, he immediately involved himself in the protests which were taking place there at that time. He tended to go about with other members of the IRSP, but he also had time for others. When anyone came back from a visit, he always asked if they had heard anything, not scandal, more the military/political sgéal. He was a fairly serious person but he would not hold back from getting involved in the craic. When he was sentenced, he went to H5. He was quite quiet in the wing, only getting up to the door to take part in discussions.

On the morning he went on hunger strike, the wing was quiet when the screws came round with the breakfast. Most of the wing would have preferred not to take any breakfast, knowing that Scatter was on hunger strike.

Eoghan MacCormaic . . .

I used to see Raymond McCreesh at mass in H5, and we would say 'hello', but rarely much more than that. Then in March 1981 when he joined the second hunger strike, he was moved over to our wing from the wing he had spent the Blanket on (the 'yippie' wing in H5). For the previous year or so Raymond had been in the cell with Francie Hughes, and when he arrived onto our wing, he was put into cell 3 (C wing) while Frank was in cell 3 (B wing).

That night the two of them were up at the windows calling across the yard to each other and giving a bit of banter. Everybody had a sort of pious respect for the stailceoirí – when one of them talked at the window, the rest of us kept quiet to give them a chance to discuss whatever it was they had to discuss. Mind you, we were all secretly 'earywigging' to hear what sgéal there was going, since the place thrived on sgéal. I'll always remember the gist of the end of their conversation. Frank was saying that he expected to be moved to the hospital the next day, and was making his farewells to Raymond. He mentioned some cryptic piece of sgéal which the two had been talking about a few days previously, and said to Raymond that he had heard some more about it. Raymond wanted to know the details, but Frank wouldn't divulge a word of it. He probably knew we were all listening and, being a bit of a raker, liked to keep everybody guessing. 'Sure I'll tell you about it when I see you up at the hospital,' he said. 'What if I don't get to see you up there?' asked Raymond. 'Well, then, you'll just have to wait until we both get to the other place'. The two of them were laughing about that. They were both prepared to die, of course, but it was a bit scary to hear it being talked about in such a lighthearted way.

Tomboy Loudon . . .

On Bobby's birthday, Monday 9 March, we had a singsong and sung all the songs he had written and we called him for a speech; he got up to the door and thanked the lads for a great concert and said he would have given us one himself. but it was too cold to stand at the door. He said he was proud to be among his comrades, especially the young ones who had come through so much in the past few years and he knew what was at stake in the hard road that lay ahead; but no matter what, he wouldn't let anybody down. When he finished he said, 'Oiche mhaith' and the lads got up to the door and cheered, and I can honestly say a lot of men shed a tear that night. As the days passed, Bobby began to feel a lot more tired, but he still talked at the window and enjoyed a smoke (the lads in the next cell held onto his tobacco). When Bobby was to be taken to the prison hospital, he went round shouting into the lads through the doors. I got out of the cell on the pretence of going to the toilet and we met each other on the landing and threw our arms around each other. His last words to me were, 'Slán, cara'.

BIK McFARLANE . . .

After 23 days on hunger strike, Bobby was transferred to the prison hospital. I managed to get up to the washhouse for a few last moments with him as he prepared to leave. I had the awful feeling that we wouldn't see each other again. The previous Sunday at mass had driven home the stark reality of our situation. We were discussing overall strategy when he asked me what I would do after his death. It had sounded so matter of fact, as if that had already been decided and nothing we could do would alter such a fearsome inevitability. I suppose it was at that moment the painful truth of what lay ahead at last settled deep inside me. The barrier of optimism I had been erecting was rapidly ripped away by a severe dose of cruel reality. As he left the wing to a chorus of 'God speed' from a collection of eager voices, I settled down to write a short note updating the Army Council on developments.

SEAN LENNON . . .

At this time the local council elections were coming up and this was also the topic of conversation among us. There was a general view that we should contest them by putting up prisoners or members of our families or H-Block Committee members. It would be a great chance to bring more publicity on the hunger strike and also give anyone supporting us the chance to register that support to the world. But there was a problem: the Movement's policy at the time ruled out taking part in any elections in the North, even though we thought that it should be changed and the path cleared to allow us to contest them. We didn't contest them, but a lot of people were put forward on an anti-H-Block ticket and won seats. This was a great boost to the protest.

BIK MCFARLANE ...

The news from outside told of marches, meetings and demonstrations. People were taking to the streets in thousands all over Ireland and abroad to support our five demands. My crystal set was an invaluable asset, as long as I remembered to view BBC news reports with a degree of scepticism. Then came the sad news of the untimely death of Frank Maguire, the nationalist MP for Fermanagh/South Tyrone. He was a fervent believer in and worked for self-determination for the Irish people and a united, Britless Ireland, and he was a firm supporter of the prison struggle. It was decided that Bobby should run in the election for Frank's seat. Here was an opportunity to cut through the censorship and to lay low the erroneous assertion that we had virtually no support.

We were extremely enthusiastic about this tactic, at the same time realising that an election victory did not necessarily mean that the Brits would accede to our demands. There were periods when everything appeared static. We knew people outside were working feverishly, but cut off from all the activity and buzz, it could be difficult to visualise just how much was happening. Perhaps a couple of weeks dragged by with nothing major occurring – waiting was always a Blanketman's worst experience. The screws could sense the enthusiasm displayed at this political manoeuvre, but dismissed it in the firm belief that the Unionist, Harry West, would be victorious.

LAURENCE MCKEOWN ...

There was little mention of the hunger strike in the media and we didn't know if this was deliberate or just that it wasn't newsworthy at that period. But being fairly cynical about the media, we mostly opted for the former. When we heard that Bobby would be standing in the Fermanagh/South Tyrone by-election, we looked on it merely as something which would focus attention on the stailc. Not knowing the area or its history, we never thought for one moment that Bobby had a chance of winning the seat; at least that was our initial feeling. As the date of the election drew nearer, however, we were getting reports from outside which said that Bobby had a good chance of winning, though Fr Faul had said just that morning at mass that 'the people will give the Provos their money, their cars, their houses but never their votes'.

We wrote letters to everyone and anyone in the Fermanagh/South Tyrone area calling on them to support Bobby. The letters were smuggled out and some weeks there would be over 200 of them going out. This increased as the election drew nearer.

KEVIN CAMPBELL . . .

Around this time Frank was taken from the wing to the hospital. Even though he was only 25 days on the hunger strike he was very weak, but his morale was sky high. Six screws came to the cell to escort him out. This was intimidation but it failed to move Frank. As he left the wing, surrounded by these six screws, he raised his crutch in the air and shouted 'Tiocfaidh ar lá! Victory to the IRA! Victory to the Blanketmen!' We all banged on our cell doors. This was our last farewell to a brave comrade and friend. We were never to see him alive again. The screws were totally demoralised by this show of strength by him and the unity among ourselves.

JOE McQUILLAN . . .

When I heard of the death of Frank Maguire, I thought it was a bit of a blow to our campaign on the outside as he appeared to us to be a hard worker. When I heard that Bobby was being proposed to stand for his seat, I had reservations. My fear was, what if Bobby didn't get elected? Frank Maguire had held the seat, so it must be a strong Nationalist area, but what would happen if the Unionists won it? I thought that it wouldn't matter to the Brits how big a vote Bobby attracted, that if he was beaten even by a small number of votes that would be good enough for the Brits. Our hopes were raised when the SDLP was embarrassed into pulling out.

FELIM O'HAGAN . . .

The first month or so of the hunger strike passed uneventfully; indeed the reports we were getting back via visits were that the local RACs were finding it very difficult to generate support and enthusiasm. An atmosphere of foreboding began to build – and then suddenly Frank Maguire died. I don't know from where the idea arose that Bobby should be put forward as a candidate but the suggestion immediately seized us. It was recognised as the best, perhaps the only chance of saving lives and winning our demands.

We learned only snatches of the manoeuvres that went on to persuade Frank Maguire's brother to stand aside and let Bobby have a clear run, but when news came that he had withdrawn his nominaton papers, our propaganda went into overdrive. POWs from Fermanagh/South Tyrone were besieged with requests for the name of every person they knew; lists of names and addresses came in from outside and before long thousands of comms were on their way. The message was simple: vote for Bobby and ask your friends to do likewise; it's the last chance he has. City men who previously thought the world ended at Dunmurry now became experts on such exotic places as Belcoo, Lisnaskea, Augher, Clogher and Fivemiletown, holding forth on demographic and voting patterns since 1922. Priests who came in to say mass were assailed with questions about the area and canvassed for opinions on the outcome. Fr Faul, I well recall, declared unequivocally that while people in the area had Republican sympathies, they would never vote for Bobby in sufficient numbers: 10,000 was his estimate.

THOMAS LOUGHLIN . . .

10 April – this was the longest day of the hunger strike to date – waiting on the result of the by-election. The Block OC in H3 warned everyone to keep quiet regardless of the result because to do otherwise would only reveal to the screws that we had radios. Sometime that afternoon between 4 o'clock and 5 the result came through. The man with the radio went to the door and in a quiet voice, speaking in Irish, he announced to the wing that Bobby had won. For a moment there was complete silence until someone let out a small 'yippee'. This was followed by another one, then another and another until someone got up to the door, piss-pot in hand and began banging the door screaming 'Up the IRA! Victory to the Blanketmen!' Then another one started and so on until the whole wing was going mad. The other wings, on hearing this crescendo, couldn't contain themselves and they began to do the same and the screws began questioning how the lads came about such information, 'It must have been one of those orderlies who told the bastards; check and see if any of them are about'. God help any orderly who was caught in the wrong place.

FELIM O'HAGAN . . .

If the ending of the first hunger strike was my lowest point, the day of Bobby's election was my highest. Throughout the day, the man with the crystal radio set listened in and passed reports down the pipes or out the door in Gaeilge. We in H4 had been well warned not to display any reaction in front of the screws when the result finally came through. After dinner, as usual, Larry (Marley) and I put our blankets on the floor and walked up and down together – little was said; reports had been already analysed and re-analysed; now there was just the waiting. After tea the screws left the wing at 4.30 and a really deep silence fell; we knew the radio would be set up as soon as they cleared off and it wouldn't be long before the result was known. When we heard cell walls being softly rapped up the line, we both immediately crouched down by the pipes and were waiting there when the rap finally came on our wall. 'Tá an bua againn' (We've won). All I remember next is the two of us dancing around the cell, punching the air, mouthing screams of delight – all in complete silence! Having passed on the news to the next cell we resumed our walk, huge grins on our faces, bursting into laughter every now and then. No doubt a similar scene of silent hysteria was played out in every cell and not one triumphant word was heard out the doors.

At 5.30 the screws came back; normally they would be talking loudly to each other, some of them half-drunk after a few pints in their club. This time there was only the sound of grilles being opened. After 6.00 they came around with the tea-urn on the trolley to dish out the supper, and to see their shattered expressions was a joy. We had a hard time of it trying to keep a straight face. After years of brutality, abuse and humiliation it was a very sweet moment, and sweeter to know that thousands of people supported us.

LEONARD FERRIN . . .

It was approaching 4.00pm. Excitement was at fever point as Paddy 'Mo' Burnside and I paced the floor of the cell. Like all Blanketmen that day, we had heard that the result would be known by 4 o'clock or thereafter. The report received that dinner-time from the man in charge of 'Maggie Taggart' was, 'Jesus lads, the Sinn Féin tally people reckon that Bobby not only polled brilliant but may actually win!' That brought whoops of delight from each cell which earned us all a ticking off from the wing OC, Tom Holland. There was vibrant conversation throughout the wing all afternoon. Predictions differed, though the quest for victory and most importantly, the added impetus it would inject into the hunger strike had the adrenalin flowing as we ambled from door to window – all six paces – and back.

Paddy Mo and I kept reassuring ourselves of victory by referring to the confidence displayed at the count by our tally people. Being a naturally nervous guy Mo began to shake in anticipation as our next door neighbour and radioman, PV Coyle, ended the conversation he was having with Spotto Devine. All would be known shortly! Minutes later the quietness of the wing was broken by PV announcing 'Cailleamar é' (we lost it) to Spotto. Paddy Mo read the result from my reaction and quickly joined me holding his head; we both sat dismayed. We cursed the tally people until we were blue in the face. One comment I recall was, 'They surely don't need any Branchmen to break Republicans in Castlereagh; all they need to do is get Sinn Féin officials to make predictions'. Our world seemed at an end.

Mo remarked it strange that the result had been unannounced to the rest of the lads. I had imagined that PV and his cellmate, Danny Clarke, were similar to ourselves – wrecked – and hadn't come to terms with the defeat yet. To satisfy Mo's curiosity I knocked on the wall and inquired, in Irish, would it not be right to inform the rest of the wing of the result. 'What do you reckon I have in here, a crystal ball?' replied PV. 'Did you not say to Spotto 10 minutes ago 'cailleamar é, we lost it'?' 'I did! But I was talking about the news. Didn't you know that the verb caill means both to lose and to miss? Cailleamar – we missed it. Don't you get it?' As it dawned on me that I had blundered badly and eased out a sigh of relief, my poor unfortunate cellmate let fly with a barrage of abuse. Within minutes what followed will be remembered by me forever. 'Tá an bua againn' (We've won), shouted a delirious PV from his cell and in unison 48 Blanketmen, led by the security-conscious OC, roared and punched the air in triumph. Amidst the laughter, shouting and crying that day, our thoughts were exclusively for the people from Fermanagh and South Tyrone and of course their MP who lay close to us in the prison hospital, 41 days on hunger strike.

Laurence McKeown . . .

Our Block hadn't cheered or shouted when we heard the result and when the screws came round that evening with the tea, they told us Harry West had won the election. One of them, a Scotsman, went to great lengths to convince us of this. It really sickened him when men stood with a broad grin on their faces and said with confidence, 'No way; we know the people of Fermanagh/South Tyrone; we know the support there is for us. Bobby will win'. One of the screws went as far as to argue with a prisoner returning from a visit the following day that Bobby hadn't won. This despite the fact that the prisoner had been discussing the election victory for almost half an hour with his family, and obviously within earshot of the screw.

We made up that day for the silence of the previous day. We sang and shouted about it. We rubbed it in with great delight. Our hope for the success of the stailc now grew. From a very gloomy beginning we now felt we had moved into a new situation. Bobby was now an MP. What clearer sign could there be that the people regarded him – and by extension all of us – as political prisoners than by voting for him as their parliamentary representative? We felt this would cause the Brits all sorts of problems and put them in a dilemma as to how to treat an MP who they were condemning as a criminal. We felt the contradictions would be hard for them to overcome.

Once again we underestimated the Brits' capacity to blatantly change the rules to suit themselves. They simply enacted a Bill which barred prisoners from standing for future elections. That taught me a lot about the Brits and politics and about power and the misuse of it. It taught me a lot about the façade of democracy which cloaks a very unjust and deep-seated system of privilege and power in the hands of a few. My hopes of a few days previous were dampened.

SEAN LENNON . . .

With Bobby's election it was impossible for the Brits to keep the lid on what was happening here, and in particular on the hunger strike. Media from all over the world were asking all sorts of questions and coming to our people seeking interviews. We were now riding on a high as far as publicity was concerned and we re-doubled our resolve to build upon it. More and more comms began to flow from here and letters of support from all around the world were coming into the Sinn Féin centres on a daily basis. All this was being sent in to us, so we were fully abreast of the situation. It gave us great strength to know that we were not alone in this, that there were millions of concerned people around the world.

There was a lot of optimism around the Blocks and our visitors were saying that the Brits wouldn't let Bobby die now seeing as he was elected and there was massive pressure on them to concede. I was hoping they were right, but I wasn't optimistic as I had no faith at all in the Brits.

JAZ McCANN . . .

The day after the election result both Raymond McCreesh and myself had visits. Early that Saturday morning we were allowed out together to wash. I was feeling really good and chatted away with him. But he looked very ill. His movements were very, very slow. He was that weak he did not appear to be able to enter into the spirit of celebration that gripped the wing. I had noticed that on the previous Sunday at mass he had difficulty getting down on his knees and even more difficulty getting up again.

I tried my best to cheer him up that morning. I remember lifting a very large scapula of Padre Pio that he left beside the sink while he washed and saying to him that he would be alright with Padre protecting him. This got a smile out of him. I talked about the great result and how things were looking good and joked with him about his not taking any chances, hedging his bets through wearing Padre Pio and rosary beads around his neck. While Raymond saw the funny side and laughed, I got the feeling that he knew everything was not going to be alright.

The two of us were called for our visits together. They put me between the grilles first to await the escort for the visit. Then Raymond followed, but he could barely walk. With each step he progressed about four or five inches and each step was very slow. He looked like a cripple taking his first steps and at each step he looked as if he would fall to the ground. I assumed that they would have transport to take him to the visits and that it was only a matter of making it to the front of the Block – which was no mean task given his condition. A couple of the screws did show some concern and I felt they would have the decency to look after him. I was amazed later to learn that they had indeed made him walk, that no transport awaited him and that, not surprisingly, he had collapsed en route. Their callousness was hard to credit. It was soon obvious that he was never going to make it. After he collapsed, a van was called for; he was taken to the visits and after that they brought him straight to the hospital. The lads were disappointed because they could not now give him a good send-off.

THOMAS LOUGHLIN . . .

At mass one Sunday Séanna Walsh produced a comm he got from Bobby outlining how things were going. He read it out to a few of the lads and when he was finished with it, Larry Marley asked him for it. Séanna gave it to him and then watched as Larry carefully folded it and put it away 'What are you doing with that?' asked Séanna. 'Sending it out to my wife,' replied Larry. 'Why?' asked Séanna. 'To hold on to it,' replied Larry, 'because this is a piece of history'. All he got was blank stares as no one appreciated the significance of such things at that time.

BIK MCFARLANE . . .

While the election victory succeeded in internationalising the hunger strike and drew a host of calls for the Brits to depart from their intransigent position, it did not move Thatcher's government towards a settlement.

There followed a variety of moves and visits by dignitaries from far and near in an attempt to persuade the hunger strikers to call off their hunger strike. The most despicable manoeuvre was when Charlie Haughey, feeling the intense pressure from grassroots Fianna Fáil to act decisively on the issue and wishing to secure his support base for an impending election, persuaded Bobby's mother and sister that the British would indeed act if the European Commission for Human Rights was brought in. This could only be achieved by lodging a complaint with the European Court at Strasbourg. Marcella, Bobby's sister, was persuaded to sign the complaint and Haughey, the ultimate survivor, slipped quietly out of the firing line, satisfied that he had thrown the ball into someone else's court.

Our solicitor, Pat Finucane, and Bobby met to prepare for the arrival of the European Commission's delegation. Pat was an invaluable asset to us in a number of ways. He worked tirelessly and played a vital role in helping to maintain contact between the hunger strikers and ourselves, as well as linking with our contacts outside. He became emotionally involved as the full horror of the hunger strike unfolded and men began to die. It was obviously extremely difficult for him as he watched our comrades slip agonisingly out of this life. I know that Bobby and himself built up a very close relationship over a short period of time. My own visits with him were an immense relief from the pressure chamber of the Blocks – even a visit with no real news to relate, a quiet relaxed yarn with a patient man prepared to listen. I suppose I then came to consider him a friend as opposed to my solicitor.

Bobby laid down some conditions under which he would receive the delegation. I was to be present and he also sought the presence of two prominent members of the Republican Movement, Gerry Adams and Danny Morrison, as advisors. It was felt that if the Brits genuinely wanted to pursue a settlement, Bobby's preconditions could easily be accommodated. Since I was of the opinion that the Brits weren't at that stage anxious to negotiate a solution, I did not expect them to grant Bobby's request for advisors from outside. So I was very much surprised when I was called to the prison hospital on the afternoon of 25 April.

I was shown into an office allocated to the four Euro-Commission members. We had a brief discussion as to their function and when I explained Bobby's preconditions for meeting them, I was informed that such was impossible – the British government would not permit Gerry Adams or Danny Morrison into the camp as they were personae non gratae. I explained that Danny had been a regular visitor until a few months prior to this and that if the Brits genuinely wanted a solution, there would be no difficulty in admitting Gerry Adams or anyone else for that matter. But I was arguing a lost cause and I knew it only too well. I then told them I would see Bobby if it could be arranged, outline our conversation and return with his response.

It was my first trip to this new hospital: everything so fresh and clean, and an unusual quietness about the place. The thoughts of seeing Bobby, 56 days into a horrifying ordeal, scared me. I just did not know what to expect, but I desperately wanted to see him. The steel grille clanged behind me as I entered the ward and an MO showed me into Bobby's room (cell). It was a frightening sight. He was propped up slightly by some large pillows but his emaciated frame appeared sunk into them.

He had difficulty in seeing who it was had entered the room. I moved round to the side of his bed and sat close to him. There was so much pain on his face that I could almost feel the agony. His eyes, dark and sunken, seemed so distant. He looked so fragile and delicate in this silent world of his that I found myself speaking in whispered tones for fear of disturbing some inner peace. It seemed irreverent to intrude upon this silence. Yet, there I was, awkwardly striding in with news that was no news – worse perhaps, because my whispered conversation confirmed only that the Brits were not willing to negotiate a settlement. He already knew this and quizzed me as to my understanding of what exactly had occurred with the Euro intervention. Satisfied that I was abreast of all developments, he asked about all the lads back in the Blocks. Everyone was fine – everyone was asking – everyone was working hard on letters – everyone was hoping and praying – I was fine too. 'Tell them all to keep the spirits up – they're good lads'. Yes, I would tell them – yes, they are good lads. We sat for a few minutes longer and I held his hand gently; there was nothing left to say. He had been right all those months ago. I wouldn't let him down when the crisis came. I would walk away and quietly wait while he slipped slowly from his life. As I prepared to leave, he looked up at me with a pained expression and whispered, 'I'm dying, cara, I'm dying'.

I gathered my thoughts quickly on my way into the office again where I simply re-stated the pre-conditions Bobby had laid down, and then politely took my leave of the Euro delegation. Nothing was achieved from their intervention, save to expose Haughey for the conniving self-seeking politician he has always been.

The lads were all eager to hear some positive news back in the Blocks – expectations had been raised when I had been called to the hospital. A sign of movement, everyone felt. But I had only depressing news for them. The situation looked dire. The visit by the Pope's envoy, Fr Magee, didn't raise any hopes, and Don Concannon's deplorable conduct – he visited Bobby to tell him the Labour Party fully supported Thatcher's stance – only angered us and outraged people throughout the country.

TOM HOLLAND . . .

On Friday, 1 May, 1981, I was in B wing, H3, at that time holding the position of wing OC. Because of that role I often received comms from the camp OC, Bik, giving me an update on developments in relation to the hunger strike. That Friday I was given a comm from Bik to be explained to all the men on our wing. It was of marked importance – it was the camp staff's opinion that there was now no chance of Bobby surviving his hunger strike. Bik stated that all possible avenues for a successful conclusion to the hunger strike had been firmly closed. The British government were holding firm and were going to let Bobby die.

Up until that point there was a degree of hope among the men in our wing that Bobby would not have to die, especially after his unbelievable election victory in Fermanagh/South Tyrone. Recognising this general, but cautious, optimism Bik was determined to prepare the men for the seemingly inevitable worst. Hence the comm. My job was to ensure that all men were made aware of the British government's final act of intransigence, and to prepare the climate for a collective and mature response to the imminent death of Bobby. I carried out this difficult and sad task to the best of my ability.

Two days later, Sunday, 3 May, Fr Faul came into our wing canteen to say mass. At that time the extent of Faul's deviousness was unknown to us. We knew he was opposed to the tactic of hunger strike, but we did not know how low he would go to undermine our position. During the course of his sermon that day Fr Faul concentrated on Bobby Sands. He said, among other things, 'The British government won't let Bobby die. They are the world's experts on brinkmanship. They will bring Bobby to the edge of death, then come in with an agreement which will be sufficient for an honourable settlement. This settlement mightn't be exactly what you are looking for, but it will be enough to end the protests once and for all'. He concluded his lengthy sermon by confidently stating, 'The British won't let a British MP die on hunger strike'.

Fr Faul's statement at mass that day caused tremendous confusion in our ranks. He had put across a forceful and articulate opinion which was the complete opposite to what Bik had informed us a few days earlier. Hope was once again raised, expectations were high. Perhaps Faul had better contacts with the NIO than Bik? The psychological preparations we had built were now destroyed.

I came into regular contact with Srón Dearg, a screw notorious among us for his unique brand of inhumanity, both physical and psychological. Each day I had to leave the wing to go to the circle for medical treatment, which meant often enough that Sron Dearg was my 'escort'. Luckily enough during this period the beatings had slackened, so few incidents occurred. However, the climate was tense and you could've cut the atmosphere with a knife. It was quite noticable that the screws were watching for signs of disillusionment or demoralisation in our ranks as the hunger strike progressed.

On Monday, 4 May, 1981, I was coming back from the circle after having received medical treatment and went into cell 26 to change from the prison trousers to the prison issue white towel to cover my nakedness. Srón Dearg followed me in through the door as normal, then for the first time in four years he did something which he had never done before – he spoke to me. 'Well, Holland, is Sands going to die?' I was completely taken aback by his words. I lifted my head, looked at him and said, 'Maggie Thatcher will decide Bobby Sands's fate'. Angrily Srón Dearg moved closer to me, lifted his finger, pointed it at my face and shouted, 'He hasn't got a fucking clamp on his mouth'. I fixed the white towel around my naked waist, moved towards the door of the large cell (pretty annoyed with myself at this stage for speaking back to him in the first place) and said, 'No, but he has principles'.

BIK MCFARLANE . . .

The days dragged agonisingly by and each night I listened to Radio Ulster's late news bulletin which gave a brief account of Bobby's deteriorating condition. We no longer exchanged banter out the windows with adjacent cells. Everything was sombre and subdued as we waited for the inevitable. Then on Sunday 3 May the prison chaplain arrived into my cell unexpectedly. 'I've some bad news for you, I'm afraid'. I was stunned. 'Oh, it's not from the hospital,' he said, 'It's your father; he passed away yesterday'. I couldn't believe it – I wasn't even aware that he'd been ill, so it came as quite a shock and left me numb. I hadn't seen any of my family since I arrived in the Blocks in 1978 – I didn't take the visits until the hunger strikes started – so I had no idea how things were at home. The monthly letter never contained details of anyone's health or well being. Sunday drifted by in a daze and I made arrangements for a special family visit.

CIARAN MCGILLICUDDY . . .

On Sunday the 3rd Fr Toner said mass in H4. He was in the hospital with Bobby each day and he was telling us how Bobby was coming and going into a coma. He told us of reading the Bible to him and at one stage Bobby stopped him and motioned for him to read over the last few lines. Fr Toner seemed to be happy that Bobby was listening to what he was reading. What he asked him to read was, 'God loves those who hunger for justice'. As Fr Toner talked about Bobby, you could have heard a pin drop in the canteen. Everyone's eyes filled with tears and some cried. Sundays were always quiet days, but when we got back to the wing no one talked for hours. I cried and my cellmate cried too.

BIK MCFARLANE . . .

That Sunday night the news told us that Bobby had slipped into a coma and we quietly waited for the end. Monday passed and after I had heard the late evening news, I stayed for an hour at the window quietly yarning with Ricky and Marty next door. I decided after midnight that I would leave the crystal set assembled and catch the next couple of news bulletins on the hour. The main item on the 2.00 am BBC bulletin was the announcement that at 1.17am on Tuesday 5 May Bobby Sands had died on hunger strike. I was simply devastated, in spite of the fact that I had been waiting for this very moment for God knows how long.

I woke Paul, my cellmate, and broke the tragic news to him, and then woke some guys in the adjoining cells to let them know. It was a sleepless night for the most part and the next morning the screws were sounding quite chirpy. Everyone was totally shattered but it was essential to ensure that spirits didn't flag. It was difficult to keep the chin up. Apart from a very brief note to Brownie, I did practically nothing the following couple of days – just lay back and drifted for most of the time. And my family visit was an extremely testing and emotional affair which did little to help matters. But we simply had to battle on.

TOMBOY LOUDON . . .

When Bik went to the hospital to see the lads, everyone waited nervously on him returning with news of the hunger strikers. As the time was starting to run out and Bobby was drifting in and out of a coma I kept saying to myself 'Where are these British bastards? They're playing about with Bobby's life'. I kept waiting to hear the screws opening Bik's cell and take him to the prison hospital to negotiate an end to the hunger strike. I kept dozing in and out of sleep on the night of Monday 4 May as I knew that one of the lads was listening to one of the small crystal radios trying to catch the news. I heard voices at the bottom of the wing and pipes being rapped and I knew then before the news had even reached me that Bobby was dead, and I just sat and cried and I cursed the bastards who murdered him.

I could hear other lads shouting 'murdering bastards'. Bik sent word around the wing that he didn't want anyone threatening or hitting any screws the next morning, that we should mourn Bobby's death with the respect it deserved and that we would have to double our efforts for our comrades following Bobby. I lay back on my mattress and closed my eyes and thought back to the comm Bobby gave me that Sunday he started the hunger strike when he said 'Don't be worrying about me cara, I will always be with you' and I just said to myself, 'Tiocfaidh ár lá, cara, tiocfaidh ár lá'.

KEVIN CAMPBELL . . .

I was awakened by the man in the cell next to me banging on my cell wall. It was around 7.30am. He told me that Bobby had died during the night. He had just got the news on the wee radio. We were all told by the OC to remain calm and not to say a word to the screws and not to show any emotions in the face of the enemy. Everyone was shattered. I remember lying in my bed still and silent; neither I nor my cellmate spoke a word. We were both deep in our own thoughts. We were shattered and demoralised. My emotions at that time were ones of deep sorrow for Bobby and his family. I grieved for him in the same way I would have grieved for a brother. I find it hard to describe just exactly how I felt. Even though I never shed a tear, I was completely overcome with grief. As I thought of our situation and what the Brits had done, my grief turned to anger and then to deep hatred. I prayed that morning – in a hypocritical manner – that the IRA would blow the Brits to hell, that we would send scores of hundreds of the bastards back in boxes and make Thatcher regret she had ever heard of the H-Blocks and what she had done to Bobby and his family.

My thoughts of hatred were interrupted when the screws came round to do the morning check. It was around 8.00am and the sun was shining outside. The screws who were doing the check were whistling the tune 'Oh What a Beautiful Morning'. One of them shouted to the screws at the top of the wing, 'What a lovely day. It's the best day in my life'. We all knew what he was referring to, even though he didn't mention Bobby's name. No one acknowledged his taunts; we just ignored him. The rest of the day passed off without any more taunts. The screws even seemed timid in a sense. When any of the lads went out for a wash the screws kept their distance and didn't speak a word. They were either under orders from a governor to say nothing or else they realised that to open their mouths might just result in them getting a pot of piss thrown round them, or something much worse.

The talk over the next few days was about what would happen next. Would the Brits let Frank die? And most of all, would the IRA blow England to hell? We heard on the radio that there was rioting all over the country. The Belfast men came back from their visits with the scéal that there were thousands already gathering in Belfast for Bobby's funeral.

LAURENCE MCKEOWN . . .

On the morning of 5 May, 1981, we slopped out, washed and brushed our cells as usual. We noticed no real change in routine. The screws were maybe a bit slower in opening the doors, but nothing really out of the ordinary. At dinnertime Fr Toner came in and went to the Dark who was in the end cell at the top of the wing. When he left, the dinner dishes had already been collected and the wing was quiet. We heard his voice, a cell door slamming shut, then footsteps going out of the wing. Moments later the Dark's voice shouted through the side of his cell door, 'Bobby's dead'. It was as sudden as that. There were no questions to be asked. We had all expected it sooner rather than later, yet it still came as a shock. I felt both sorrow and rage. There wasn't a sound to be heard in the wing. Few spoke in the cells and when they did, it was isolated, disjointed comments rather than dialogue.

Later that day, when the lads exchanged views out the windows, the general consensus was that we couldn't stop now. We had to go on. It was a battle of wits between them and us. Mingled with these comments were anecdotes about Bobby: something he had said to someone or things he had done. Sympathies were expressed for his family and we wondered just how they would be taking it. His death was a major blow to us, and somehow unreal because we were isolated from what was going on. Those outside had up-to-the-minute radio and TV reports on it – we had to rely on information from visits and the few news items we could hear on our radios.

Felim O'Hagan . . .

It's odd, but I don't recall much of the day Bobby died, though I know that in those last few days before his death we were all resigned to its inevitability. A rap on the wall early on the morning of 5 May, a whispered 'Fuair Róibeard bás' and that was it. The Block was sombre and quiet all day; even the screws were subdued (in our presence at least), apart from one who could be heard gloating at the top of the wing.

Some men have since told me that they cried that day – I didn't, nor did I cry upon the deaths of any of the lads. I say that not in a boastful, macho way – far from it; it worries me that it's evidence of an uncaring attitude or a lack of emotional involvement. The strange thing about being in the Blocks then, and increasingly as death followed death, is that I experienced a sense of detachment and it was more than a cliché about being in the eye of the storm. Comrades were dying in the prison hospital only a few hundred yards away, children were being murdered by plastic bullets, whole nationalist areas across the North were in turmoil, yet here in the focal point of the situation all was calm. It was unreal.

Sean Lennon . . .

Even though I was prepared for the death, it came as one massive shock to me when we heard. I shed a few tears that morning for Bobby. The silence in the wing was eerie. I remember the screw coming to the cell and offering me a bath, which I took. I wanted out of the cell to be alone for a while to think. As I went up the wing to the shower area, not a sound could be heard; there was only one screw on the wing at the grille and the rest, orderlies included, were not to be seen. It was frightening. I could sense the tension in the Block; it was as if the screws were expecting us to pull the place down bit by bit. They must have been told by the governors to play it cool and to give no aggro. I don't think I could have held myself back had one of them said a bad word about Bobby or any of us that morning.

I showered and took my time. When I got back to the cell, my cellmate and I talked about the death. It was a sad yarn; we were bolstering each other's confidence and we needed to. During the first lock-up, when the screws left the wing, we had a meeting and we decided not to allow ourselves to go downhill and allow the morale to flag. Remembering the last message Bobby had sent to us, to lie moping would be a dishonour to Bobby and all he had lived and died for, so we told the lads to act normally and not to stop talking out the windows or the doors to one another, to carry on with the ranganna. We had to lift the wing from the doldrums; should our heads go down, it would be disastrous for us all and especially for the hunger strikers. So the wing started to get back to normal, but it was a false type of normality. After a few days life had been restored to the place and we were all back fighting fit and ready for anything they should hit us with.

THOMAS LOUGHLIN . . .

I remember my cellmate and I discussing what it would mean to us; would we get status? It was during this discussion that our door opened for a cell search. The two of us were put into the cell with Jake McManus and Peter Whelan.

We looked upon Jake as someone who had a bit of savvy as he was always telling us about socialism and Russia, so we asked him what he thought was going to happen. 'Well,' he said, 'it's obvious the Brits have declared their intentions so we can expect a few more lads to die. But it's the repercussions that need to be considered. If you ask me, there could be a civil war.' 'Jesus Christ,' I said, 'What the fuck are you talking about?' I always remember those lads who were in the Cages talking about how they used to be on their guard at night in case of civil war breaking out and the UDR coming in and shooting them. Visions of this happening flew through my head and I actually felt afraid.

'Here Jake, how do you work this out?' I asked. 'Well, put it like this; the Loyalists have always been looking for an excuse. Now they have got one. Anyway, as we all know, the districts have been stockpiling food for weeks'. 'Okay Jake, what's going to happen?' 'Well, the Short Strand will get the gutty (be destroyed) as will all marginalised Catholic areas, particularly in the country. What's been happening to date will seem like a children's picnic. But the sooner it happens the better because it will bring a speedy end to the struggle.' Jake went on to say that he felt such a situation would give the Brits the opportunity to put the Loyalists in their place by moving thousands in and imposing a settlement on them, which would be a united Ireland. The Brits would pull out, leaving a UN peacekeeping force to hold the fort until things settled down.

I remember saying to him that would be great, but in the meantime we in here wouldn't get to see the fruits of our work, not if the UDR had their way. As we left the cell my cellmate turned and said, 'Here Jake, next time we get a cell search I'm asking to get put into another cell – you're full of bad news'. This talk frightened half of us to death. Apparently this was the scenario painted in many other wings.

RAYMOND McCARTNEY . . .

In 1982 I found myself back in the hospital for a few days. I can remember walking down the corridor, a million memories flooding my brain. Accompanying me was Bobby H, a prison orderly. He had been orderly throughout the hunger strikes of 1980 and 1981. He pointed out the cells each of the lads had been in when they died. He pointed out the room set aside for the families so that they could be near as their son, husband, brother left them. So much had happened in those eight small rooms and yet so little had been said about the personal stories that each possessed.

Old Bobby told a few of his recollections of the period. He is a very warm and genuine man. He was a few months from his release date when I spoke to him. He told me that some newspapers had approached him to be interviewed on release. He declined because in his words, 'What I shared with the hunger strikers was not for selling newspapers'. I am confident he would not mind me doing it now. This man, a Protestant, imprisoned for tax irregularities, was perhaps one of the closest observers of those tragic eight months. He affirms that he witnessed unparalleled courage unfold both in the lads and in their families. He also bore witness to some amusing incidents.

Old Bobby always ensured that the lads in the hospital had whatever comforts were possible: books, papers, tobacco and cigarette papers. The first day that Bobby Sands came to the hospital, the sean fhear (old man) made it known to him that anything he needed 'ol' Bobby will do the rest'. So, quick as a flash Sandsie replied, 'Can you get me some fag papers?' Old Bobby got him an ounce of tobacco and three or four packets of cigarette papers.

Next morning: 'Bobby, any more fag papers?' Once more, no problem, the sean fhear was back with three or four packets. The following morning the same story. Only this time old Bobby said that he noticed that the ounce of tobacco had remained relatively untouched. So the sean fhear found himself in a bit of a quandary. He was worried that Bobby was in some way harming himself with the cigarette papers. He thought to himself that he was perhaps using them as some form of hunger breaker by chewing on them. So he looked in the waste paper bin and elsewhere, but no sign of any spat-out or half-chewed papers. Then old Bobby was left to ponder on whether he was swallowing them. If so, it would hardly be doing him any good. There was no way the sean fhear would share his concern with the screws or the MOs. He said that he was really worried.

So, the following day he was in Bobby's cell, cleaning it out. (Those rooms were the best kept cells in the world. Old Bob's excuse to get into the cells for a chat or pass on the tobacco was the pretence of brushing, mopping, polishing or whatever – three or four times a day.) He was chatting to Bobby and was building up the nerve to hit him with his concern. Finally it came: 'Here Bobby son, would you answer me a question?' 'If I can I will,' came the reply. 'What do you do with all the fag papers? Like (and pointing to the tobacco), you are not smoking all that much.' He said that Sandsie started to smile, then laugh, 'Simple, Bob. I write on them'. Old Bobby breathed a sigh of relief but he was equally baffled. He said that using up that many papers for writing would have been as difficult as smoking them!

He spoke of the day Bobby was elected. He said that there were a couple of governors and NIO people in the hospital around teatime. The result had been in an hour or so earlier. Old Bobby said their faces told the story. He said it was a lovely sight. He mentioned to one of the MOs that Bobby's cell needed cleaning (again); 'After all, we have an MP in the wing now'. He said that the NIO entourage just glared at him. The sean fhear went into the cell and shook Bobby's hand, saying simply, 'Well done, son; you deserve it'. In return Bobby joked, 'Sure, if you have any problems you can always ask for an MP's visit with me!'

Bobby's family had been at his bedside for a few days, and the day before he died, old Bobby said there was an eerie atmosphere hanging around the place. The Sands family were very strong throughout this period and every time old Bobby went into the room where they were, they always spoke to him. They were very chatty, despite the trauma they were experiencing. That night the sean fhear was sitting in the TV room when one of the chaplains came in and said that Bobby would like to speak to him. He walked down the wing and into the cell. Some of Bobby's family were at the bedside. It was easy to see that Bobby's body had been depleted of all the physical resistance; only his remarkable spirit held him. Once Bobby was aware the sean fhear was in the cell, he put his hand out and spoke. 'Bobby, I'm going to die but I want to thank you for all you have done for me and the other lads. We will never forget you; you are a real gentleman'. The sean fhear said he held Bobby's hand as if he was his own kin. He was full of tears. He said he felt so proud but at the same time utterly useless. He told me, 'Despite all his own suffering, the prospect of imminent death, this man whom I met hardly a month before this remembered me and thanked me. For what? A bit of tobacco and some papers. For a man so noble and brave that he gave his life for his friends and in a strange way, even for me, they let this man die. May God forgive them'.

Eoghan MacCormaic . . .

I have a strong memory of Bobby from the Crum which was a big influence on me. I learnt Irish at school, but I don't think I ever spoke it outside the classroom. Irish was a school subject and I had never learned it in a living environment. Then one day in the Crum there was a bit of trouble on the 3s (the top landing); the screws were going slow in opening the doors to let the men out. We were already in the yard and Bobby called out the window to a fellow called Mickey Lenaghan and the two of them started this whole discussion in Irish. I was spellbound because for the first time Irish wasn't just a dry school subject.

I spent a few months on remand with Bobby, then when he and the rest were sentenced (and after three of them had spent six weeks on the boards in the Crum due to a fight with screws at court), he came onto our wing in H5. Straight away he picked up where he had left off in the Crum, organising publicity and a basic campaign to raise the issue of the Blanket in the public eye. He asked me to give him whatever poems or scribblings I had done about the Blanket and was soon sending this all out for the Republican News. He took over as PRO and at the same time began taking ranganna; the first one he took was for Tony O'Hara and me, and in turn we were expected to take a rang a step behind us.

He used to talk, talk, talk like all the rest in our wing. We would have these great debates which lasted for days and days, debates about politics, history, sport, football. Bobby was a fanatic about Aston Villa, or at least to enter the spirit of the arguments he became a fanatic. I remember the time he 'stole' two points for Villa. The football followers used to go buck daft on a Saturday to get all the results and work out a league table from memory. One Thursday morning Bobby got up to the door and announced that a screw walking down the yard had told him that Aston Villa had an away win the previous night. That put Villa on the top of the table according to the wing league table, so for the next few weeks whenever an argument would arise about the relative merits of this team over that team Bobby would always say, 'Well, I think the League table speaks for itself'. When the true table was finally obtained after about three weeks Bobby got a lot of stick over his 'theft' of the two points.

The last time I saw Bobby was the night the first hunger strike ended and he came around the Blocks to tell the OCs to inform the men. He was walking down the yard on his way out, surrounded by a lot screws and huddled up into himself against the rain. The weight of the world was on him, no doubt. I can still hear him an odd time, singing 'Band of Gold' and 'The First Cut is the Deepest' or one of the Irish songs like 'Gleanntan Glas

Gaoth Dobhair' or 'Baidin Fheidhlime'. He was a great 'chanter' and always a man for the singsongs. I think he had an instinct for knowing how morale could rise and fall and was therefore always conscious of finding ways of keeping it up whether by smuggling snout or by concerts and so on.

LAURENCE McKEOWN . . .

A comm came in from outside stating that in the event of Bobby or any of the three others on hunger strike dying, no one would replace them. I don't know if it was written to test our resolve and commitment to the stailc or if it was seriously intended that the hunger strike tactic should be limited in use. But it certainly provoked a response. I was one of those at the door 'biting the angle-iron off' in rage at such a suggestion. My view was that if Bobby died and no one replaced him, it would be immediately obvious to the Brits that they had only to weather the storm of four deaths and the entire issue of the H-Blocks would be resolved. It was crucial to show the Brits this was not the thinking among the prisoners. We had to show that there was determination to achieve our demands and that the determination did not falter when faced with the reality of people dying. Many others expressed a similar viewpoint and the consensus in our wing among those who put forward a view was that there should be replacements for those who died. Some felt they couldn't put forward an opinion as they themselves were not prepared to go on hunger strike. I didn't think that a valid reason for not arguing the merits of a particular strategy, but I was happy with the outcome.

It is difficult to describe the feelings of those in the Blocks at the time in terms of the depth of strength and determination there was. This was as a result of the protest which had gone on for over four years; it had shaped our thinking and built our solidarity. We had taken on the consciousness of those at war and our battle was with every manifestation of the system and its administrators, especially with the screw who opened and locked our doors. Our view was that, if we gave in now, that screw would have a massive grin on his face and would rub it into us for the rest of our time in prison. We knew that a lot of us had a lot of time still to do and no way were we going to allow these people to make that life a misery. We were steeled for the conflict.

KEVIN CAMPBELL . . .

On 7 May Bobby was buried with over 100,000 in attendance. It was said to be the biggest funeral seen in Ireland. It was another clear message to Thatcher and the world that the Nationalist people were fully behind us and backed our five demands. We were all hoping now that the gap of two weeks between Bobby and Frank going on hunger strike would give us enough time to force the Brits to give in and save Frank's life.

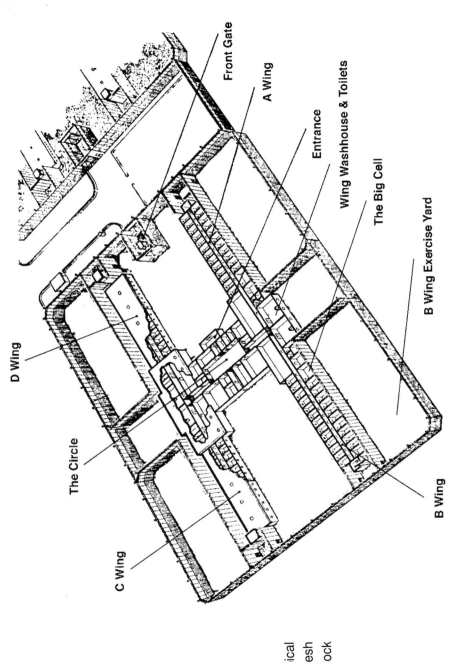

Front Gate

A Wing

Entrance

Wing Washhouse & Toilets

The Big Cell

B Wing Exercise Yard

D Wing

The Circle

C Wing

B Wing

A typical
Long Kesh
H-Block

KEVIN CAMPBELL

PETER CUNNINGHAM

KEVIN DEEHAN

LEONARD FERRIN

NED FLYNN

BERNARD FOX

DAVY GLENNON

MICHAEL GORMAN

LEO GREEN

TOM HOLLAND

SEAN LENNON

MARTIN LIVINGSTONE

TOMBOY LOUDON

THOMAS LOUGHLIN

JAZ McCANN

RAYMOND McCARTNEY

EOGHAN MACCORMAIC

BIK MCFARLANE

CIARAN MCGILLICUDDY

LAURENCE MCKEOWN

JACKIE McMULLAN

JOE McQUILLAN

HARRY MURRAY

FELIM O'HAGAN

JOHN PICKERING

JOHN THOMAS

SÉANNA WALSH

PEADAR WHELAN

Ciaran Nugent, the
first Blanketman,
leaves Long Kesh,
May 1979

*Photograph by
Derek Speirs*

The first march
organised by the
National H-Block
Committee
from Clonoe Church
to Coalisland
February 1980

*Photograph by
Derek Speirs*

March in support of the first hunger strike, Dublin

Photograph by Derek Speirs

Riot during
first hunger strike

Pacemaker

The banging of bin lids
announces the death
of Patsy O'Hara

A Dublin march
passes the GPO in
O'Connell St.

Suporting the
hunger strikers in
Derry

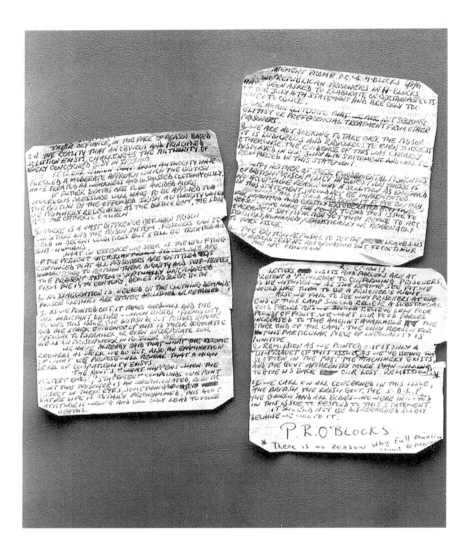

Comms elaborating
the prisoners'
4 July statement
(see page 196)

10

A Time of Dying

5 May 1981 – 8 July 1981

F̲ollowing the death of Bobby Sands, all moves towards mediation in the prisons came to a standstill. The British government, despite turmoil on the streets of the North and international condemnation of its stance, seemed ready to weather the storm which further deaths would bring. Within two weeks of Bobby Sands's funeral three more hunger strikers were dead: Frank Hughes, Raymond McCreesh and Patsy O'Hara.

Each of the dead hunger strikers was replaced and there would now be a gap of two months before the first of the replacements, Joe McDonnell, reached a critical stage. It was decided that other volunteers would join the strike at weekly intervals so that no longer would there be lengthy gaps, but rather a continuous stream of hunger strikers, each entering a critical stage immediately upon the death of the previous striker. The prisoners realised that it was an extremely high-risk strategy: it was designed to put more pressure on the British but it would also inevitably place enormous strain on the hunger strikers themselves, and on their families.

June brought a General Election in the South and the prisoners again seized the opportunity to highlight their cause. Two prisoners were elected to the Dublin parliament, while other prisoner candidates and those standing on the H-Block/Armagh ticket polled strongly in many areas.

In the wake of the electoral successes the Catholic church became directly involved in the prison crisis. The Irish Commission for Justice and Peace (ICJP) had a number of meetings with the hunger strikers and with the Blocks OC Bik McFarlane in early July. It quickly emerged that the ICJP was interested not in addressing the fundamental issues nor pressing the

British government, but in pressurising the prisoners to end the hunger strike at any price and saving the face of the Irish Establishment. As the ICJP intervention ended in fiasco and recriminations, a second cycle of deaths in the H-Blocks began.

BIK MCFARLANE . . .

With Frank, Raymond, and Patsy entering the critical stages there was no substantial pressure brought to bear upon Thatcher to seek an end to the terrible situation. Everything seemed to freeze after Bobby's funeral. Nothing moved – not even a hint of an opening for dialogue – no offers from the British that would go some way to negotiating a settlement. It was like living in a vacuum. We had no direct contact with the hospital, but even if I had been able to gain access, I could only have been able to deliver sombre and painful news – the Brits were holding firm and there was every probability that each of the three lads would die. It was a prolonged nightmare as we watched while Frank, Raymond and Patsy followed the same torturous path as Bobby; Frank died a week after Bobby; Patsy and Raymond nine days later on 21 May. Four comrades dead in 17 days. I wrote the same type of sympathy and condolence letter to each grieving and heart-broken family, and we stood silently and sadly behind our doors as we paid tribute to our selfless courageous comrades. We did not know where it would end – we only believed we had the determination to succeed.

EOGHAN MACCORMAIC . . .

During the whole of the second hunger strike my cellmate and myself had the responsibility for the 'Rud Eile', the crystal radio which was our lifeline to news. My cellmate had a bit of trouble with his hearing so I used to listen to all the news to make sure we got it right.

After Bobby and Frank died I think Tony O'Hara must have started to accept that his brother Patsy was going to die too. Tony had always been within a few cells of me during the Blanket and we used to talk a lot through the windows. On the night before Patsy died, Tony (or Scatter as we called him) was given a final visit to the hospital. When he returned, it seemed pointless to ask how Patsy was. How do you ask how somebody is when you know the person is about to die? We talked for a while, then Tony said he wanted to lie down for a while. 'Our Patsy isn't going to make it through the night,' he said and I think our whole wing was breaking their hearts with him.

In the early morning, maybe about 6 o'clock, I wired up the radio. The news came on. It said that another hunger striker, Patsy O'Hara, had died. I wound up the radio quickly and whispered out the window, 'Scatter.' Straight away he replied, nobody in those days slept, it seemed. 'Fuair Patsy bás le linn na h-oíche. Ta brón orm, mo chara.' (Patsy died during the night. I'm sorry, my friend.) 'Maith thu, Gino. Tchífidh mé thú ar ball.' (OK, Gino. I'll see you later.)

BIK MCFARLANE . . .

We had discussed and agreed upon a strategy for the replacement of hunger strikers. This was an extremely difficult task to perform and of necessity it had to be addressed in a very clinical manner. But it was quite impossible to turn aside from the shattering emotional impact it carried. When Bobby quite calmly asked me at mass what I would do after he had died, I was speechless for a while. How do you tell a man facing an horrific ordeal on hunger strike, 'It's alright; when you die, Joe McDonnell will take your place'? I suppose if anything steeled my nerve to perform what was the the most unenviable and heart-breaking task of my life it was Bobby's very direct and unemotional injection of harsh reality. Decisions, however unpalatable, had to be taken and I was the one who had to select those people to replace dead comrades.

We brought this strategy into operation. Joe McDonnell was selected to replace Bobby. And with his introduction to the hunger strike the die was cast for a prolonged and gruelling hunger strike campaign. The British government was now fully aware that we were absolutely committed to attaining our goal of an honourable settlement.

RAYMOND MCCARTNEY . . .

I had been on the wing with Joe McDonnell from January to October 1979. I had come to know him as well as one could, given the circumstances. One of the things I had noticed since his time on remand was that he had put on a lot of weight. The lads were by this time calling him Fat Joe, Seosamh Ramhar – a name not suitable in remand days. Joe didn't take visits, and obviously he was always keen and anxious to maintain good written contact with his wife Goretti, the children and the rest of the family. Goretti visited some of the lads form the Andersonstown area, and in doing so, it allowed her to send on personal messages to Joe.

I had started the appeal visits around September 1979, and women from the RAC would have visited me regularly, often two or three times a week. Therefore I was fairly competent at the visit ploys – getting scéal, comms and the odd tobacco beart. Joe asked me at mass one Sunday if I would take an appeal visit with Goretti. I readily agreed, and so most Friday afternoons for about five months I took a visit with Goretti.

Appeal visits lasted only 15 minutes. Technically you were supposed to converse only on matters relating to the appeal. For a period the administration and the screws didn't really bother with interpretation of the guidelines. Then in late 1978 a new visiting complex opened. The guidelines changed, so that a screw sat in on the visits to ensure that only the appeal was spoken about; if not, the visit was terminated. Of course, this only applied to those on the Blanket – other prisoners' visits continued unsupervised. Therefore on these visits we had to be careful, and we had to build up a method of subterfuge to camouflage what we were saying; for example, 'The witnesses John and Mary can't make the appeal as they are in the US at the minute' could have meant that John and Mary are in Castlereagh. Goretti and I built up our own forms of camouflage. Some of the screws weren't always as diligent as most of their colleagues, and the odd time they didn't care what we said. These visits were obviously excellent, and a good 15 minutes of scéal was to be had.

I had a couple of these 'free' visits with Goretti so I was able to give Joe a good half hour about the visit – with Joe everything had to be described in full detail. Was she laughing? What colour was her coat? I was able to bring the McDonnell family news into the H-Blocks. One of Joe's favourite quirks was the Donegal Celtic club, of which he was an ardent member. I reckon that if a table was moved Joe was able to report it out the door to the other DC revellers in the wing. If anyone ever told a story about the DC and got the geography wrong, Joe would correct the story teller. Men were always surprised at this, but they soon learnt Joe's wily ways.

I can recall the first appeal visit I had with Goretti. At the best of times it is not a straightforward task meeting someone for the first time on an ordinary visit, never mind an appeal visit with my screw escort. So I was a little nervous. When I reached the visiting area, Goretti was already seated in the visiting box and before I had time to be seated and say, 'Hello, I am...', this beart of tobacco came flying across the table and onto my lap. Goretti was as quick as a flash; she noticed that the screw had gone to hand in the pass. It wasn't the best introduction for my nerves. On return to the Block, tobacco secured, the story told – Joe was very proud of Goretti indeed.

Even on these brief encounters I got to know a very warm, generous person in Goretti. You could always detect in both of them the emphasis they placed on each other, on their children and family. They had little nuances and questions which brought this to the fore. They are difficult to describe, but even if it were possible, they would remain private and my personal memory of Joe.

The last time I saw Goretti was on 14 March 1980. At the end of one of the visits she slipped the tobacco into my coat pocket. Unfortunately it was spotted by a screw. So off to the boards I went. It was through this incident I saw another side to Joe. He was fond of telling all the stories of his youth, a real Jack-the-lad. Apparently he hung about with people a lot older than himself, worked on the boats, and saw himself as a real 'toughie'. (Indeed they say he was that alright.) When I was on the boards (which at this time were notorious for beatings and forced washes) he went to my cellmate (his ol' mucker on the wing) and said, 'I hope the wee pig will be alright.' Fortunately I did return unscathed and all was not lost, I had managed to retain Joe's wee notes from Goretti. The following Sunday he said to me, 'I hope you weren't annoyed that there was tobacco up on those appeal visits'. I wasn't, but Goretti was banned from visiting me and I knew I'd miss my wee Friday afternoon sorties.

The last time I saw Joe McDonnell was October 1980. I was on hunger strike and we spoke at mass. He said that Goretti had tried to come that week on appeal visit but had been refused. He wished me all the best and said, 'We will all be thinking of you'. Six months later it was Joe on hunger strike. By this time I had left H5 and was in H4. The scéal came back from the visits that Joe had been seen on the visits with Goretti, their children Bernadette and Joe Óg, and his mother. From my experience as an onlooker in their life for that short period I could empathise with the deep emotions they were sharing that day. It would have been over three and a half years since he had seen them last. The circumstances were not as joyous as they should have been after such an absence.

BIK MACFARLANE . . .

There was now a considerable period of time leading up to the critical stages for Joe McDonnell. Three others had joined him in the meantime: Brendan McLaughlin, Kieran Doherty and Kevin Lynch. We decided that an increase in numbers would help to add further pressure. We felt that to close the gap between the crisis periods for hunger strikers would mean a more constant and concentrated form of pressure on the Brits. As it stood, a lengthy gap existed between the deaths of Bobby, Frank, Patsy and Raymond and the time when Joe McDonnell would reach a critical stage. By increasing the numbers of hunger strikers by four at regular intervals we ensured that if the Brits wanted to ride out the storm of Joe McDonnell dying they would have to be prepared for a succession of potential hunger strike deaths and each of these to be replaced in turn by very eager and dedicated volunteers. It was a calculated risk, taken in the firm belief that we could definitely exert further pressure both on the Brits to seek a settlement and on the Irish Establishment to do something positive to get Thatcher's government off their intransigent line. It was also taken with the knowledge that the already immense pressure under which we struggled would soar to astronomical heights. But we needed to act positively and decisively. And pressure, regardless of its severity, could never balance against the sheer hell of an agonising death for those on hunger strike.

MARTIN LIVINGSTONE . . .

Kieran Doherty – Big Doc – was the perfect gentleman. He had a brilliant attitude and was always the first to offer advice or help to a comrade – very staunch and committed and right from the start had a clear insight to the struggle and what it was all about. He never had one doubt what he was doing and it showed in his actions, as he had held several staff positions and was always to the fore. In the Crum some people saw him as aloof and elitist, but I knew him from internment and the outside and he was just very serious and systematic about what he was doing, and as such always had a very professional approach to the struggle within the jail. He took real pride in being a Volunteer – his life was in the Republican Movement and he was completely devoted to it.

He always drew the attention of the screws because of his size and the way he carried himself. Someone once described his movements as similar to a big cat as he was always on his toes and he was always very dignified, no matter what he was doing. He took no nonsense from the screws. One incident that sticks out was when they tried to bend him over during a mirror search and he got into a corner and defended himself. He held them off well, until an SO grabbed him by the testicles and squeezed until he lost consciousness; that was the only way they could overcome him.

He was on our wing for a period on hunger strike and it was really tragic to see him literally wasting away in front of your eyes; his size and stature added to the enormity of his sacrifice. He used to get really irritated with all of us asking him how he was and would always play down his obvious suffering.

EOGHAN MACCORMAIC . . .

I had heard a lot about Big Doc long before I ever saw him, and when we did get to meet, in October 1979, it was in the back of a van with both of us going to the boards. On the boards we were put on separate wings and at that time the boards were packed with Blanketmen and remands. At night we were calling across the wings to get scéal about other Blocks, but the screws used to make a lot of noise to prevent us from talking. On the day I was coming back, a Sunday afternoon, a PO and a couple of screws from the Block arrived down with a van. Standing in the circle of the boards was a screw called Armour, known as the Red Rat. He was down to collect Big

Doc. 'Pick up that bag of clothes,' he said to me. I told him to 'bain as' (clear off). At that time the screws used to order the men coming off the boards to carry the prison clothes back with them knowing they would refuse. They would charge us with 'refusing an order' and we would be kept on the boards for another three or four days. The PO came out of the office when he heard the argument between the Red Rat and me and settled the issue by picking up the bag and handing it to one of the screws from H5 to carry back. The Red Rat was ripping, and then started to boast about how he was 'going to make Doherty carry his bag down' and threats about what he would do if he refused. I was in the circle but Big Doc was still locked up in his cell. The next thing I hear this voice shouting up from the wing, 'Is that the Horse up there? (H4 used to call Armour the Horse) Is that you Armour?' And the Rat shouted down that it was and what he was going to do and what he wasn't going to do. 'I'll shove you into that the bag, you wee bastard, if you don't give over your slabbering,' was the answer Doc gave him, and the Red Rat was fit to be tied. The PO came back out of his office again to see what all the shouting was about, and told him to pick up the bag and make sure there was no more hassle about it. Doc was laughing away down the wing, but I think the Red Rat was actually relieved. Doc had a bit of a reputation for taking no nonsense from the screws.

Ciaran McGillicuddy . . .

I used to watch Big Doc and was afraid of him; I don't know why because I had never talked to him. I used to look at him; he was very big and dark-haired. One day, when talking to my next door mate, I mentioned my fear of Big Doc. He told him, but I didn't know that he had.

So there I was one day at mass and I saw Big Doc walking over to me. I looked around to see if there was anyone else he could be looking for, but I was the only one there. I nearly fell through the floor. When he got to me he stood above me – I'm only 5 foot 5 and he was over 6 feet. He just looked down at me and said, 'Hi boy; I hear you've been talking about me.' I went out of my way to say I'd never said a bad word about him, then I heard everyone laughing. Doc was laughing as well. He told me I'd no need to ever fear him and gave me a friendly slap on the back of the head.

John Pickering . . .

The night before we got caught was a scorcher, 24 August 1976, a truly hot summer. Brendy and I were sitting in a car outside a clubhouse in Andersonstown, watching the spectacle of Big Doc trying to win over the Battalion OC. Judging by the hand waving and hand shaking that was going on, he wasn't having everything his own way.

Although Doc was a good operator, he was also an experienced organiser; this was the crux of the matter. Having been involved in the planning and preparation of the following day's operation, he also wanted to take part in it. The OC obviously didn't go along with this. As far as he was concerned Doc was too resourceful an organiser to risk losing on an operation if anything went wrong.

Only a few months earlier, along with Sean McDermott, Mairéad Farrell and another, Doc went on a bombing mission to the Conway Hotel on the outskirts of Belfast. They were confronted by the Brits and the RUC and Mairéad was captured. Doc, Sean and their comrade made their way on foot to a nearby Loyalist housing estate. They entered and secured a house and demanded the keys of the family car. The man of the house replied that the keys were in an upstairs bedroom. While Sean accompanied the man to get them, Doc and the other Volunteer guarded the rest of the family and kept watch on the street for pursuing Brit/RUC patrols. Time was of the essence and the lads were working quickly.

In the bedroom the man (who was an RUC reservist) opened the drawer where the keys were supposed to be, drew a firearm and fired, critically wounding Sean. Although Sean managed to return fire, hitting the man's hand, he couldn't move and lay on the floor. Their weapons were aimed at each other in a stand-off.

Doc was already half way up the stairs and shouting to see if Sean was alright. Sean weakly told Doc he was badly wounded and warned him not to open the bedroom door. The man had both Sean and the door covered. Again Sean warned Doc not to enter and ordered him to leave the house before the Brits arrived. Instead Doc shouted he was coming in; he wasn't leaving. Sean repeated the order to leave, warning that the man had the door covered with a firearm. He told the two Volunteers to make good their escape before it was too late. The other Volunteer shouted up the stairs that everyone must have heard the shots and they'd better hurry. Reluctantly, Doc and his comrade left, escaping through the nearby fields and eventually getting picked up in a sympathiser's car, their only good fortune that morning.

Sean McDermott died from the wounds received in the house. Mairéad Farrell served ten and a half years for her part in the Conway operation, and was later killed by the SAS in Gibraltar. Brendy O'Callaghan was shot dead by the British Army at the Hunting Lodge in Andersonstown; he was on active service at the time.

At the clubhouse Brendy and I speculated on Doc's chances on this job. We knew the OC didn't want him on it, but Doc wasn't easily discouraged. Minutes later we watched him return to the car, grinning broadly. He was on the operation.

EOGHAN MACCORMAIC . . .

Kevin Lynch was known as Barrabbas when I knew him in Crumlin Road, the name coming from the beard and long hair of the mid-seventies. He came in in the latter part of 1976, charged with a group of others from Dungiven, and when we talked, as everyone did walking around the yard, we found that we knew people in common. He was connected with the IRSP and so spent most of his time with the others in that organisation, but there was also a lot of common ground because we were all involved in the same protests at Townhall Street remand court, or in the parades and protests in the wing. I have a picture of Kevin in my head as being part of a colour party marching around A wing yard just after Máire Drumm was murdered.

BIK MCFARLANE . . .

We learned that Brendan McLaughlin had become seriously ill with a perforated ulcer almost immediately after going on hunger strike and he was forced to terminate it on medical grounds. Martin Hurson joined the hunger strike in his place.

KEVIN DEEHAN . . .

The first time I saw Martin Hurson was in the Crum in 1979/80 when he was up for a retrial. We were in A wing and he was charged with the responsibility of giving us the insight into what we could expect when we arrived in the Blocks. Even then, you could see he was committed to the H-Block/Blanket struggle.

One Sunday Fr Faul was saying mass. All of a sudden he announced during the mass he wanted to congratulate a certain man on his engagement. Of course Martin Hurson – who had kept everything under wraps – took a reddener. Heads started to turn towards Martin and at that second Faul announced his name. The place was in an uproar but Martin, who was the type who took reddeners easily, was shattered with embarrassment.

When Patsy died, Martin, who was close to Frank, was up at the door talking to one of the other lads about the deaths. Martin was clearly very shaken. The emotion that he felt spilled over to his voice, and it was a suppressed cry.

The last time I saw Martin he was washing himself and he looked weak. I asked him how he was, and he said he was fine, considering. Few words were spoken because they could never express what I was really feeling at that moment. This man is on hunger strike, others have died; is Martin going to die? Is this going to be the last I'll be with him? Is all this worth such a sacrifice? Of course, we could not unwrap such feelings at the time.

EOGHAN MACCORMAIC . . .

Martin Hurson was in the wing across from us and so we would have a passing acquaintance. He was the sort of boy who always seemed to have a smile, and was well liked. I talked to him just before he left the Block to go to the hospital after about four weeks of his hunger strike. I had already seen some men who had been on strike up to three weeks. During the first strike Raymond McCartney had lost a lot of weight and seemed to be suffering badly from coldness in the canteen at mass on Sundays. Raymond McCreesh also lost a lot of weight quickly. Brendan McLaughlin was moved out of the Block before the visible signs occurred but was, even at that early stage, seriously ill. Joe McDonnell lost weight and it was very noticeable, but he still looked OK. In Martin's case the weight loss was both noticeable and really grim looking. He was skeletal; his bones were sticking out, his face was a skull and for me the saddest sight was that his eyes seemed to have taken on separate wills of their own and were wobbling about in his head. He was weak and tired and sick and it was a burden to talk. Burden or not, he made the effort to talk to each of us who came over to him to say a few words. For most of us it was a shattering experience and one that wouldn't be forgotten. I can't say I said goodbye; it's ironic but the thing most of us said in those sort of circumstances was 'slán leat'. When I hear slán leat today I always think of it as being the final farewell.

BIK MCFARLANE . . .

Our escalation strategy commenced on 8 June with Tom McElwee, to be followed by Paddy Quinn, Mick Devine and then Lorney McKeown. It was around this period that the authorities began to move hunger strikers onto my wing in H3. As each man joined the hunger strike, he was transferred to D wing, H3 where he spent an average of three weeks before being moved to the prison hospital. It was my own belief that this was an attempt to weaken me – watching each comrade through three of the last weeks of his life was bound to have an emotional impact. Unquestionably it did have an effect, but the resilience and determination displayed by dying comrades and friends also gave me a tremendous inner strength and a great resolve to stay solid.

EOGHAN MACCORMAIC . . .

Being in Crumlin Road on remand was like being a day behind the news. One day you would hear about someone appearing in court, and the next day the same person would be walking out through the gate into the yard. In 1976 a lot of men and women comrades were charged in groups. They used to have collective titles. The 'ABC', for instance, were caught at the ABC cinema in Belfast; the 'Ballymena squad' were men and women caught after bombs had exploded prematurely in that town, badly injuring some of the men. A few days after that incident, the first of them arrived in the Crum. Their injuries were serious but the RUC wanted them out of Musgrave and into the jail as quickly as possible. Tom McElwee arrived in with a still badly-scarred face and one eye missing; one of his comrades had a leg blown off and another had part of a foot blown off. They soon fitted into the swing of things. At that time the Loyalists were on a 24-hour a day lock-up and so we were out for the two exercise periods and a couple of hours association each night until seven o'clock. There were about 40 of us on the first landing on A wing and so at night you got to know everybody else very soon. I used to sit and talk to Tom; he was a take-a-hand sort of boy and very popular. I remember that somebody told him the name of the girl I was going with, and we'll just say that it rhymed with Argentina. Every time he saw me he used to sing 'Don't cry for me...' to the tune of that song. In turn everybody used to sing to Tom, 'Don't cry for me Ballymena', which fitted the tune just as well.

In later times on the Blanket, Tom was to show the screws that he would take no aggro from them and he spent a lot of time on the boards for hitting any screw who stepped over the line of tolerance which he had set. Up in the Crum you could see that Tom had laid down a particular role for the screws in his captivity – he wasn't ignorant to them, but he didn't show them any recognition or friendliness at all. They were the enemy who were keeping him in prison and as such, contact was on a very limited basis. There was one screw, however, that Tom used to wind up a bit. Everybody called the screw Marley Mouth because he used to shout everything in a very excited fashion. When we'd be called to lock up at night from the canteen the OC would call 'faoi ghlas anois' (lock up now). Marley Mouth used to be ripping at this blatant undermining of his 'authority' and Tom used to goad him on by telling him that it was 'Free Long Kesh' that was being shouted.

Mickey Devine, Red Mick, was one of the people that I would rarely have been talking to except to pass on some news from a visit from Derry or to swap some comms or writings. He was in a different wing from me but we would get a full report on their wing activities on the Sundays when we were at the same mass as them. The main memory I have of Mickey is that at Christmas 1979 he wrote and organised a pantomime. I think it was Cinderella but with the whole story line changed to local politics. Red Mick had a bit of a name as a writer, as did Raymond McCreesh who wrote the odd poem and did the odd cartoon. When I was doing PRO, I would be given a lot of bits and pieces at mass from men and these in turn would be sent to the Republican News. Micky's panto was said by those in his wing to have been very funny and witty, and in those grubby conditions it would have taken something to make a body laugh enough to forget where he was.

BIK McFARLANE . . .

The election in the 26 Counties took place on 11 June, a main focus of which was the inclusion of hunger strike candidates. We were hopeful of gaining a number of seats, thus highlighting the dire situation in the H-Blocks even further, and possibly forcing the 26 Counties Establishment into taking a more positive line in confronting Thatcher.

TOM HOLLAND . . .

When it came to our attention that the H-Block prisoners were to go forward as candidates in the elections there was a lot of misunderstanding and general surprise in our wing. Up until shortly before the elections we were not aware that we would be intervening; nor did we know who would be standing, where they would be standing, how many would be standing and perhaps more importantly, we were not altogether certain why we were standing. This was understandable. Detailed communications about decisions taken and events about to take place were a rarity in our special circumstances. Reliable news was a valuable commodity and so much was happening in a short period of time that it was inevitable confusion would arise. On top of this was our political naivety.

Our only experience of electoral intervention by prisoners was Bobby's victory in the Fermanagh/South Tyrone seat. We had succeeded in raising the prisoners' cause way beyond our expectations. Our plight had been transformed from page five of the *Irish News* onto the international stage of the world media. The hunger strike and the reasons for it had been raised onto a higher plane. However, Bobby's death and the subsequent deaths of Frank, Patsy and Raymond during May shattered us all. The significance of Bobby's victory at the polls was diminished by his eventual death. Votes didn't seem to mean much when they failed to change opinions and influence events. Our short-lived faith in the power of the ballot box died in the early hours of 5 May, and on 12 May and again on 21 May. It is in the light of this that the cynicism of 11 June arose.

June was a quiet month in the Blocks. None of the hunger strikers was expected to reach a critical stage, therefore our necessary pressure appeared to be missing. Questions were asked among the men in our wing as to the wisdom of our tactics which had now allowed the British government a considerable breathing space. Others believed a climate was being deliberately created in order to allow the British government a way out of the impasse – if they so wished – a period of relative calm away from the glare of the world media being the best possible circumstances for a negotiated solution. In our wing June was viewed as an uncomfortable time, with no apparent urgency and little sign of a breakthrough. This frustration, coupled with the cynicism about the effectiveness of the election tactic, led to growing scepticism among many men in our wing about the election. A prominent question was: 'If 30,000 people in Fermanagh/South Tyrone could not force Britain to work out an honourable settlement, then how were 5,000 in County Louth going to change things?'

Such pessimism was not accepted by us all. The possibility of a prisoner being a TD in Leinster House offered us the opportunity to put the H-Block issue on the political agenda more powerfully in the 26 Counties. Pressure from that quarter was essential in deciding the outcome. We could use any election victory as a platform to prick the conscience of a nation into forcing the unwilling Free State Establishment into action in order to break Britain's intransigence. Arguments and discussions went to and fro between us: in our cells, out our doors, out the windows and on the pipes. A new angle seemed to arise every day. Opinions changed with the summer weather we were supposed to have. Why weren't all the hunger strikers involved in the elections? Why wasn't Bik standing? Why could a proxy candidate not be put forward to directly represent the hunger strikers views at Leinster House? Could our intervention possibly be enough to encourage Haughey to negotiate with us to prevent Fianna Fáil losing votes? If Fitzgerald gets in as a result of our intervention, were we not throwing away any chance we may have had with the 26 Counties politicians? How would a H-Block prisoner TD affect a hung Dail? One thing was clear – our understanding was limited. Despite this, we all knew that now we had intervened, we needed to do well; a prisoner getting elected would be a victory; a hunger striker getting elected would have the potential of determining the conclusion of the whole issue.

The 26 Counties election results did not have the same impact on us as did Bobby's election two months earlier. Yet it was acknowledged as an advance in our campaign for political recognition. The total vote notched up by our prison comrades' election was way beyond our expectation, and undoubtedly the icing on the cake was the actual victory of Paddy Agnew in Louth and Kieran Doherty in Cavan-Monaghan. The cynicism and scepticism surrounding elections seemed to fade as we debated the possible effect of two TDs from the H-Blocks 'sitting' in Leinster House. What exactly did it mean? None of us was fully aware of the answer. Would Paddy and Kieran have an input into the proceedings at Leinster House? Could someone represent them on their behalf? We didn't know the practical realities. The strong feeling that was emerging in our wing was that Kieran Doherty's success could be the source of a conclusion to the H- Block tragedy. The view centred on the opinion that the 26 Counties Establishment could not sit idly by as one of its TDs slowly neared death in the H-Blocks. We were all aware that a primary part of overall strategy was the targeting of the 26 Counties, the Catholic hierarchy and the SDLP to force them to abandon their cosy position and confront the British. We now believed Kieran Doherty spearheaded this attack on constitutional Nationalism. Our general impression was that, if Kieran Doherty was allowed to die, then our strategy had failed; if a dying TD couldn't move them then nothing would.

MICHAEL GORMAN . . .

The artificial light that shone off the shiny black floor and clean, speckly cream walls created a cold, lifeless atmosphere. An eerie place. As I entered the hospital wing I sensed a strong, sickly sweet odour. Some sort of air freshner or strong disinfectant? Or maybe the fat MO who was taking down my particulars had thrown half a bottle of after shave over himself? Whatever the source, it wouldn't cleanse this place or my mind of the fact that Bobby died here and that Fat Joe and Big Doc were here now, also dying. I wondered if I would get a chance to see them.

As I sat pondering these thoughts, a hard retching noise loudly rang out, causing me to start. It was in a voice I barely recognised. I asked, 'Is that one of the lads?' The fat MO turned to look at me and replied, 'Yes, that's one of the prisoners who is starving himself to death.' Anger rose in me and I shouted at him, asking if he was trying to be funny. He said, 'Take it easy. I didn't mean anything.' He stalked off, flustered, and called for a PO. I thought to myself I could be out of here quicker than it took them to get me in; I had better watch my mouth.

I shouted up the corridor, 'Joe? Doc?' No reply. Before I could shout again keys jingled and a grille opened and clanged shut behind me. 'Right lad, there's no need for that racket. Your friends are probably resting.' Turning in the chair, I watched as the PO and MO approached, benign smiles on their faces. 'Let's get you into your room and clean that foot up,' said the PO. I followed him, hobbling awkwardly. Halfway up the corridor a muffled voice from behind a closed door echoed in the quietness, 'Who's there?' 'Is that you Joe? It's Dikel here.' 'Are you alright, Nail-in-the-boot?' 'Aye, I'm okay'. 'Do you want a smoke? I'll see if I can get a couple up later.'

Later that evening Joe and Doc shouted out the window to me. I was next door to Joe; on his other side was Doc. 'I take it they are finally going to cut that foot of yours off?' asked Joe. 'Naw, they've already done it.' 'What's he saying?' asked Doc. 'He has cancer of the arse,' was Joe's quick reply. 'Did you say a beart stuck up his arse?' asked Doc. Joe's laughter and my own mingled and echoed in the still evening. In the background Doc mumbled something about two smart Alecs.

The lighthearted moment ended as quickly as it began and the sound of harsh coughing sent a tingle like ice-cold fingers running up my spine. I shuddered and anguish filled my heart for my comrades.

Silence descended suddenly like a heavy blanket over the place. Time passed slowly. How long I stood perched on the pipe I don't know. I could do nothing and I didn't know what to say. I shouted out, 'Hey, Joe, are you there?' 'Naw, I'm away home, you headcase!' I was embarassed by this retort, but I smiled to myself, for that's just Joe. 'Nail-in-the-boot?' 'Yes?' 'We're away to lie down here, but we'll try to get in to see you in the morning'. 'No problem. Oíche mhaith'. 'Same to you, kid.' I moved back delicately to my bed and climbed in. Turning on to my side, I thought of them.

The noise of a trolley wakened me in the morning. Apart from the rubber trolley wheels squeaking in the distance, the place was deadly silent. The spy-slit in the door opened, prying eyes locked with mine for an instant, then the flap slammed down.

Later that morning an orderly came into the room with his mop and brush and cleaned the place. The mechanical way of life in jail goes on, it seemed. I tried to start up a conversation and asked how the lads were, but I got no response. Then on the way out the orderly, to my surprise, gave me five cigarettes and whispered, 'Joe says don't be smoking them all at once, and give him a shout during lock-up.' He then hurried from the room.

Lock-up was at 12.30pm. I went to the pipes and rapped the wall, first gently then harder. 'Here, do you want a fucking hammer in there?' shouted Joe. He's in form. Moments later he thumped loudly on the wall. 'Are you there, Nail-in-the-boot?' I resisted the urge to tell him I was away home. 'Aye, I'm here'. 'Just as well you didn't say something else, for I'd have killed you if you had,' he chuckled. 'Listen,' he said, 'with a bit of luck you'll be getting out tonight to see 'Top of the Pops'. We've had a yarn with a big MO and if he's on tonight, you'll get down to see us for a yarn, OK?' 'That's great.' 'Right, kid, I'm away over to the other side to spoof with Big Doc. See you tonight then?' 'Aye, I'm looking forward to it.'

The rest of the day flew by. I did nothing but pace the floor since getting the scéal about that night. Before I realised it, evening had come and I was trembling with nervous anticipation. I could feel my heart thumping. What if that MO isn't on? Please be on so I can see them, I wished to myself.

The door opened and an MO shouted 'Association time!' Before he could say another word, I was out through the door and halfway down the corridor the wrong way. 'Here, kid,' said the MO, 'it's this way, second on your left.' As I turned to head in the right direction I saw Big Doc and Joe at the far end of the corridor laughing and shaking their heads. I moved slowly towards them, my legs and feet like lead. As I got closer, I saw the smiles on their faces.

Waves of emotion flowed through me. When I reached them Joe and Doc put their hands out. Reaching out, I touched and gripped them in my own. It was all too much; my feelings took over, my bottom lip quivered and the tears flowed, tears of joy at meeting them, tears of pity for the suffering they and their families were enduring and tears of caring for two dying comrades with whom so many others and I share a bond which no amount of time will erase. Arms enfolded and comforted me; I lowered my head, ashamed. Big Doc told me to let it out. Joe said, 'Hey, guerney gub, don't be wiping your snatters on my fancy bath robe,' then laughed, lightening the mood. In the TV room we sat down at a table and lit cigarettes. They both wanted to know who was in H6. So, one by one I went through the names; between the three of us, I'm sure there were some ears burning in H6 that night.

I asked them how they felt things would go in the forthcoming weeks and months. Joe looked at me and quietly said the Brits wanted to think they would break us; 'They haven't since the Blanket started and they fucking won't now.' I looked at Big Doc who smiled gently and nodded his head in agreement. For a few moments everything went quiet and we sat there just looking at one another; my eyes roamed their faces, their eyes roamed mine. The sound of boots in the corridor intruded upon the moment. The MO entered the room, 'Time to lock up, kid, there's a governor coming down.' I rose wearily, touching them both on the shoulder lightly as I did so, 'Get to flip out of here before you have the both of us gurning,' said Doc. 'See you on Sunday at Mass,' said Joe. At the doorway I paused and looked back, then turned and walked up the corridor to my room.

Sunday came none too soon; the days between had been agonisingly slow. I shouted to the lads a few times and got no replies but they sent me newspapers each day. The coughing sound had become my constant companion and it had got steadily worse over the last few days. I couldn't stop from shuddering each time it rang out. Mass time came and I headed for the TV room where it was being said. As I walked through the doorway, Doc and Joe were seated directly in front of me; to my left I saw what looked like a pile of blankets on a wheelchair. As I passed by, a slight coughing sound came from the blankets, stopping me dead in my tracks. I cast a puzzled glance towards Joe and Doc. Joe told me it was Martin Hurson and that he was very ill. In the foreground Fr Toner was kneeling, saying prayers softly; candles burned on top of the makeshift altar, their flickering cast shadows and their burning smell filled the room. I searched with my eyes for Martin's face. Reaching out I touched it – he was warm and looked peaceful and at ease. I moved away and sat beside Joe and Doc. 'Why is he so warm and wrapped up like that?' I asked. Doc replied that Martin had picked up some sort of bug and had to be kept wrapped up to keep him warm, and that he had been coughing badly.

Mass was a somewhat solemn affair. Very little of what Fr Toner said registered with me because my thoughts were on the three men next to me and my prayers were for them. I lifted my head to see Fr Toner come round the altar with a little platter and move towards Martin. I watched as the communion was lifted and touched to Martin's lips. Lowering my head, I felt a deep sadness sweep over me at the sight. Then Fr Toner was in front of me, sorrow etched on his face. He lifted the communion; I closed my eyes and offered my tongue.

After mass I passed a few words with Fr Toner. In the middle of our short conversation a harsh wheezing cough filled the room. It was Martin. On their knees one on each side of the wheelchair were Joe and Doc talking to him, their voices seeking to soothe him. What a sorry, pitiful, moving and heart-breaking sight. I felt humbled at it, yet so proud of them for their loving and comradely gesture.

Big Doc rose, called me to the side and handed me a beart of tobacco, 'That should keep you going for a while, Dikel. We don't know when we'll get to see you again but hopefully it won't be long.' We shook hands. Joe and Martin were already back in their rooms.

That evening, sleep didn't come easy; the sound of coughing wakened me continually through the night. Monday morning came and so did the doctor to examine my foot. My heart sank at his words, 'You can go back today'. When he left, I rushed to the window and called out to Joe and Doc. No reply. Half an hour later an MO arrived with my clothes and stood guard as I dressed. As I pulled on my prison-issue boots another MO joined him. They flanked me on either side as I left the room. Down the corridor I turned quickly and walked to the door of Martin's room and lifted up the flap. In seconds they were upon me but not before I looked through to Martin lying on his side and shouted goodbye. I hope he heard me. The same goes for Joe and Doc; as I was pulled along the corridor I shouted out to them. I want to believe they heard me because that was the last time I was to see them alive.

KEVIN DEEHAN . . .

About two weeks after Martin Hurson left the wing, I was sitting in the cell with Geordie O'Neill when Fr Faul came in. He was obviously concerned about Martin, who had developed complications. He described to us how Martin was in agonising pain, and said that he should be pulled off the strike because he would not last. He pleaded that we should take him off. This encounter hurt me as it brought another dimension to the experience – the hospital dimension which we never got to see.

BIK McFARLANE . . .

Throughout the entire period of the hunger strike action and even prior to us commencing the first hunger strike, the British government had consistently defended their intransigent position. They frequently stated that political status would not be granted and that they would not introduce a prison regime for one set of prisoners demanding preferential treatment. They made great play of the 'fact' that no political prisoners existed in 'Northern Ireland' and therefore no such status could or would be afforded to anyone pursuing such demands. They conveniently ignored the fact that hundreds of Republicans and Loyalists were treated as political prisoners and enjoyed POW status in the cages of Long Kesh. Their particular conditions of imprisonment actually went further than our five basic demands would entail. And this was readily pointed out to the British government in, of all places, the House of Commons at Westminster by none other than Enoch Powell, Official Unionist MP for South Down. Needless to say, he raised it not in suport of the five demands, but rather as an indicator of British government duplicity. It was more than ironic to hear frequent denunciations of our five demands as being 'tantamount to political status' – Mrs Thatcher's chosen phrase. The contradiction was stark, so we decided to exploit it to the full.

Our first suggestion to the Army Council was that a direct reference be made to the POW conditions in the Cages and that the Brits be asked to square this with their pronouncements concerning our five demands. This wasn't acted upon and our comrades in the Cages who enjoyed POW status were not to be drawn into the equation. They had sought permission from the AC to engage in a variety of protest actions, but were refused, primarily on the basis that it could not match the severity of the hunger strike action in the Blocks, and it could possibly provide an element of confusion and detract attention from the central and crucial issue of the hunger strike.

Since we were not able to promote that approach, we had to look for other avenues to exert more pressure on the British government. An opportunity, or at least what appeared to us as something worth a shot at, emerged during

one of our regular yarning sessions out the windows. Ricky O'Rawe, the
PRO, had been a little troubled about the constant rantings from British
spokespersons, from Thatcher right down to NIO press officers, that
preferential treatment would not be considered. We didn't appear to be
making loud enough noises on the propaganda front in explaining the exact
nature of our five demands. Possibly because they were simplicity in
themselves, no one really considered a major elaboration to be necessary.
We talked it over for a long time, with contributions from Butch Butler and
Colm Scullion, our respective cellmates. Our cells were separated by another,
occupied by Marty McManus and Ta-Buck Bradley, and we had some
interjections from them. Finally we agreed that a comprehensive explanation
of the five demands should be drafted. So Ricky set about the task eagerly.

I believe also that in our isolated situation and during a period where little
of great substance in the way of reaching a settlement had unfolded, we felt
an even greater need to be doing something positive. The limbo-like
existence, with nothing happening, was more than intolerable and only
added to the sense of utter hopelessness. But here was a chance, a small
one, to demonstrate our positive side with a little bit of action.

It was three or four days in the moulding, some aspects being re-worked
for better emphasis, bits of toilet paper shunted back and forth between our
two cells, until we agreed on the finished product. I was happy with some of
the angles we had introduced, because no longer could anyone level criticism
at us for seeking preferential treatment. We declared that our demands
should be applied to all prisoners, regardless of their status, and that by
implementing them there was sure to be a significant improvement in the
quality of life within prison.

Our statement was released on 4 July and was received in a manner which
astounded us. The media carried lengthy articles, hailing it as a major
conciliatory move by the prisoners. The British government was urged to
move and on the basis of our statement to negotiate or implement a settlement.
A variety of prominent Church and political groups and individuals were
now saying that the prisoners had signalled good faith in seeking a solution
and with this statement had moved substantially from their previous rigid
position – the way was now open for an honourable end to the crisis for
both the British government and the prisoners. It was beginning to look as
though we had pulled off something of a coup, albeit a minor one. We were
congratulated by the leadership of the Republican Movement for our 'master
stroke', which of course pleased us immensely and helped to raise spirits a
great deal.

We expected an immediate response from the British, but nothing emerged
the following day, which made us all the more confident that we had caused
more than ripples. Then, when an NIO spokesman publicly declared that

the government was studying our statement carefully, we knew that our efforts had been well worth while.

When the British response did finally come, several days later, it was almost lost amidst the furore and recriminations following the tragic death of Joe McDonnell and the shabby treatment suffered by the Irish Commission for Justice and Peace, whose intervention, lauded by the Irish Establishment as the most positive attempt up to then at finding a solution, was simply swept aside by the Brits in contemptuous fashion. The British government response to our statement was of course negative in the extreme – they saw nothing in what we had outlined which signified any major shift in our position. Despite the considerable and broad welcome our statement had received, the British chose to ignore it as the basis for a negotiated settlement.

4 JULY STATEMENT

We, the protesting republican prisoners in Long Kesh, having replied in short to H. Atkins' statement of 30 June, wish to expand our view of this statement.

1) *The British government are responsible for the hunger strikes in Long Kesh. The ending of special category status was a political tactic used by the British government in its attempt to criminalise the republican attack on British imperialism in Ireland.*

   The existence of special legislation, special courts and special interrogation, plus the British administration's refusal to acknowledge a special category of prisoners, all contribute to the placing of the responsibility for this issue on that administration's shoulders.

   Furthermore, the British government have had ample opportunities during the course of this issue to avoid the occurrence and recurrence of hunger strikes. The Cardinal O'Fiaich/NIO talks, and the refusal to honour the 18 December agreement, are prime examples of this.

2) *Lord Gardiner, like so many other Brit-appointed examiners, was sent to Ireland to do a specific job: to recommend the ending of special category status so that legal credibility could be attached to the criminalisation policy.*

3) *It is wrong for the British government to say that we are looking for differential treatment from other prisoners. We would warmly welcome the introduction of the five demands for all prisoners. Therefore, on this major point of British policy there is no sacrifice of principle involved.*

4) *We believe that the granting of the five demands to all prisoners would not in any way mean that the administration would be forfeiting control of the*

prison, nor would their say on prison activities be greatly diminished; but the prisoner could have his dignity restored and cease to occupy the role of establishment zombie.

5) *The European Commission on Human Rights criticised the British government for being inflexible and for allowing such an impasse to develop. Flexibility is in not perpetuating protest but, rather, trying to remove or resolve the cause of dissent which foments such protest.*

6) *Mr Atkins outlines the present work routine under the title 'prison activity'. It is a crude system which Mr Atkins disguises with flowery jargon. Yet, it should not be a major point of contention between the administration and ourselves. What the British government recognises as 'prison work' we do not. Therefore, with goodwill, 'work' and the achieving of a compatible arrangement should be available without loss of principle. Besides self-education, which would be the main prop in any agreement, we are prepared to maintain ourselves, wings, and Blocks and engage in any activity which we define as self-maintenance.*

7) *Mr Atkins is either misinformed or exaggerating the free association demand. Free association means that there would be freedom of movement within the wings. Supervision need not be restricted. That is a matter for the regime's discretion. There would be no interference with prison officers, who would maintain their supervisory role. It must be remembered that H-Blocks are control units, and each wing is built to accommodate 25 prisoners. So it is rather a red herring to speak of the regime losing control of the prison if the prisoners had freedom of the wing.*

Equally, it is misleading to quote figures of 100 prisoners presumably associating together. We believe there should be wing visits but we do not envisage ourselves (although Mr Atkins does) running around the Block as we please in large numbers.

It is unrealistic to expect loyalists and republicans to integrate satisfactorily together. Forced integration, or the deliberate creation of a confrontation between those who bear arms in respect of their highly conflicting political ideologies, is wrong and can only lead to trouble. Even Mr Paisley recognised this fact several years back.

If studied carefully it will be seen that our definition of free association is far removed from what seems to be Mr Atkins'.

8) *Prison clothes are prison clothes. It is illusory to minimise the wearing of prison clothes to half the week. Prisoners, like everyone else, sleep, and for most of the other half are forced to wear prison clothes. The women in*

Armagh wear their own clothes, and there is no objective reason why all prisoners should not be allowed to wear their own clothes.

9) *If we accept that toiletries, and to a lesser extent reading material are essential, then the weekly parcel amounts to 4lbs of fruit. That speaks for itself.*

10) *Lost remission is a result of the protest and is not connected with the cause of it. As the British government says, the machinery exists to reclaim it – yet, for some reason the British government is being ambiguous on this matter. What constitutes a 'subsequent good behaviour period'? What does one-fifth return of remission mean?*

This should not be an area of disagreement, for it does not directly affect the running of the system. But it is of mutual benefit to all whom it affects that full remission is given back to we prisoners.

CONCLUSION:

In giving our views on what Mr Atkins said, we have outlined what should be the basis of a solution, without loss of principle to either side in this conflict.

It could well be that Mr Atkins has been misinformed about our demands. It certainly appears from his 30 June statement that this is so. We ask all parties involved to study this statement closely. We particularly ask the British to study it. It should not be taken lightly.
By asking the British administration to come in to discuss a resolution we ask nothing unreasonable. It is common for officials from that administration to visit this prison and converse with prisoners. It has been done before.

Comrades of ours have died and eight of our other comrades presently face death on hunger strike. Our people on the outside have died and more may die. That is why we seek immediate talks with the British administration to seek a solution to the H-Block protests. It is a reasonable request.

BIK MCFARLANE . . .

As we had approached July, there were moves afoot amongst the Irish Establishment to attempt to bring an end to the crisis. The SDLP and the Church were heavily involved in this and it materialised in the shape of the Irish Commission for Justice and Peace. Initially, overtures had been made to us via Fr Crilly, a member of the ICJP and a cousin of Tom McElwee. During a visit with Tom, he outlined his own position and that of the ICJP, offering their services as a potential mediator in the crisis. He indicated that they, as a reputable body, had considerable influence and would be prepared to use this in seeking an honourable settlement. He assured Tom that they would do nothing to undermine the hunger strikers and the prisoners. They would deal honourably with us at all times.

I had absolutely no idea what the ICJP was, but any group which was representative of the Irish Establishment always raised a certain degree of suspicion in me. We already had recent bitter memories of Haughey's despicable manoeuverings with Bobby Sands' family. We dearly wanted to avoid a repetition of that disastrous episode.

After discussing the situation with Tom, we decided to make the ICJP fully aware of our own position regarding a settlement and who would negotiate it for us. We were more than capable of handling that end of things ourselves. We did, however, welcome their concern and expressed our view that, if they wished to press the British government to introduce a prison regime which would allow a way out of the crisis, then we would be extremely pleased with that. But we felt, and stated, that the best possible lever they could employ was to publicly declare their support for our five demands and press the British to negotiate on that basis. Fr Crilly had assured Tom that he believed our demands were reasonable and that he supported them himself.

A series of meetings were held between the ICJP and Michael Alison of the NIO. Speculation began to mount in the media and rose to fever pitch when the ICJP was granted permission to visit the hunger strikers. Expectations among our people outside were high – surely this was a clear sign that the pressure had finally forced the British to open negotiations and implement a solution? In the Blocks also there was a sense of something in the air. After such a long period, with four of our comrades already dead and no movement from the Brits, and now an intervention by the ICJP, hopes were building rapidly. Although we urged everyone not to be too optimistic and to view this intervention with extreme caution, there was a buzz among the lads.

TOM HOLLAND . . .

The month of July had serious implications for the hunger strike. Our hopes based once more around a popular mandate – this time from the people of the 26 Counties – were relatively high despite entering July with four of our comrades dead. Pressure was beginning to mount again; more hunger strikers approached the critical stage in their protest and on top of this came the intervention of the ICJP. Initially the lads in our wing dismissed the ICJP's worth, but after a while it began to emerge that things were beginning to happen. We knew that negotiations were going on through them with the

NIO. Suddenly our understanding altered. The ICJP was basically a 26 Counties grouping; therefore could it be that this was the 26 Counties' reaction to our election success? Was Fine Gael (then in power) going to get this issue settled before Kieran Doherty's life was in danger? Everything seemed to be fitting into place. 11 June had been the turning point in our campaign – or had it?

BIK McFARLANE . . .

It was Saturday 4 July when the delegation arrived at the prison hospital to speak with the hunger strikers. The Brits stipulated that I could not be present, so the first meeting took place while I remained in my cell. I was pretty annoyed at being excluded because we had already agreed amongst ourselves that negotiations about a settlement would not take place without me being there to represent the views of all the POWs. In fact, our original position, as established by Bobby Sands, that negotiations would only take place in the presence of three advisors (Gerry Adams, Danny Morrison and myself), had not been dispensed with. However, some of the hunger strikers felt that, since they weren't actually negotiating a settlement, but only hearing what the ICJP had to say, then to possibly jeopardise the meeting by insisting on my presence would, in their opinion, have been foolhardy. But we had allowed a wedge to be driven in which would be difficult to remove. The hunger strikers did inform the delegation that, in the event of a settlement being negotiated or agreed upon, I would have to be consulted, and they urged the ICJP to seek a meeting with me as soon as possible.

LAURENCE McKEOWN . . .

I was on hunger strike a week when the Irish Commission for Justice and Peace arrived in the camp. On the Saturday, I was taken to the hospital about noon. Mickey Devine was the only one there, in the canteen, having been brought over from H5. Those on hunger strike in the hospital were locked up in their cells at this time.

It was the first time I had talked with Mickey. He had been in the Crum while I was still on remand, but we never had any contact and during the Blanket protest years our paths had never crossed. We asked each other how we felt physically, what our weight had been when we first started the fast and after that shared yarns about the Blocks and some of the characters in our wings.

At 2.00pm the lads in the hospital were unlocked and came down to the canteen: Paddy Quinn, Tom McElwee, Kieran Doherty, Kevin Lynch and Martin Hurson. These all walked in. A few minutes after that, Joe McDonnell was brought in on a wheelchair. Only I knew that Joe was the last one to come I wouldn't have recognised the figure in the chair. He was slouched over, his head resting on his shoulder; his lips were cracked and saliva trickled from the corner of his mouth which seemed to be twisted. I had remembered him as 'Fat Joe' and this person before me resembled a third of the Fat Joe I knew. The image which came to my mind was of a physically handicapped person and what has stuck with me since is the lesson I learnt about physical disablement. While Joe was not actually disabled, he appeared to be and I found I was talking to him, treating him, as if he was in some way mentally retarded. Joe was very lucid and when I heard his voice, though it was low, the character of Joe came through clearly. He was strong. He was interested to hear what was going on, what Bik thought of this 'crowd' (the ICJP) and he was concerned that everyone was getting a cigarette or drink of the spring water they had. His hearing was affected and often he would ask for something to be repeated, but Big Doc stayed beside him and ensured he was getting everything that was being said.

The ICJP arrived shortly after this and introduced themselves. We first asked that Bik be allowed to attend, but they said they had no authority over this and had been told he wouldn't be allowed to attend. However, they would be meeting him later. There was nothing striking about them, except for Logue whose language and manner I noted to be much more forward than the others. I asked Tom if he had caught his name when they had introduced themselves and he said he hadn't. I said he sounds like a politician. Tom agreed: 'I was just thinking that myself.' The other notable thing about him was that he smoked small cigars, so we helped ourselves to a few of those.

The day's discussions went over a lot of ground, toing and froing. They described their meetings with the NIO and what they had agreed upon. They seemed happy with their achievements and felt they consisted of the 'basics' of the five demands as listed by the prisoners for a successful resolution of the hunger strike. Bishop O'Mahoney sat in the middle and said very little. Fr Oliver Crilly sat on his immediate right and did a lot of the speaking. A lot of our questions were directed towards him as he was Tom's cousin, had visited the jail a few times and we probably thought that he had a grasp of the situation. Logue sat on O'Mahoney's left-hand side, with Brian Gallagher between them. Gallagher and the other member of their delegation, Jerome Connolly, rarely spoke throughout.

Discussion went on for two to three hours. All of it was fairly amicable. We reiterated our five demands but said we would discuss with anyone how these could be implemented. Talks ended with us shaking hands all round and them promising to return the next day. They left, Bik rejoined us and all of us then discussed the meeting before Bik and I returned to H3 and Red Mick to H5. We told the lads that night out the door what had taken place and discussed the general situation. What did we make of this group? Why did they suddenly arrive now? What agenda were they working to? What tie-in/authority did they have from the Southern government, the Church, the SDLP? (We had by then discovered Logue was a member of the SDLP.)

BIK McFARLANE . . .

The following day I met with three of the ICJP delegation. The manner in which this visit was arranged was preposterous, to say the least. The Brits had informed the ICJP that as an official delegation they could not meet me, because that would be tantamount to affording recognition to IRA structures within the Camp, which HM Government 'could not possibly countenance', whatever about the official meeting with the European Human Rights delegation. I was then to be informed that three named individuals sought a visit and I was to indicate if I would accept such a visit. All 'wink, wink, nod, nod, you know how these things are' baloney. The Governor even looked a little embarrassed as he told me of the NIO arrangements. 'The ICJP are not permitted to meet you, but will you take a visit with three members of the ICJP?' The logic of this appeared to be in a simple mathematic equation: five members = delegation = recognition of IRA structures; three members doesn't constitute a delegation and so no recognition of the IRA. Everyone breathed a sigh of relief, everyone excluding ourselves that is. We had too much previous experience of Brit machinations and their tinkering with terminology to be impressed by this latest little intrigue. But one thing the manoeuvre did reveal which was important – it gave us an insight into the degree of forcefulness (or rather, lack of it) inherent in the ICJP delegation. Either the Brits had the measure of them from the outset and would string them along as far as was necessary; or the ICJP were not genuinely interested in securing an honourable settlement, but wanted an end to the crisis on whatever terms they felt suited. Perhaps even both aspects applied.

One or two of the screws on duty in the visit Block pressed me for some scéal. Were these mediators who were coming to see me? Would we take what was on offer? Would it all end soon? How long could this go on? I engaged in some small talk and threw out a few evasive remarks as I waited for the ICJP delegation to arrive (or three-fifths of a delegation, depending on one's sensitivities). It was the end room in C Block – normally used for legal and ecclesiastical visits – so the visit would be spared the customary harassment from screws hanging over the box. The door would be closed and a degree of privacy afforded (although a constant healthy dose of paranoia had me firmly convinced that those visits had their fair share of bugging devices, as I suspected was the case in the hospital also).

My wait was fairly brief. The quiet was disturbed by approaching voices and a tap on the rear door, followed by the shuffling sounds of bodies edging past each other in a narrow corridor. The door of my visit room was pushed gently open by the screw as he ushered the delegation in. I rose from my chair to welcome the first – attired in traditional clerical black, with a wide extravagant smile and both hands outstretched as though to embrace me, Bishop O'Mahoney moved towards me. I offered my hand in greeting, which he clasped between both of his, and speaking in soft tones told me how he had been longing to meet me. I felt a little discomfited at such an effusive greeting and was inclined to draw back a little, if not physically, certainly mentally. I was introduced to Hugh Logue (SDLP economic spokesman) and Fr Crilly in turn. We positioned ourselves around the table and immediately launched into the business of examining exactly what form of settlement they had been proposing and discussing with the Brits and hunger strikers.

During the course of our lengthy discussion we covered every conceivable aspect of the protest and hunger strike action. There had been a suggestion that we suspend the hunger strike to allow the Brits some space to manoeuvre without the pressure hanging over them. This was totally unrealistic considering the Brits' record of not moving without pressure being brought to bear. The delegation indicated that they supported our five demands, but stated they would not publicise this position as it could damage their 'independent' stance and credibility as a mediation force. They felt it would serve no positive purpose and they would therefore refrain from public pronouncements.

Elaborating on their talks with Alison, they assured me that the issue of clothing would be resolved in an instant – in fact, Alison had as much as told them our own clothing was guaranteed, according to Bishop O'Mahoney, and was no longer really an issue. He went on to suggest that a major stumbling block to a successful resolution was our insistence on five demands as a package. The British authorities, he pointed out, would have immense difficulty in saving face if they had to concede openly to a package of five demands. He was convinced that a much better approach would be to reduce our demands to a package of three – to wear our own clothes, work to be 'defined constructively' and better facilities for association – as this would be clearly observed as a genuine compromise by the prisoners and a demonstration of our goodwill in searching for a solution. This sounded absolutely incredible, especially in light of repeated British statements that they would not yield in the face of such pressure to any demands. Their position remained that prison reforms would be favourably examined if and when all protest action had been terminated. So they were hardly likely to jump for joy and introduce a package of three demands. In fact, at one stage Thatcher had vociferously defended her murderous intransigence by declaring that yielding to even a single demand would be to grant political status to terrorists and criminals. I refused to agree to isolating any of our demands. They were basic, reasonable and provided a sound foundation – as we had elaborated in our lengthy explanatory document that very day – for an honourable settlement.

Bishop O'Mahoney and Hugh Logue were at great pains to convince me that what they had obtained from Alison, and which they felt should be couched in less severe demands – that is, their package of three – was in fact the very substance of our five demands. I was somewhat bewildered by this assertion because there was no evidence to suggest that they had obtained anything of the sort. But I made it very clear to them that, if they were able to produce a settlement, the basis of which contained the substance of our five demands, then I would most certainly jump at it. I didn't have to jump too far though – in fact, I didn't jump at all, because the only thing I'd have landed on was the issue of clothing, and I wasn't even sure of how solid that 'guarantee' had been. Their redefinition of work and association/segregation fell far below our base line and could not have provided an avenue for real progress.

The debate continued and I outlined our position again. I expressed my view that the Brits were simply using this intervention of the ICJP to create an illusion of negotiation and movement towards a successful resolution of the crisis. I pointed out that our position could be greatly undermined by such interventions which attempted to sell us short, and that the best course of action the ICJP could take would be to publicly declare their support for our five just demands. With Joe McDonnell in a serious condition and not far from death, I asked if they thought it a little strange that the Brits had waited until now before admitting them to the Blocks. The pressure would now be very heavy on us to accept half solutions as we battled to save Joe's life.

Fr Crilly listened patiently and attentively to everything I said and told me he would do nothing to undermine the hunger strikers – he had the greatest admiration for them and dearly wished to be of assistance in bringing the heartbreak to an end. Tom McElwee, he told me, was a relative and so he personally felt the pain. He agreed that our views should be represented correctly and that we should not be pressed into accepting a settlement which was not an honourable one. I had the feeling that I could talk with this priest without worrying about him digging pitfalls for me. He was unquestionably a very reasonable man and I somehow felt that his decency and honesty did not belong in this sordid and murky business of dealing with Thatcher and Co in full flight. The chief concern, however, of Bishop O'Mahoney and Hugh Logue seemed to be in getting me to acknowledge that their three-package deal was the ultimate answer to the nightmare. I was sure they didn't absorb what I had been explaining. They even told me that the hunger strikers had listened carefully and favourably to their proposals. Their role as self-appointed mediators was fast becoming one of frantic salesmen with a deadline to get rid of some cheap product. There appeared to be no interest whatsoever in moving towards our position. I left the meeting after thanking them for their concern and stating clearly that further negotiations would have to be conducted with the hunger strikers and myself in attendance.

LAURENCE MCKEOWN . . .

On the Sunday morning I was again called to the hospital. I didn't know what to expect and certainly wasn't expecting Danny Morrison to be there. He was banned by the NIO from visiting the Camp on ordinary visits and, as this was a Sunday morning when no normal visits take place, all sorts of rules had been set aside to allow him in. The first thing he said to us was that the screw who opened the front gate for him had sworn: 'Bastard!' He soon learnt though that this wasn't directed at him but at Maggie Thatcher who, the screw reckoned, must have conceded to our demands given this extremely unusual visit with someone who was banned from visiting.

Danny told us the history of their contact with the ICJP and also mentioned other contacts with the British Foreign Office (none of the communication between the Republican Movement and the British government at this time has ever been admitted to by the latter). We outlined our position to him and told him that we had heard nothing so far to make us believe there was a resolution to the staile in sight. The ICJP would, however, be returning that evening. We split up after that and Danny went to see Bik who hadn't been allowed to be present with us during our meeting. I was happy with what had taken place. It seemed there was movement. Why else would the NIO agree to Danny's visit with Bik and us? I felt we were in a strong position.

The ICJP delegation arrived back that evening. A few moments were passed in exchanging small talk, then we got down to business. From the start Bishop O'Mahoney played the dominant role. He gave a breakdown of their negotiations, saying what they had 'achieved' and what was on offer to us. This was no different from the previous day when we had been told we would be allowed to wear our own clothes, work would be looked at in a constructive manner and better facilities for association would be introduced.

Logue came in to back this up by saying that what they had achieved was the basis of our five demands and in fact they had even gone further and got us a sixth demand. I looked at Logue a bit incredulously and said, 'Go ahead, tell us what this sixth demand is.' He said, 'A recognition of the Gaelic culture and Irish language, and as a goodwill gesture, we have been given permission to present you with this Bible written entirely in Irish.' He said this as if we were to fall down at his feet in praise for what he had 'won' for us. I don't think that he was too pleased with the response he did get – total disinterest in his Irish Bible.

We asked a number of questions and attempted to involve Oliver Crilly in the conversation, without success. It was obvious he had been 'nobbled' by O'Mahoney. His whole demeanour portrayed a reluctance to involve himself in discussion. At the end of a period of frustrating dialogue about the status of what was on offer, Big Tom put it straight to Crilly: 'What's being said is that our own clothes are on offer and that's the heap, isn't it?' Crilly didn't respond for a moment, then looked up at Tom and said, 'Yes'. At this point Logue burst in saying, 'It would be criminally irresponsible to say that that is the only thing on offer. We have outlined what is in fact the basis of your five demands and have indeed included a sixth.' Oliver Crilly didn't reply, obviously aware that he had spoken out of tune and against what the rest of the delegation had planned to say. He has to be given some praise for his integrity in this instance. Whether it was because of the family connection – Tom being his cousin – or just that, looking across at the faces of men most likely to die within a few days, he couldn't bring himself to lie to them or paint a much better picture of the situation than what it was, I don't know. But it has to be said he was the only one to act with some integrity.

Logue (who this day had decided to leave his cigars out in the car) was prepared to push through any duplicitous deal, no doubt hopeful of the political kudos it would bring him. Being a member of the ICJP delegation which negotiated an end to the hunger strike when everyone else had failed would no doubt do his political future in the SDLP a world of good. I would sum him up by saying he is one of the most treacherous people I have ever had the misfortune to meet.

Bishop O'Mahoney must take full responsibility for the role the ICJP played. He was fully aware of how he was being used by both the Dublin government and the NIO officials. He could not have been unaware of this. It would be interesting to know what brief the Church had given him on his role. What he was clearly intent on doing was forcing through a package which would have been a sellout of our demands. He knew that.

The discussion between us went on for many hours, even after it was very clear it was getting nowhere and that we had rejected outright what was on offer. Maybe they thought we would tire. I know they were certainly frustrated and angered that we had cut through all the frills of their speech and exposed just what the reality was. No doubt O'Mahoney was not accustomed to having people speak back or asserting their views or belief in themselves, in their comrades and in their commitment to a struggle. Logue was certainly not amused that his fancy way of packaging the 'deal' was exposed as being just so much crap. Oliver Crilly looked sad, very sad, as if he knew what had been attempted and now knew what the outcome of it would be.

BIK MCFARLANE . . .

I met the ICJP at midnight. They had just spent a gruelling four hours trying to break the resolve of the dying hunger strikers in an attempt to get their proposals accepted as a final solution. I had been whisked up to the hospital sometime after 8.00pm and informed that my presence might be required at the negotiations. I was installed in a single ward at the end of the corridor. Everything was so quiet – there was no evidence of any activity. I paced the floor for a considerable period and when nothing had materialised, I climbed into a very comfortable bed and just lay there wondering what was going on, if anything.

The door opened at midnight and in trooped Bishop O'Mahoney, accompanied by two other members of the ICJP (Jerome Connolly and Hugh Logue, I think, possibly even one other; so long as it wasn't the full five, they were on safe ground). They looked quite exasperated as they positioned themselves around my bed, Bishop O'Mahoney sitting at the bottom and Jerome Connolly in a chair beside me. They began to relate how they had been in session with the hunger strikers for four hours, trying to get them to see the 'value' of their proposals. I felt a sense of outrage creeping through me at the thought of weak and dying men being bombarded and harassed by these people with their partial solutions. If they had badgered Atkins and Alison as ferociously as they had just done with our comrades on hunger strike, then perhaps something positive would have emerged. They then asked me if I couldn't somehow persuade the hunger strikers to accept their package. 'Are you people serious?' I asked. After spending what must have been a torturous four hours with the hunger strikers, cajoling and arguing, only to be told that their entire package amounted to nothing other than a vague promise of our own clothing, they actually believed they could persuade me to go along and do exactly as they had done. Jerome Connolly was practically pleading with me and at the same time asking if I realised the international standing and clout which the ICJP had. It was with some effort that I managed to avoid erupting, but the knowledge that the hunger strikers had dealt very firmly with this delegation was more than enough to calm me. I simply refused to pressurise my comrades into something which they wouldn't accept. Nor would it have been acceptable to myself or the rest of the POWs. My answer was direct and very short. They left and I was locked in for the night to reflect on the events of that hectic day. I couldn't help feeling somewhat astounded at the naivety of these 'learned and professional men of experience'.

The members of the ICJP appeared to me to have an over-inflated sense of their own importance and clout. The Brits had a long history of dealing decisive blows to those out of their depth in such affairs. And it was only some days later that the ICJP was simply dismissed as having totally misinterpreted the NIO minister's views on how a settlement could be implemented. While they were hopping back and forth between Stormont and the Kesh in supposed negotiations with Alison, the British government had secretly opened a link to the IRA and begun negotiations to attempt to resolve the issue. My first knowledge of this came when I had been summoned to the prison hospital that Sunday morning only to be confronted by Danny Morrison. I was completely flabbergasted at seeing him there; my mind was racing through all sorts of computations. It transpired that the Brits had agreed to allow him into the Kesh to consult with us and to explain the nature of the contact which had been established. There was definitely an air of optimism gripping me, but I was urged to be cautious, as it was possible that nothing would emerge to satisfy our demands.

As I sat with all the hunger strikers in the canteen discussing what was on offer, I felt very much humbled by the dedication and determination of those around me. I was very moved by Joe McDonnell who was troubling himself so much to ensure I was seated comfortably and had cigarettes if I needed them. He was in an appalling condition and could barely hear what I was saying. He was almost 60 days on hunger strike and was confined to a wheelchair, in which he sat with head crouched low to one side. He looked to be in immense pain, but joked with me as he grabbed my hand to shake it on this our first meeting. He was at pains to assure me that his commitment was strong and cautioned me not to be thinking of him if negotiations were in progress. There were hundreds of Blanketmen to look after, he said, and my responsibility was to obtain a proper settlement for them. 'Don't you worry about Joe McDonnell. I might only last a few days but I'll hang on as long as I can and buy all the time we need.'

THOMAS LOUGHLIN . . .

When the ICJP got involved, no one gave it much thought, thinking it was just another concerned group. However, as it became clear that they were making progress, we were led to believe by everyone except those most closely involved that a settlement was imminent. Even the deputy Secretary of State Michael Alison indicated that the hunger strike was about to be resolved and that he would be sending in a message to wrap the whole thing up. This was the feedback most of us were getting at the time. So morale was sky-high in the knowledge that it would soon be over and that no one else would die, although we were all aware that Joe McDonnell was in a bad way. On 8 July it really appeared to us that it was over.

This was the first time during the whole hunger strike period that the wing had any sense of normality. In fact, it was much more than that; there was a genuine buzz. It reminded me of the day before the ending of the first hunger strike when we were told that we were on the brink of victory. We felt like that because it seemed a settlement was really on the cards. The ICJP had been talking to the Brits for quite a while and to our knowledge were getting a very positive response. I'm not sure if we were told to brace ourselves for the end, but we knew that a messenger from the NIO was due in at any time with the necessary documents that would offer a solution. We were aware that Joe McDonnell was at a crucial period, but to our knowledge he was not yet critical, so we were very hopeful that he would live. That night a few of the lads were at their doors talking or having a bit of craic. My cellmate was talking to Hugh Rooney (Hugh never spoke English – only Gaelic – and my cellmate couldn't understand a word he was saying, so there was I translating the Gaelic for my cellmate who answered in English; it was weird).

Before the night got any later, one of the lads got up to the door and asked for silence; we all knew it was important and immediately shut up. 'Fuair Joe McDonnell bás,' he said. That was it, nothing more, not another word was said. I remember looking at my cellmate for a while, totally stunned, then we both sat on our beds. There was a feeling of hopelessness; what do we do now? Very few of us knew or even had met Joe McDonnell; all I knew was that he was married and had two kids; all I could think of was how close he came to winning, to achieving victory. I must have sat on my bed for a long time thinking and sometime during that I felt tears sliding down my cheeks. Those tears were for Joe and I suppose the lads who had died before him, but they were also for those who had yet to die. If there ever was a period when hope for us had finally run out, it was then. The only words heard in the wing for quite a while were those of the lads with the radio telling us the latest news. It said that Michael Alison had not expected Joe McDonnell to die so soon, but he went on to talk about the futility of the hunger strike. Yes, we thought, you always intended him to die.

The next morning the NIO went back to their 'not an inch' mentality. It was then we understood the magnitude of difficulties we faced.

LAURENCE MCKEOWN . . .

The ICJP stayed in the news on the Monday. On Wednesday morning Joe McDonnell died after 61 days on hunger strike; then the recriminations began. The ICJP claimed publicly that the NIO had promised them such and such, the NIO said they hadn't and the British government, to back up this position, pointed out that no junior minister could have promised anything of the sort. The whole episode appeared very messy.

This was possibly the last serious attempt the Church or the Dublin government made at intervention in the stalemate. After this their public pronouncements became more weighted against the hunger strike, calling on the hunger strikers to come off it and more or less agreeing with Thatcher's line that 'no government could be seen to concede to such pressure'. I think it was at this stage we began to realise we were very much on our own and that our actions were having a wider political effect than we had first imagined. We were exposing the so-called nationalist politicians and cutting through their rhetoric. We were posing a threat to the status quo, no longer prepared to bend the knee and accept moral control from the Church, thinking for ourselves and acting in our own best interests. We had to be stopped. Soon Fr Faul stepped up his anti-hunger strike campaign of vilification of the Republican Movement and its leadership.

BIK MCFARLANE . . .

Back in the Block, I waited for news that would end the nightmare, but the comms I received from the Army Council showed the Brits still hadn't gone beyond the position we had agreed and had reaffirmed on Sunday in the hospital. Then on Wednesday we received the heartbreaking news that Joe had died early that morning. It was more than tragic because I had been holding out hope that this was the chance we had longed for. And I could only think of Joe holding on grimly with every last ounce of his energy to buy us that precious time he knew we so badly needed. It was a stunning blow to us all and it appeared that we were now into a second cycle of deaths.

JAZ MCCANN . . .

Joe McDonnell was one of the toughest people I have ever met. A couple of years ago, while in conversation about old times with a screw from the Blanket days, the screw, with a hint of admiring respect, divulged that Joe was the toughest prisoner that he had ever come across. He related to me incidents where Joe had fiercely resisted the mirror search. He admitted that to his knowledge they had never once succeeded in bending Joe's legs. We refused to bend so they would kick the backs of our leg until they buckled and we fell down. The more the prisoner resisted the more he would be kicked. Personally, they had only to give me a couple of kicks and I was down. This wasn't that I had weak legs in the physical sense; they were metaphorically weak. I think most of the resistance to the search was token but Joe's was principled. In retrospect I would say Joe's attitude to the search epitomised his life – he quite literally refused to bend. Therefore it was no surprise that he was to become one of the key men on the hunger strike. He was never a man for taking a back seat.

It must have been about September or October 1979 when a rumour circulated in H5 that some of the leadership in H6 had planned a hunger strike to coincide with the Pope's visit ot that year. I remember Joe was furious. He made his view known that all the Blanket Blocks should have been consulted, that the protest was not the preserve of H6 and that if a hunger strike was agreed to, all Blocks must be permitted to participate. Joe approached the staff and let it be known that, if there was a hunger strike, he wanted to be part of it. There was no hunger strike that year, but talk of hunger strike became more and more common and it seemed inevitable that there was going to be one. Around May 1980 I noticed Joe while at mass on several occasions in deep conversation with the staff. He told me later unoffically that there was to be a hunger strike, ten men were going on it and he was to be one of them. However, as far as I know the Church learned of the impending hunger strike and asked that it be stopped. Knowing what lay ahead, Cardinal Ó Fiaich and Bishop Daly (Derry) made approaches to the British government in attempts to find a resolution to the prison issue. Their talks were to last several months and they raised many hopes, but to no avail. In September we were officially informed that there was to be a hunger strike. Volunteers were asked for, and the staff emphasised that before anyone volunteered, they must accept that they could die. Joe put his name down.

I rather foolishly put my own name down. I did not and could not come to terms with death – that is, my own death – but I wanted to be part of the hunger strike. So I decided to put my life in the hands of fate – if I'm picked, I must go on it; if the Brits don't give way I must... but I couldn't come to terms with that last link in the causal chain that I had initiated by forwarding my name. Some say I was influenced by Joe – which I certainly was to some extent. But I think that even if I had been removed from his influence, I still would have been foolish enough to put my name down without coming to terms with the consequences.

Approximately a week later we were informed of the seven names who were to go on hunger strike. Raymond McCartney was the only one from our wing among the seven. I think Joe was a bit surprised that he was not included because he had been one of the main pushers for hunger strike. But the strategy of picking seven men from different geographical areas to maximise support consoled him. As only one man was chosen from Belfast, Joe was not so arrogant or lacking in humility to believe that he should have been the 'chosen one'. However, there was no hiding his disappointment on 14 December.

That December night as Sean McKenna lay critically ill, word was shouted to our Block from H4 that we were to put more men on hunger strike. I think we were to provide seven volunteers. Joe was confident that he would be selected, but this was not to be. I think the staff preferred to select from the abundance of single men who had volunteered, rather than select Joe, who was married with two young children. He was peeved at this, not just because he was not allowed to join the hunger strike but because for months he had lived with the idea of a hunger strike, had probably spent many sleepless nights trying to come to terms with death, had sweated blood psyching himself in readiness for a hunger strike and yet apparently all along the staff's preference for single men ruled him out.

I felt for him that night. He was hurt, and I'll never forget what he had to say. In a rare show of humility he confessed that it was probably best that he didn't go on hunger strike because he was not made of the quality that makes a martyr and patriot. He laughed at the idea that anyone could ever hold him in high esteem and he ridiculed himself for having the audacity to try to gatecrash membership to that gallant band of Plunkett, Pearse and Tone, etc. He had no desire to be a martyr; he enjoyed life and wanted to live it to the full. But living to the full for him meant fully committing himself to Republicanism and this brought the inevitable side-effect – not aim – of threatening that very life that he wanted to live to the full. Now that he was removed from the situation, he was able to step back and look at the consequences that might have been and believing that they were absurd, that it was inconceivable his name could be honoured, it helped to relieve his disappointment.

I ended up on hunger strike myself. Luckily enough for me it ended three days after the group and myself embarked on it. During those three days Joe made a fuss over me. He would regularly shout to me and enquire how I was. He enjoyed conversation with those in the cells near to him (of which I was one) and listening to someone 'doing a book' out the door. In fact, when I look back now and recall how he used to beg, cajole and intimidate a man to do a book, a man who told nothing but excruciatingly boring stories in a monotonous dull tone that nearly drove the (reluctant) listeners to suicide, I realise that Joe just liked to hear the sound of a human voice. Yet he was prepared to forego this love if it disturbed me. I appreciated Joe's fussing, but I wanted everything to run just as normal and since the story teller (if I can stretch the imagination to infinite limits to call him that) disturbed me when I had a full stomach, he could not disturb me any more or less while I had an empty stomach.

Joe would not intentionally hurt anyone (except the enemy of course), and if he was aware that a person was particularly sensitive about something, he would not refer to it. For example, one of his many slags with me concerned my relationships with a couple of women. One day at mass he took my cellmate to the side and said that he had heard that I was taking it bad about his slagging me about an ex-girlfriend. He was concerned, enquired how bad I took it and promised the cellmate that he would never mention her name again. I don't know where he had heard that I had taken the mention of her name bad; it was nonsense. I lost my sensitivity in the first year on the Blanket.

Outsiders would have found the humour strange. We could always laugh at ourselves. Providing there was no malice, it was open season. Sometimes when the slagging got hot and heavy and did cause anger or hurt, Joe could never let the night end on a sour note. Every night, every single night (except when that bloated bore of a storyteller had put him to sleep) he would end his day by shouting into me 'oíche mhaith' or 'goodnight Big Jim'. If I didn't return the greeting he would shout again and again until I did. Had he overstepped the mark with the slagging, my responding 'oíche mhaith, Fat Joe' meant that all was forgiven and the day ended well.

When word was shouted across from one of the wings about who would follow the four on the second hunger strike, silence gripped the wing. It was explained that a pool of twelve men had been selected to replace dead hunger strikers. They would join the hunger strike in numerical order. Joe was to be number 1, Brendan McLaughlin number 2, Martin Hurson number 7 and I was to be number 11. This meant that Joe would replace Bobby, should he die first. Bobby and Joe had been captured on the same bombing mission and therefore he took some pride in being with him again on this very important mission. There was some confusion as to whether Joe would replace Bobby or the first hunger striker to die, but apart from that, there was not a great deal of talk. I think Joe's attitude was more or less to take a big deep breath and say to himself, 'Let's go'. He probably believed (as I did myself) that Bobby had selected him to replace him and I could sense he was touched and honoured by this.

But when Bobby died, word was sent to Joe that he was not, as planned, to go on hunger strike. At first neither he nor any of us knew what was happening. Joe was annoyed. He had prepared himself for hunger strike and now he was informed that he was not to go on it. Later he received a comm informing him that he was going on it but not just yet. Following this he received further word that he might not be going on it. We were to hear that the IRA (outside) was against the plan to replace dead hunger strikers. They had said that four men were enough and there was to be no more. Joe was very angry at this. He felt that they should have voiced their opposition before the hunger strike began (it is possible they did) and that they had no right to scuttle the strategy now that it was in progress. He may also have believed that not to go ahead with the strategy would be to abandon Frank, Raymond and Patsy and to give up hope of winning our demands.

For three or four days the conflicting messages continued – don't be going on it; hold tight, you'll be going on it later. The confusion was taking its toll on Joe. I can remember him writing a comm to his wife in the morning informing her he was going on hunger strike and giving her directions what to do, and then writing another comm to her in the afternoon to cancel out what he had written that morning. To compound his own ordeal he was worried about the distress it would cause his family.

The confusion for Joe ended not through a comm from Bik or the IRA but via Radio Ulster. On the night of 8 May (I think) the radio man shouted across to Joe that it had been on the news that he was to join the hunger strike the following day. Joe asked the OC what he was to do, and the OC informed him to go ahead and join the hunger strike and that confirmation of this would probably arrive the following day.

That night we talked about his wife and family and how they would handle the news that he was to go on hunger strike. Joe had not seen his wife and family for almost four years. He had refused to take visits because it meant wearing the prison uniform, which he refused to do. Now that he was going on hunger strike he had to have a visit with his family, and he was excited about seeing them at last. I joked that his wife wouldn't want anything to do with him after she saw how fat he was. While the banter flowed that night and the thought of the visit lifted him, I was hurt for him. I was hurt for him because of what he had to endure over the previous three or four days, and I was hurt for him because the visit he had dreamed and talked about down through the years was not to be. The visit was supposed to be a joyous occasion. He was supposed to wear his own clothes because we would have won our demands and his wife and family would have been overjoyed at seeing him and overjoyed that the protest was successfully concluded and the future looking bright. But now that visit was to take place under a cloud of foreboding.

The following morning Joe refused his breakfast. The PO came to see him and made arrangements for a family visit. After the visit Joe admitted that

he had cried during it, and we teased him that he was a wimp. He may have
been one of the toughest persons I ever met but inside he was as soft as
putty. He was not one for walking away from a fight or challenge and this
characteristic was not to help him on his hunger strike. Hunger strikers had
to endure jibes, and cheap and insulting remarks from screws. This abuse
was at its height when they were out of their cell, usually when on the way
to or from the daily medical check in the MO's room in the circle. Screws
would talk about delicious meals they had or were going out to have, they
would speculate whether the hunger striker would stay on the hunger strike,
how long he would last and if anyone apart from Adams and Co would turn
up for the funeral. They actually placed bets on how long a hunger striker
would survive and would ask him to time his death to coincide with the
prediction. It was best to ignore them, especially since they wanted a
reaction. But Joe could not always ignore it.

One day, when he was locked between the grilles a couple of screws had a
look at him to see, as they said, how their bets were going. One of them said
to the other that he had Joe down for 60 (days) and that he was looking good
for it. The other one laughed and said that he had no chance of doing 60. Joe
was livid, and such a mouthful he gave them. He couldn't get at them
because they were outside the grilles – they would not have said anything
had it been otherwise.

Most of the regular screws on the wing did not bother him because they
knew what a tough nut he was. However, there was one screw in particular
who never missed an opportunity to taunt Joe. Of course he would make
sure that there was a locked door or grille between them when he said these
things and he always made himself scarce if he was on the wing when Joe
was about to be unlocked. One day this screw appeared at a grille when we
were at mass. Joe spotted him, and myself and Gino MacCormaic had a
difficult job calming him down. Lucky enough, the screw realised that Joe
had seen him and once more made himself scarce. Joe stated that day that if
he was to come out of the hunger strike alive he would get that screw.
(Some time later that particular screw was shot.)

Several days after he went on the hunger strike, he was moved to a cell at
the top of the wing. So I could only get talking to him at mass and on an odd
occasion I tried to see him by getting out of my cell to go to the toilet while
he was at the washhouse.

Frank Hughes died on 12 May and Brendan McLaughlin took his place
on hunger strike. Brendan was also moved to the top of the wing, and this
was some comfort for Joe. But Brendan became very ill, deteriorated very
fast and had to be moved to an outside hospital. Raymond and Patsy died on
21 May and Brendan became the focus. He was only days away from a
certain death caused by peritonitis brought on by his hunger strike. A

hunger strike to have maximum effect must be long and drawn out. Brendan's early death therefore would not be effective in putting pressure on the British and he was therefore asked to end his hunger strike. He agreed to do this.

This now left Joe the front runner and he most definitely felt it. After the conflict that preceded his hunger strike, Joe settled down and carried on life as if he was not on hunger strike. I was amazed at his strength. At mass he was the same old Joe running about scrounging tobacco, gleaming bits of scéal here and there, slagging, laughing and cracking jokes. Nothing was difficult, or at least outwardly nothing was difficult. Physically too Joe looked in good shape. His body appeared to be bearing up to hunger strike very well. This was in complete contrast to Raymond. At 20 days Raymond could hardly walk and looked very frail, whereas Joe at 20 days looked in good condition and was running about as normal and burning up energy. Given that Raymond had died after 61 days, I thought that Joe would last way beyond that. When the ICJP was negotiating with Alison I was hopeful that Joe could hang on because it appeared that a breakthrough that would save his life was close at hand. But I suppose if the Brits had been determined not to give way, whether he was able to last 60 days or 100 days made no difference. But I was surprised that he survived only the same length of time as Raymond.

On Holy Thursday we were at mass again. Brendan had come off the hunger strike on the previous day, I think, and Joe for the first time showed signs of being under pressure. He knew that he was going to die and as I sat beside him, talking and listening to him, I realised myself that he was going to die. Naturally I didn't give him the least indication that he was right. I made light of his fatalism; I told him that he would feel different tomorrow when he was in better form. I changed the subject and slagged him about the publicity he was receiving and how he would have no trouble now getting the leather jacket he was after. (Joe was a man for fine clothes. He wanted a leather jacket, but he kept changing his mind whether to ask a friend in the States to buy him one.) The mention of the leather jacket had always provoked an animated response but not only did it fail to spark anything in him that day, he turned to me and said with a definite air of finality that momentarily had me lost for words, 'I'll never wear it'.

It shook me. I felt like crying; for seconds I could think of nothing to say to him. I wanted to deny the truth of what he was saying both to myself and to him. I admired this man. He was strong, he was tough, he was staunch and he was likeable. He had been a source of strength to me down through the years, as well as a good friend. Now I wanted him to be strong enough to deny the truth because I was not strong enough at that moment to deal with it and give him the support he needed. All I could say to him was that he would be alright. Even though he sat between myself and another friend in a packed canteen, I could sense that he was all alone. I could feel his loneliness. A subdued and dispirited Joe McDonnell was alien to me. It was an imposter! I wanted the boisterous, high-spirited Joe McDonnell to return because his absence was killing me. I felt for him but was powerless to do anything. It was one of the lowest points I have ever experienced.

I had a visit that afternoon. I had to tell my parents that I would be going on hunger strike sometime in the future. To make the task even more difficult, it was a closed visit (I had been caught with a comm on a previous visit and for two months my visits were 'closed' – a partition separated me and my visitors). The screw could hear nearly everything that was said. My mother pleaded with me not to go on hunger strike. She was crying and the screws were witnessing this. To end this terrible scene I promised her that I'd pull out. At the time my conscience was eased with the belief that I was doing it for her. But I know I was less than honest with myself. The truth was I didn't want to die. But the thought of Joe was heavy in my mind that day and I felt I was abandoning him by pulling out. On my way back into the wing I rapped Joe's door to ask him how he was. He shouted out to me, 'How did the visit go?'; in other words, how did my parents take the news that I was going on hunger strike? He knew that I would be telling them. A lump came to my throat. The screw pushed me on. I couldn't tell him. I was shattered.

I was never to see Joe again. He was unexpectedly moved to the hospital that afternoon. He shouted out farewell to me and I shouted back all the best to him. I was close to tears. I kept saying to myself he must come back, he must not die, I must see him again. He wrote me a comm a couple of weeks later and I was really pleased and relieved that the Joe McDonnell of old clearly shone through. He wrote about the TV programmes he had been watching and how good the visits were.

There was only one note of complaint. He informed me of British Liberal MP David Steel's visit and wrote that Steel had misquoted him to the media. I wrote back to Joe but he never received the comms. I gave one to Martin Hurson who was also on hunger strike and asked him to take it with him when he was going to the hospital.

I'll never forget the morning I handed him that comm and asked him to bring it to Joe. As I turned to walk away, Martin asked me when I was going on hunger strike. I was that ashamed I could not turn around again to face him. I pretended that I did not hear him and walked away. Given the noise in the canteen and that most of it was going on around Martin, who was the centre of attention, I'm sure he believed he wasn't heard rather than ignored.

Martin gave it to a friend in the next cell to look after until he was moved, but he too was moved unexpectedly and wasn't able to get it back.

My hopes were raised with the entry of the hunger strikers and other POWs into the Dáil elections. Unfortunately Joe missed being elected by about 500 votes and the brutal irony of it was that one of the candidates in the same Sligo/Leitrim constituency stood as an anti-H-Block candidate and took precious votes away.

The ICJP gave cause for hope, but Joe slipped into a coma and the anxiety became unbearable. I lived from one news bulletin to the next; hoping and praying that it would tell us that an agreement was reached and Joe was off the hunger strike. The raised hopes and tension was to come to an abrupt and agonising end on the morning of 8 July.

I was awakened at about 6 am by the voice of Gino MacCormaic trying to contact the person in the cell facing him. His sombre tone sent a shiver down my spine, I knew what news he had before he said it. I wanted to block it out but I heard it nonetheless, 'Fuair Seosamh ramhar bás ar maidin' (Fat Joe died this morning). I felt weak, almost paralysed and an emptiness enveloped me. In the background I could hear walls being rapped and the whispered tones of 'Fuair Seosamh bás ar maidin' being passed from cell to cell, but I felt removed from the whole scene. It just didn't seem real to me. Joe was still alive in my mind. Memories of bantering and slagging matches with him were still fresh. It was difficult to replace these palpable thoughts of him with the incomprehensible news that he was dead. How could he be dead? I had not witnessed him die nor had I seen his body.

I lay in my bed, thought about Joe and tried to absorb the fact that he was dead. It was like a tide ebbing and flowing – at times I could feel it and I was heartbroken but at other times I could not feel it, it was unreal. Then my conscience began to annoy me. Joe was dead. I was in despair – but it wasn't total. While there was pain, I began to feel that it was not biting as strongly as I thought it ought. I owed it to Joe to be completely and utterly devastated. The pain had to be brimming to its full otherwise I did him an injustice. I almost willed pain on myself.

I know now that I could not fully accept that he was dead. I had not witnessed him die nor seen his body nor attended his funeral and therefore the reality could not sink in. Even today at times I still feel it strange. For example, after the escape in 1983 the screws took all my and the other recaptured POWs' clothes and this effectively put us back on the Blanket. Being back on the Blanket for those two weeks, there were one or two occasions when I actually forgot myself and thought 'Seosamh ramhar' was next door to me and once when calling the man in the next cell I unthinkingly called him Seosamh.

When I look back and think of him, I always recall that night he said that he wasn't made of the stuff that makes a martyr and patriot. He could never have been more wrong. My abiding memory of Joe is that he never, ever bent.

11

"We could cry no more, curse no louder, pray no harder"

8 July 1981 – 8 August 1981

Following the false hopes raised by the involvement of the ICJP, Joe McDonnell's death was a bitter blow. The prisoners were just coming to terms with it when they received the shock of the unexpected death of Martin Hurson after only 46 days on hunger strike. It brought home the sober realisation that there was no guaranteed length of survival. Death could come at any time.

At this stage there emerged a serious threat to the whole viability of the prisoners' strategy. The Catholic church stepped up its campaign against the hunger strike and Fr Denis Faul in particular agitated among the families. The prisoners were extremely angry at his manipulation of the families' natural concern, and his channelling of their concern into opposition to the Republican Movement instead of directing it against those who held the key to a solution – the British.

At the end of July the hunger strikers had an unexpected meeting in the prison hospital with three leading Republicans, among them Gerry Adams. Optimism at the outset was dashed as he laid out the chilling reality of their position: the British were quite prepared to let more hunger strikers die and the subsequent pressure upon the prisoners to call off the hunger strike would be intense. However, the hunger strikers remained firm in their resolve to continue.

In one week at the start of August, Kevin Lynch, Kieran Doherty and Tom McElwee died. These deaths, coming in such quick succession, shook the prisoners. In the H-Blocks a terrible sense of resignation to the inevitable prevailed.

Laurence McKeown . . .

When Bik told me one Sunday I would be going on the stailc and when, I was delighted. I had written to him a few weeks earlier inquiring how men were selected and if he had my name amongst those on the shortlist. It wasn't a case of bravery or a sense of ego; I simply felt I could go through with it. I wasn't married and was serving life, and I felt I had a responsibility to those around me and to the struggle. I wasn't unique in that sense, as I knew my views and reasoning were shared by a large number of others.

I was to begin the stailc on 29 June. Well before then I received a comm from the Army Council. It read simply, 'Comrade, you have put your name forward for the hunger strike. Do you know that this means you will most likely be dead within two months? That means, comrade, that you will be no more. Reconsider carefully your decision. AC.' Those aren't the exact words but it was as blunt as that. I hadn't expected it and the words did startle me at first. Seeing my 'death' written in black and white appeared very stark, but it didn't cause me to rethink my position. Earlier examination of it had been done from a very serious and responsible attitude. I was ready to go ahead.

I had moved in with Mackers during the first stailc and stayed with him until 29 June 1981, the day I joined the hunger strike. We had hotly debated the pros and cons of the ending of the first stailc but as things became clearer, we settled down, like everyone else, to write letters campaigning for support.

We talked a lot in the cell, though conversation often involved others next door because we would talk at the window. There wasn't a lot said about my going on hunger strike. We both knew the seriousness of it, knew how the decision had to be thought through carefully to be fully sure of our commitment to it, but after that, it was put to the back of the mind. We didn't want to envisage that in two months or less I would be dead because we didn't want to think that several more friends would die in the intervening period or that our demands would still not have been granted. So in many ways our chat revolved around the same topics as were common in the Blocks: our visits, our families, our adventures while outside, and the friends we had come to know since being imprisoned. A degree of the usual backstabbing of others in the wing was also commonplace.

What sticks in my mind clearly is that Mackers did not eat his breakfast. Whether this was because he simply didn't want it or he knew that I was later going on hunger strike, I don't know, but I took great pleasure pouring the two bowls of cornflakes into one and eating the heap. Since the ending of the no-wash protest and particularly since our move to H3, the grub had improved a good deal. At least now we were getting more than the previously common five or six spoonfuls of cornflakes and the milk didn't seem to be watered. I looked forward to and enjoyed breakfast time.

When I began the hunger strike, I weighed ten and a half stone, about two stone under weight. My heart, lungs and blood pressure were checked and I was generally in good shape. I had never been in hospital or suffered any serious illness in the past so I wasn't too concerned in that regard. I was asked to read and sign a form which stated I was aware of what I was doing and that doctors would not intervene medically unless I so requested.

I moved that morning to Bik's wing. A couple of the lads, Denis Cummings and Phil Rooney, were assigned to look after me, that is brush my cell out and get me anything I wanted. They also took down the details of my weight and blood pressure each morning when I returned from the doctor. These were sent to the Sinn Féin centre outside and a record was also held in the wing. Big Tom McElwee and Paddy Quinn were already there, though they moved within a few days to the prison hospital. Tom looked fairly well, but Paddy even at that early stage was showing the effects of his fast.

Coldness was what I felt first, my feet especially. The heating in the Block was off for the summer and when I complained about this, I was told the boiler was being renewed. I got extra blankets. At one time I had seven of them covering me and some of these were doubled over, making it about 10 or 11 layers of clothing over me. Only then did I feel warm enough. No doubt drinking the cold water didn't help where heat was concerned, though I noticed that when I moved to the hospital, which also had no heat on, I didn't feel the same degree of coldness. In fact, I slept with just the usual issue of bedclothes covering me. Possibly I was becoming accustomed to it, though my feet still felt cold.

While in the Block, I would be out washing each day. The screws would leave me until everyone else was finished, then let me out. Apart from that, the only time I was out of the cell was to go to see the doctor daily and to mass on Sunday. The lads would all be around me, eager to find out how I was keeping. Their comments were always positive though no doubt they noticed the effects even by then. Mostly this would be apparent in my slower pace of movement. I had also to be careful rising, that I didn't get up too quickly or I would go dizzy.

The Assistant Governor who did his rounds of the Block each day would look into my cell. He would ask if I had any complaints or requests. I wouldn't have, except for the heating to be switched on. Most of the Governors would confine themselves to these formalities, though an odd one would make a comment. McMullan asked me one morning what date my birthday was on. I said, '19th of September'. He said, 'You'll not be seeing your next one, then,' gave a laugh and walked out. I was raging with myself for giving him the opening. I should have realised what was coming, but after I had silently cursed him for a while and got it out of my system, I realised just how insignificant he must feel and the only way he could have any effect on the situation was to try and annoy someone on the staile, so I just dropped him and the incident from my thoughts.

Apart from isolated remarks such as that, I didn't experience too much verbal abuse from the screws. I think by that stage they realised they were living through a very tense and dangerous period and, as no one was telling them anything, they felt very vulnerable. They had done the administration's bidding down through the years and now they were dropped when no longer of assistance.

One morning, when I was out with the doctor for the usual daily check-up, I inquired how Martin (Hurson) was keeping. Dr Ross was on the Block that morning. He looked up from what he was writing and said, 'Martin's dead; he died early this morning'. The shock was great. Martin had been nowhere near a crisis stage. I knew he had been sick for a while, but that was considered an inevitability in some cases. No way did I think he was near death. The MOs with the doctor said nothing. He himself just stared at his desk and rolled a pen about in his fingers. I got up and walked back into the wing, stopping at the washhouse when I heard Bik's voice. I shouted over to him and as he walked towards me, I said, 'Fuair Mairtin bás' (Martin has died). Bik said 'What!' and as I went to repeat what I had said, a tall screw grabbed me by the shoulder and said, 'Come on you; you're not out here for association.' At the same time he tried to push me down the wing.

It could only have been a case of him having momentarily taken leave of his senses, as instantly all the lads who had been in washing, Dennis Cummings, Marty McManus, Jake Jackson and a couple of others besides Bik came running out. Feelings were already fairly high in the Blocks and all it would have taken was a spark to ignite it. Laying a hand on a hunger striker was like taking a flame-thrower to the situation. Seeing the lads racing out, the screw immediately took his hand off my shoulder. By this time Bik was in front of him shouting, 'If you ever lay your hands on a hunger striker again . . .' Some of the other lads were not so much interested in providing advice; they were intent on showing him that he had crossed the line. At that point Gilmore, the screw in charge of the wing, appeared and asked Bik what was happening, slowly manoeuvring himself between Bik and the other screw. For a few moments everything hung in the balance. Gilmore kept reassuring Bik that it would never happen again and that he would guarantee it. The other lads just stood and stared at the big screw.

Gradually the tension eased. Bik called them back in to finish washing and we all had a few words together. We reckoned the screws had learnt an important lesson from it and it was unlikely there would be a recurrence.

For a few moments the news which prompted the incident was forgotten, but it soon returned to us. The lads asked what had happened and I told them the little I knew. All were shocked. Word was shouted over to the other wing and I walked back to my cell wondering just what had brought such sudden death to Martin. I began to realise that there were no definite patterns anyone on hunger strike followed. Each one would be unique.

BIK MCFARLANE . . .

We were just about getting ourselves on to firm ground again when we were totally rocked by the news that Martin Hurson had deteriorated rapidly and had died a very violent death. This was only five days after Joe's death and Martin had been on hunger strike 43 days. We couldn't fathom this at all, and everyone was visibly shaken. We had thought that nothing more could shock us after the tragic losses we had already suffered, but the unexpected is always sure to shock.

THOMAS LOUGHLIN . . .

That night a group of Orange bandsmen gathered outside the camp and beat Lambeg drums for hours. To many of us this was really ironic, considering that Loyalist prisoners were demanding the same rights as we were, and that the hunger strike was all about achieving those rights for all prisoners. We couldn't understand them. Their attitude of 'die, you bastards' was probably coming from the relatives of Loyalist prisoners.

BIK MCFARLANE . . .

In the aftermath of Martin's death Fr Faul appeared to have decided that he would work feverishly to bring about an end to the hunger strike – not by rallying support around our five demands, but by undermining us at every possible chance and driving a wedge between hunger strikers and their families. On occasions at mass in the canteen we had fierce rows; once he accused me of being responsible for the death of Martin Hurson. I almost resorted to a physical attack over that incident, but was calmed by Ricky O'Rawe, Jake Jackson and others. If it was his intention to get me to explode and run off the rails, he almost succeeded, but using Martin's tragic death as the pillar to lash me to was probably the most despicable and devious manoeuvre he attempted.

He was impossible to argue with, because he set his sights on a target and nothing was going to budge him. I suppose the only occasion I witnessed him left speechless was when he approached Pat Sheehan, who had joined the hunger strike in August, and asked how he was feeling. Pat ignored his outstretched hand and barked at him, 'How am I keeping? I'm dying on hunger strike and you're trying to kill me.'

In the middle of July another important intervention took place, which was to be the last of its kind. Three members of the International Red Cross arrived, ostensibly to examine prison conditions in the Six Counties. They would act as mediators in an attempt at finding common ground for a final settlement, if we were in agreement. They were completely professional in their approach and at no time tried to sell us short. We outlined our position thoroughly and they in turn spoke to the Brits who made their own position clear. It was still far off our five demands and would go nowhere near achieving a final settlement. We had a series of meetings over a couple of days which yielded no further improvements.

During these meetings, I became very concerned about Doc, who appeared to be fading. He seemed to have deteriorated significantly and was unable to join in the discussion. He did not attend the final meeting as he was too weak at that stage.

LAURENCE McKEOWN . . .

I was happy in the wing and the lads looked after me the best, but I wanted up to the hospital with the others. I had been pushing for this since about the 20th day, but I wasn't moved until about the 30th day of my hunger strike. I had a yarn that afternoon with Tom and Paddy in the yard of the hospital. It was good to see them again. As before, Tom looked OK whereas Paddy's condition had deteriorated rapidly. Big Doc and Kevin Lynch were confined to bed at this stage and as their families were with them, I didn't want to disturb them by going in to see them.

In the Blocks I had been showering, but in the hospital I thought I would rest in a warm bath. It was then I discovered just how much weight I had lost and from where; my hips had totally disappeared. I felt as if my hip bones themselves were resting on the bottom of the bath and bound to cut through my flesh. This was even when resting on a rubber mat. One of the MOs had told me to be careful and not to run the bath too hot as I would feel the effects of it. Being none too fond of cold baths, however, I made sure the water was fairly warm. I almost collapsed. I was lying back in the bath when suddenly I felt really faint; I tried to pull myself up and I thought for a moment I wasn't going to make it. I did eventually get myself up into a slouched-over position. I was sweating heavily and my head felt really heavy. I reached down and pulled the plug then sat long after the bath had emptied. When I had cooled down and felt more clear-headed I got out of the bath, dried myself slowly then shuffled back to my cell and into bed. I was exhausted.

The regime in the hospital remained very much as normal. There was no big difference made because we were hunger strikers, except when practical difficulties arose. We were locked in our cells during the usual times and allowed out for association in the evenings. Most screws adopted a clinical and distant approach to us and simply went about their duties as if our circumstances and ailments were something they were accustomed to seeing every day. Possibly they had been schooled in this approach. Some, however, did show their hostility towards us. It would come out in minor ways, such as constantly locking grilles and doors even when they knew we would be going back in or out in a few moments. On one such occasion when I asked the screw why the grille on the canteen was locked when the door itself was locked, he remarked to me, 'Never forget, Laurence, you might be in hospital but you are still in prison.' This was the same screw who was later to steal our cigarettes.

Other examples of pettiness were seen in relation to the yard. It had been agreed with the Governor that chairs and pillows would be allowed out. This was commonsense, as only in the early days of hunger strike could anyone walk in the yard and then only for a few laps. In later days we would only want to sit in it. To do so we needed chairs and as these were of the hard plastic type, pillows were needed as the bones of our hips would be pressing through the skin. Although an arrangement had been reached over the use of chairs and pillows some screws would continually challenge this. Their argument was that the yard was for exercising in, so no one should be allowed to go out with the intention of sitting down. There was no point in trying to rationalise with these people that those going out to the yard were unable to walk. We would just send for the Governor or PO to direct the screw to open the yard and let us out.

Our day would begin with the doors being opened to see if we had any requests – for letters, welfare, Governor and so on. The PO of the hospital also did his rounds, asking if we had any complaints or requests. We slopped out and the urine was chemically checked. We were then weighed and this was documented. We were locked again until after 10 o'clock, when we went to the yard if the doctor had done his rounds. His examination consisted basically of asking how we were, as there wasn't much else he could do. Dr Ross would stop and talk for a while about working on his family's farm on his days off or about his fishing trips. He was in charge of the hospital and of medical treatment in the camp and he was generally pleasant to talk to. He could become excited though, and a few times I saw him being very abrupt with the MOs. Years later I found when I had cause to see him that he had become very short-tempered. One day we were told he had committed suicide.

Another doctor was Dr John Hopper. He was also a qualified dentist and it was as a dentist that he was employed in the jail. He was an excellent dentist and following the end of all protests, when he had over 200 prisoners who urgently wanted their teeth examined, he accomplished this very quickly and very competently. At the time of the hunger strike he would occasionally come down the ward during his dinner break for a chat with one of us and he got on particularly well with Red Mick. His visits were not in his official capacity but because he had an interest in what was happening.

There was another doctor who was despised in the Blocks for what we saw as his total lack of interest in providing treatment or proper medical care. At the time of the forced washings he was the doctor who signed the forms saying men had head lice and required haircuts and bathing. He 'examined' the men from about six feet away after they had been dragged up to him by the screws. He also witnessed the bruises, cuts and scrapes on them two days later following the forced washings, but he passed no comment. For his role in this we nicknamed him Mengele after the doctor who experimented on prisoners in the Nazi concentration camps.

We were talking about him one night in the hospital and Paul, the MO, had listened to the names we were calling him. The following day Mengele was the doctor on duty and when he was examining me, Paul said, dead innocently, 'What was that name, Laurence, you said you called the Doctor?' He probably thought I would be embarrassed but I replied 'Mengele' and when Paul asked, 'Why Mengele?' I explained. Paul stopped talking and looked at the Doctor who said he always heard it shouted at him when he was going in an out of the Blocks but couldn't make out what it was. I didn't tell him we all reckoned he was really a vet, or someone who had made a tragic blunder on some occasion for which he should have been struck off the register, but was offered the job at Long Kesh as it was known he would be a willing and trustful ally for the administration. It didn't matter that there was no proof for these allegations; his attitude and behaviour confirmed our worst suspicions of him.

The Governor in charge was AG McCartney. We believed he was specially appointed to the post during the hunger strike period because he had an amiable manner and would be pleasant when meeting families and other visitors to the stailceoirí. A lot of focus was going to be on the jail and hospital and they needed someone who could look after things well. I found him to be polite and someone who didn't come out with nonsense.

He didn't recite prison rules in robot-like fashion, but tried to adapt them to the unique circumstances and events. He would grant extra visits, or 'special' visits as they were called. No doubt he had the go-ahead from the NIO to do this but I think it would not have been his nature to limit us to the one visit a week which we got by virtue of the fact that we were in hospital.

He came in one morning to tell me three letters had arrived for me which I would receive soon, but there were two others he wouldn't be giving me. He described them as not coming from 'friends'. They were wishing me a 'slow and painful death' and were what he called 'poison pen letters'. I was going to argue to be shown them just out of curiosity, but then let it drop. He said the sentiments in one of the other letters were none too favourable towards the 'staff in the prison'. He gave a broad smile at this, but added that I would be getting it anyhow as it was not his intention to hold back mail which came from family and friends. Later, when I did get the letter and read about the 'dirty Loyalist scum bastards', I took a bit of a reddener myself.

After several weeks on the fast, my sense of smell grew much stronger. This increased as other senses such as sight and hearing became impaired. One aspect of this which became loathsome was that I found it hard to tolerate the smell of the floor polish the orderlies used in the ward. When I pointed this out to the hospital orderly, Bobby H, he limited its use or on occasions didn't use it at all. Air fresheners had to go as the 'fumes' from them were overpowering. One morning Paul brought me in a jug of water, the first jug of the day. As I reached for it I detected the scent of after-shave. As I put it to my mouth it seemed as though the jug was full of 'Old Spice' after-shave lotion and I was almost sick with the smell. I called Paul, who couldn't believe it at first as it had been the previous night that he had shaved and used the lotion, and he had washed his hands several times since.

Water itself had its own smell and taste. Drinking so much of it became very tiresome, but I knew it was best to drink at least six pints a day. So I would stagger it. One pint early in the morning, one at dinnertime, another in the afternoon and one in the evening, one before lock-up that night, then the last before going to sleep. The last two pints became a real battle in the latter weeks of the stailc, but I was lucky in that it was staying down. I had watched others being continuously sick, throwing up water and a green bile from their stomachs. It was a depressing sight to watch them bent over a kidney dish, their chest and stomach heaving every few minutes. It was evident that it was physically exhausting.

The spring water was something introduced during Bobby's fast. At a time when he found it impossible to drink tap water, they tried spring water.

He found he could drink it a lot easier, so after that they bought case-loads of it. I found there were times I preferred it and other times when I preferred the ordinary tap water. A routine I had for a while was to drink tap water in the morning and spring water in late evening. The change made the last two pints a bit easier to drink.

Taking salt was easy. When I first began the fast, I put it into my water-gallon, then poured it into a cup to drink. I was sick with the first mouthful and after that I could only sip it in very small amounts, but I caught on within a few days that it was best to wet the tip of the finger, dip it in the salt, then put that in my mouth. It didn't taste half as bad. I soon grew accustomed to it and probably was taking far more than was needed, but it helped taste my mouth if nothing else.

One smell I found difficult to detect was the smell of my own body decaying. It's a definite type of smell, not a smell of body odour nor a smell of dead rotting animal flesh, but a smell of flesh which is still alive but decaying. Others noticed it when they entered my cell. To them it was overpowering.

I started to smoke when I was ten years of age and went through much worry in years after that trying to scrape up enough money for 20 fags – or, as was more often the case, 10. During the Blanket, when weeks could pass without a smoke, my commitment to the weed never weakened – until 1980. For some inexplicable reason I began to realise I was being dictated to by this habit (as opposed to wanting to smoke) and simply stopped it there and then. To those who reckoned that at times I would sacrifice an arm and a leg for a smoke this came as a major shock; and not a few reckoned that I had obtained some secret supply of snout and the best way to hide this from the lads was to say I had stopped using it.

I continued to bring it back from visits though, as I knew how much I had enjoyed a smoke at times and besides, there was the satisfaction of getting one over on the screws. A visit didn't seem truly worthwhile if I didn't 'touch' (get a package of snout), plus there would be other items such as pens, cigarette papers and articles in Gaeilge that I wanted.

The next time I smoked I was just three or four days into the hunger strike. It wasn't a case of feeling I needed a cigarette, more a case of something to do, something to taste my mouth with, even. Besides that, it was still an illicit activity, so there was the act of rebellion connected with smoking. Indeed, this was the most satisfying aspect of a smoke during the Blanket and may be the reason why a lot of ex-Blanketmen gave up smoking in later years – no more fun with it.

I went out on a visit on my fifth day into the fast and as usual brought back the snout. The wing I had just moved into apparently wasn't the best for bringing back snout, so that night the OC, Pat Mullan, got up to lecture the lads about how they must do better and pointed to me as a means to embarrass the lads '. . . a hunger striker is even bringing back snout for the wing . . .' I was all chuffed about this until Bik got up to the door and gave me a lecture about what I had done, how it was dangerous with me on the stailc and not to do it again. There never was a problem with it after that anyway and the most I would have smoked was six cigarettes a day. I had the luxury too of real cigarette papers not the 'bog-roll jobs' (tobacco rolled in prison-issue toilet paper) everyone else had to smoke. Having said that, the bog-roll jobs were a powerful smoke, like steel claws gripping your lungs when you inhaled deeply.

When I moved to the hospital, they had already worked out a system which suited all concerned. Those on hunger strike were still not allowed cigarettes left in in a parcel, but visitors could carry 20 in with them, then leave them in the ward. In this way a store of cigarettes built up and there were always enough (except for one occasion). It seems the system had been introduced to resolve a contentious issue. It could be publicly embarrassing that those dying on hunger strike were not even allowed a smoke, but that's exactly how it had been initially.

One screw who took great pleasure in enforcing the no-smoking rule was the class officer of the ward for a while. On a daily basis he would search Bobby Sands's cell hoping to find the tobacco which he was sure Bobby had. One day, in the later stages of Bobby's stailc, he discovered a half-ounce in Bobby's bed. He came out into the ward highly pleased with himself, holding up the 'contraband' and shouting about how he had captured 'Sands's snout'. Bobby H went up to the screw, stood facing him for a few moments, then said, 'I suppose you're really pleased with yourself? That makes you a real hard man, doesn't it? Taking snout from a dying man. Well, I can assure you of this – I'll be giving Bobby Sands a half-ounce of snout before I go off here tonight and you won't be taking that off him'. Other MOs who had listened to the goings on took no part in it. Most of them were probably embarrassed by the incident.

Ironically enough, Bobby H had discovered that he once worked with Bobby Sands for a few weeks in East Belfast, but it wasn't this which prompted his response. It was simply a basic solidarity which exists between all prisoners despite any other differing views they might have. Besides that, there was sympathy for a man who was dying. In this instance Bobby put up a direct challenge to the screw. He could easily have been charged with an offence against the 'good order and discipline' of the prison, with a resultant loss in remission and other privileges. He acted in a selfless manner and displayed a strength of character which contrasted greatly with the meanness and petty-mindedness of the screws. And this was how Bobby treated all the stailceoirí throughout the hunger strike. He would always be there to assist someone in or out of bed, fetch water, newspapers or anything else that was requested. Those who could barely stand he would help walk by placing his arm around their waist and their own arm around his shoulder. If you ever get round to reading this, Bobby, thanks for everything.

On one occasion we suddenly ran out of cigarettes. We were sitting in the yard, a few of us on hunger strike plus two orderlies and Paul, the MO. Out of the blue Paul said to me, 'Keep an eye on your cigarettes.' I asked him to repeat it. I knew this had to mean that someone was stealing them or tampering with them in some way, but I couldn't work out who or why. I knew the orderlies weren't involved because they were forever offering us snout.

That night, when I asked for a cigarette during association time, I asked how many were left. The screw said there was one half-empty pack of Embassy. I thought it strange, as I had assumed there would be more but thought I could be mistaken and possibly it was just what Paul had said that was making me suspicious. The next morning I told Paul we were out of cigarettes and he gave us a 20-box of Benson and Hedges. Fr Toner was in to say mass and I asked him if he would bring in 60 Regal. He said he would have them in by dinnertime. That evening Pat, Matt and myself had three visitors each, all of whom left 60 cigarettes. This totalled 240 cigarettes, plus the 20 Paul had given us that morning.

Just before lock-up that night I asked the screw on duty to check how many cigarettes we had left. He said we had two 20 packets, one half full – about 30 cigarettes. At least 200 cigarettes had gone missing. I couldn't believe it. I knew they couldn't be anywhere else, as they were all kept together in a drawer of the desk at the top of the ward. I called Paul and sent for the SO. I told him what had happened, or what I believed had happened, that someone had stolen 200 cigarettes on us. I know I was fairly agitated and probably incoherent at times as I simply couldn't comprehend how someone would go and steal cigarettes on people who were dying and had nothing else but a smoke. Even if they had been stuck for a smoke, they could have taken a packet to tide them over. If they had asked, they would have been given a packet, no problem, but stealing them and stealing so many.

The SO, who was new to the hospital, listened to what I had to say, asked some questions, attempted to say that possibly we had smoked more than we thought – 200 more! Paul spoke up to say the cigarettes had been in the drawer earlier. He confirmed that our visitors and Fr Toner had left 60 cigarettes each. The SO, clearly embarrassed by what was being implied, said he would look into it in the morning.

What happened was simply a cover-up. A book was introduced in which a record would be kept of how many cigarettes each stailceoir smoked. This in no way tackled what lay at the heart of the problem, but no doubt all the screws were warned about what had happened. It didn't recur, at least to the best of my knowledge. When the hunger strike ended we discovered that the screw who had been harassing Bobby, along with another one, were responsible for stealing them.

The visits during the hunger strike were mostly uncomfortable, not in the sense that there were arguments between myself and my family, but because it was difficult to know just what to say with a screw present; we just never got the right opportunity to sit and talk. It must be remembered too that the hunger strike followed over four years of Blanket protest, the first year of which I took no visits, and after that visits were once a month for a half-hour. During that time little of relevance was spoken of. What could you say really? 'I'm OK, food's not so bad and we're having good craic?' One look was enough to say we weren't getting it OK; gaunt faces spoke volumes about the food and they read and heard of the mirror searches and the beatings that took place there and elsewhere. Nevertheless, I would have ensured that I put across as good an impression as possible and shown that I was in good form, which I was most of the time anyway.

I can't recall much about the first visit I had when it was decided I was going on hunger strike. That may seem strange, but as I had already prepared my family for such an eventuality during the first hunger strike, I suppose the shock was lessened. Nevertheless, I'm sure the strain was powerful. I only discovered once I had begun the stailc that my mother had had a heart attack in 1978. I hadn't been aware of it, as she had made others ensure I wasn't told, no doubt trying to save me from worrying. I was angry that I hadn't been told, though I understood the motivation behind it. I know also that, had I been told, it would not have affected my decision to go on hunger strike, yet I would have given it more attention in that regard. If I recall correctly, my visits were spent trying to put a light-hearted tone to it all. I wasn't yet on the fast and anything could happen between now and then or even a number of weeks into the stailc.

Jim Gibney (Sinn Féin) was present on the first visit I had after I began my hunger strike. He was along with my mother and we talked mostly of the political situation at the time and the lobbying and campaigning which was ongoing. I had met Jim in 1976 when he was on remand in the Crum, so he wasn't a stranger to me.

The first visit which was emotional and uncomfortable was the one I had with my father. I was in the prison hospital by then and on hunger strike about 30-odd days. He hadn't seen me since my arrest. Like his brother, he suffered a bit from claustrophobia, but I believe it was more to do with the inability to come to terms with just what he thought of me and how he would respond to seeing me in captivity. His views of life and the Republican struggle were so much different from mine and I know that in many ways I was a disappointment to him in terms of what he had hoped for me. He would have wished for me to have a good career, something he felt had never been available to him when he was growing up. I could understand that, so would mostly listen to what he would say without openly challenging it. I would then go and do what I thought best for me. This was the type of relationship we had had before my arrest and now I was seeing him for the first time in five years.

He came with a friend of his, a retired doctor. It wasn't that he was close to Dr Cosgrave – he had closer friends – but possibly he thought him best suited to help him through the experience, or maybe he wanted the doctor to give him some idea of my physical condition.

The visit took place in the afternoon. It was sunny and I could watch the lads in the yard as I was sitting on the bed, while the visitors sat on chairs alongside, with their backs to the windows. I thought my da didn't look much different. He was always heavy and his complexion was never pale; his face not so much reddish as having a weather-beaten appearance. He wore a cap which he now held in his hand and throughout the visit he twisted and screwed it. He looked about the place nervously, would look at me then look away again. Dr Cosgrave was very calm and did most of the talking, much of it about local events, happenings and such like. Conversation was always a problem on such visits as no one knew what to speak about and there would be prolonged and awkward pauses.

At one stage my da blurted out, 'Do you know what you're doing? Do you know the effect it's having on your mother?' I said I knew what I was doing and yes, I did know the effect it was having on my mother. I said I didn't wish that and I hoped that she would be OK . He listened to me, then just looked away and tossed his head. Dr Cosgrave went on talking as if nothing had disturbed the flow of conversation.

The half-hour seemed more like an hour and a half but eventually the screw whose presence was always in my thoughts called time up. A screw always stood inside the cell during all visits; the really zealous ones sat right against the end of the bed. A number of them were known to intervene on visits and pass some comment on what was being said. Although an occasional one showed embarrassment about being there and tried to be as unobtrusive as possible, others carried out their orders to the dotting of every i and the stroking of every t.

John and Mary, two friends, visited me in the hospital when I was about 50 days into the fast. Again, talk revolved around very mundane matters:

how John was getting on at work, how fast the children were growing and the list of who was asking for me. No mention of the stailc was made until they were leaving and Mary suddenly burst out, 'Do you know what you're doing? You're going to die. Do you know that?' She appeared angry with me, but at the same time I could see the tears forming in her eyes. I knew it was Mary's way of expressing concern for me. I just said, 'I'll be OK. Look after yourselves,' and they left.

On one visit I was asked if I wanted a military funeral. It was asked in all seriousness though I knew it had to be a bit ridiculous, given the manner in which all the hunger strikers had been buried. I simply said 'yes'. I think it meant something to the person who asked. I've no doubt he would've carried out the arrangements with great precision as 'Lorney made me promise that I would look after things'. In some way I suppose it was to give me an assurance that things would be looked after in that regard.

Although I was always glad to see my family and other visitors and looked forward to these occasions, visits were something often endured rather than enjoyed. The conditions did not allow for privacy and the circumstances did not encourage carefree conversation. The look on their faces as they said goodbye always lingered with me, as did the tight grip of their hug or handshake.

One evening during lock-up the AG came to tell us that Gerry Adams, Owen Carron and Seamus Ruddy would be coming to visit us in about one hour's time. It was something out of the blue. There had been no talk about it nor had any of us requested such a meeting. I had been lying on the bed but now I got up to pace the floor – an old habit of mine formed during the Blanket. I thought this must be a positive sign. If Gerry Adams and Owen Carron were coming, it must mean some approach had been made to them by the Brits. At the same time I didn't want to get too optimistic. I had experienced the fiasco of the ICJP and knew the Brits would do anything. Nevertheless, I couldn't stop my spirits from soaring and imagining that we had at last achieved our demands. Besides that, I was excited about meeting Gerry Adams. I had heard much talk about him from others who knew him and of course he was prominent in the media.

We were unlocked shortly before the usual time and made our way to the canteen, all except Big Doc and Kevin Lynch. At this stage Kevin Lynch was lying in a coma, alive in the sense that his heart was still beating but dead in every other sense of the word. A machine was wired up to his chest to record pulse and heartbeat and it's in this manner that his last few days were monitored.

Those of us who did meet – Pat Beag, Big Tom, Paddy, Red Mick, Matt and myself – were in good form, curious about what was happening and speculating on what could be behind it all. The fact that Seamus Ruddy, an IRSP spokesperson, was also coming with Adams and Carron added to the speculation that a possible deal had been worked out with all involved. We didn't have too long to wait before they arrived. Bik was also present by now, arriving just around the same time. Everyone was introduced, though Bik and Pat were already known to Adams from their time spent together in the Cages. The rest of us soon became acquainted. It was explained to them that the other two lads were too weak to attend, one of them being totally unable to. They said they would look in on them once they had talked to us.

The meeting came together fairly quickly. We gathered around a few tables and Adams began by explaining events leading up to his visit and hence the reason for it. He outlined how Fr Faul had called the families together to talk about their relatives on hunger strike and claimed that the hunger strikers were unaware of the true situation, that they did not have any knowledge about feelings or events on the outside and that Gerry Adams should make this known to them. He would personally see to it that Adams be granted admittance to the jail from the NIO. All of this was of course to put Gerry Adams and the leadership of the Republican Movement under moral pressure to end the hunger strike.

Faul better than anyone had a very good insight into the feelings of the men in the Blocks. He was still coming in on Sundays to say mass and on at least one occasion had a blazing row with Bik and others in H3 after a statement he made saying that letters supposedly written by prisoners had in fact been produced in the Sinn Féin centre on the Falls Road. This particular row lasted about two hours and when he left the prison, he spoke to the media saying that the prisoners had approached him and clearly shown that they were up to date with events on the outside, and he was now assured that statements released by them were in fact written in the Blocks and sent to the Republican Press Centre for release. Despite this, he was, however, attempting to force a wedge between the families and the leadership of the Movement.

Gerry said that, when asked, he readily agreed to visit us and give us an appraisal of the situation and how he saw our position in relation to the possibility of the Brits conceding our demands. It was a grim picture. There were no ifs or buts. Really he was spelling out for us what we in a sense knew but didn't like to think through. The Brits had already allowed six men to die and they would likely allow more to die. Certainly there was no movement to indicate that they desired a speedy resolution to the protest. All three of them pointed out the great admiration felt by the people in the community outside for those on hunger strike and that nothing but respect would be shown if we decided to end the fast now. We said we didn't want to. We believed as firmly as when we first joined it that our demands were just and should be granted. We had also lost too many comrades to stop now.

Once these serious points had been covered and we knew there was nothing further on that line of things to be covered, there was some light banter. Big Tom wanted to know why the IRA couldn't hit Prince Charlie's wedding: 'about 500 pounds of blowy gear under the reception table' and a few other remarks along the same lines. There was general laughter amongst the stailceoirí, but I'm not so sure if the other three felt just as comfortable sitting in company which was (in a light-hearted though no less serious way) debating the merits of wiping out most of the English Royal Family. It made us feel good anyway.

Soon it was time to go. Gerry had told each of us about meeting our families and how they were keeping. He then said that they would go to see the other two lads, shook hands with us and left the canteen. They went into Kevin Lynch's cell first. They then went to see Big Doc who was still lucid and who could speak. Gerry explained the reason for their visit just as he had done with us. Doc was told that what it would mean for him if he continued on hunger strike was that he would be dead within a few days. Doc said he was very much aware of that, but if our demands were not granted, then that is what would happen. He knew what he was doing and what he believed in. On their way out of his cell Doc's parents met and spoke with Gerry, Bik and the others. They asked what the situation was and Gerry said he had just told all the stailceoirí, including Kieran, that there was no deal on the table from the Brits, no movement of any sort and if the stailc continued, Doc would most likely be dead within a few days. They just listened to this and nodded, more or less resigned to the fact that they would be watching their son die any day now.

On their way back up the ward they called into the canteen with us again. Owen Carron was crying and no doubt all three had been deeply moved by the experience, though it wasn't the time or place to sit and philosophise about it. We shook hands again and they left.

I don't think there was much conversation between those of us left in the canteen. Gradually we drifted back to our cells. Our earlier high spirits had dropped sharply. Each of us knew that the picture they had painted was the cold reality of it. The Brits were intent on crushing us. There would be no humanitarian gestures and appeals for goodwill would fall on deaf ears. We had also witnessed the duplicity of other groups who could have used their muscle, the Dublin government and the Church, even the SDLP and knew we would get no support from them. We were isolated and on our own. But then, that's how we had been, and felt, during the four and a half years of the Blanket protest.

TOM HOLLAND ...

In the latter days of July the Catholic Church began to actively intervene in the protest by creating dissent and doubt among the families of the hunger strikers and encouraging them to prevent their loved ones from dying. This manipulation caused much anger and frustration in our ranks. We believed if the Church had been as energetic about getting the British to the negotiating table, there would be no need for anyone to be on hunger strike. When we were informed of the hunger strikers' meeting with Gerry Adams and of Gerry's outline of the situation, we were disappointed, if only because it was a further indication that our hunger strike tactic was failing.

SÉANNA WALSH ...

In the days when so many of my comrades had died and another batch were psyching themselves up for the final battle, I simply lost faith in our ability to break Thatcher's determination. I had talked it over with friends on the visits and had also had a few letters telling me that it was certain death to contemplate a hunger strike at that late stage. One friend explained it thus: 'What we succeeded in doing before Bobby died and in the weeks following was to make a giant snowball of pressure. As we keep pushing it forward it keeps getting bigger and bigger. However, the problem for us is that we are pushing it uphill and the danger facing us is, if we take the pressure off, it runs back and crushes us all. So far the Brits have taken everything we could throw at them. At some stage the people are going to see it as our responsibility to end the hunger strike and all that pressure is going to come back at us.' I was very much affected by this line of reasoning. It may be termed personal fear or cowardice, but once the chalice was passed to me to sup, I wasn't able to handle it. I withdrew my name from the list of volunteers for hunger strike. I no longer felt that we would be dying for 'political status' or for the struggle, but we would be dying because we couldn't let Bobby, Francie, Patsy, Raymond, Joe and Martin down. They hadn't let us down and now it was our turn, one by one, to follow them.

LAURENCE McKEOWN ...

Pat Beag and I were sitting in the corner of the yard. It was a mild day, warm but not sunny. We knew Paddy Quinn was going through a bad period, being sick and unable to keep the water down. We both knew how important it was to drink at least six pints of water a day to flush the system.

There was no warning sound of its approach, just a very loud bellow. The only thing I can liken it to is the sound a cow makes at times. It was very low, very deep and long – an inhuman sound. R G, the MO with us in the yard, looked up and said, 'What was that?' 'It's Paddy Quinn,' I said. 'What's he doing?' he asked. 'Dying,' I replied.

The roar was repeated a number of times and it had an unnerving effect on both Pat and myself. We could only guess at the pain Paddy was going through. The roar would subside a while, then be followed by a high-pitched scream, then what sounded like giggling or chanting in a very high-pitched voice. There would be an interval of silence, then it would start all over again, slowly building up to a very loud scream. We could hear the MOs in the cell with him trying to calm him. This went on for about half an hour and it was then time for us to lock up.

Paddy had been silent for a while or at least not as loud, but shortly after I was locked up, he started again. It began like a chant which in a sense was funny as he used to be slagged about resembling a North American Indian, and that's the image that came to my mind when I heard the chant. As it grew progressively louder I tried to shut it out by wrapping the pillow around my ears, but it was impossible to deafen it. It was becoming much worse than earlier. There were less breaks in between the screams and now more deep sighs or moans, possibly as a result of his body being totally exhausted.

Shortly after being locked up, I heard a woman's footsteps in the ward and soon heard her calling Paddy's name in a soothing way: 'It's alright Paddy, what's wrong son?' I remember thinking that she was remarkably calm throughout what must have been a very horrifying and heart-breaking experience. I knew the effect it was having on me just listening to him. It must have been heart-rending watching him, knowing that he was not in control of his mind and frantically struggling with himself, doing his body damage. I discovered he had also been hallucinating. He saw people outside the window shooting at him, British soldiers and RUC men trying to get in the window. Then Raymond McCreesh appearing at the door armed with a rifle fighting off the Brits. At one stage his screams and yells built up to a very loud pitch and continued for some time, then they were muffled. I learnt later that Paul, the MO, had noticed that Paddy was hyperventilating. This is the result of rapid deep breathing which takes in a lot of oxygen but carbon dioxide is lost from the blood. It produces dizziness at first and if not controlled, can have very serious consequences. Normally, hospital wards would have proper equipment to cope with this but without these facilities Paul improvised by placing a brown paper bag over Paddy's face. A number of MOs were holding Paddy down on the bed by this stage as he twisted and jumped about and Paul had to lie across him and hold this bag over his mouth. In the middle of this a Governor happened to be doing his rounds of the ward and he looked through the flap of the closed door. God only knows what he thought when he looked at the scene in the cell, but he didn't interfere.

Soon the improvised equipment took effect and Paddy's breathing began to slow and become more restful. He still talked and muttered, mostly unintelligibly, but more quietly. At this stage his mother authorised medical intervention and he was removed to Musgrave Park Hospital.

From my cell I could hear his moans subside, then the sound of talking. I could still clearly hear his mother speaking to him. Just over and over again saying, 'You'll be alright, son; you'll be OK, Paddy.' I then heard what I took to be the trolley coming through the top grilles into the ward and a bit of a commotion outside Paddy's cell, followed by total silence. I realised what had happened and this was confirmed about half an hour later when I was unlocked. My only thought at the time was that I was glad Paddy – and his mother – had been spared any further suffering and I hoped the effects of whatever damage had already been caused would not be permanent.

SEAN LENNON . . .

Kevin Lynch died on 1 August. I had held out a lot of hope until big Doc's death on 2 August, but I guess that with his death my views on the hunger strike began to change. He had been elected to Leinster House by the people in the 26 Counties, and until then I was hopeful that, because of that, the Dublin government wouldn't allow him to die, and they would begin to put direct pressure on the Brits both publicly and in closed sessions. I was working on the theory that they couldn't afford politically to let not only an Irishman, but an elected member of Leinster House, die. Sadly, my theory was proved wrong. That was my turning point. The Free Staters, the Church, the SDLP and others let the Brits murder him and our other comrades on hunger strike.

JOHN PICKERING . . .

The last time I saw Kieran Doherty was in the prison hospital in June 1981, when I was there overnight before moving to the RVH for an ear operation. The hunger strikers were less than 10 yards down the hall. On the way to the hospital I was full of anticipation and excitement hoping for a few words with them, or better still being allowed association with them. The screws firmly nailed this idea down: 'no association for NCPs' (non-conforming prisoners), they said, thus denying me the chance of stealing a few precious moments with the lads.

Minutes before the rest of the hospital wing was locked up for the night, there was a thunderous thump on my door which scared the life out of me – much to Joe McDonnell's amusement. He slammed down the cell flap and, along with Kevin Lynch, was having a good chuckle at the fright he had given me. When I went to the door, we bantered away good-naturedly; they asked about the craic in the Blocks and why I was in the hospital, but brushed aside all queries concerning their condition, except to say they were in good form and spirits. A few feet behind them stood Big Doc; he was leaning against the wall, a small impish grin in his face. It was really brilliant to see them again. Doc said he was fine, with no problems at all. It was difficult to say anything meaningful; I wanted to but couldn't find the words. The two of us stood silently looking at each other; very little was said between us; small talk was out of place. Doc was laughing. Joe and Kevin joined in too; they sensed what was going through my head and their resilience was a humbling experience for me. Because of our close bonds of friendship and comradeship I felt embarrassed at having nothing adequate to say. Even today those words still escape me.

The weight loss was obvious in each of them, but despite that, they really looked in good form. They asked if I wanted anything: newspapers or tobacco for the night. Through the side of the door Joe, ever the schemer, whispered that there was milk and cheese in the canteen fridge and to make sure I asked for some. What could I say to that? It's hard to describe this scene; I've thought about it many times over the years. It was kind of bizarre. Here were three friends, one of them very close, whom I had known many years, and yet I didn't know what to say. Of course, they sensed this, understood it and laughed about it.

As the screw shouted to them that it was time to go, Joe and Kevin bade me farewell, leaving Doc and myself alone. Doc moved closer to the door and I asked again how he was doing. 'Fine,' he smiled. 'Everything is sound with us. Look after yourself and I'll see you in the morning, OK.' Then he strolled off, looking back at me once before going into his cell. The next morning I was taken out early to the RVH; the screws told me the lads were still sleeping. I never did see them again, but these memories of my three comrades in such good spirits will remain with me always.

LAURENCE MCKEOWN . . .

As I got up to slop out on the morning of 8 August, my mother's birthday, I sat for a moment on the edge of the bed. At this stage into the stailc this was the way to get out of bed. Rise up first on the elbows, sit with the back against the pillows and wall, then slowly move up into a sitting position, put the feet over the edge of the bed, then rest there for a few minutes until the body and circulation grew accustomed to the new position. To rise quickly would very easily lead to a blackout or at the very least a feeling of faintness and nausea. I learnt from experience.

My door was open that morning, as was the one into Tom's cell just across from me. We exchanged 'maidin mhaith' and a few words. An MO was sitting with Tom, as he was very weak by this stage, but able to sit up in bed and still very lucid. The night before, he sat with us in the canteen for a while. He was in a wheelchair and had to be assisted when he wanted to move position in it. A lot of pillows were placed in the wheelchair to soften the seat and mould it to the shape of his body to give the best support, but despite his physical condition, he was in the best of form, having had a visit from Dolours O'Neill from Armagh Prison that day. He described seeing her and the visit itself and went on to talk about his family, how he hoped to see Benny, his brother (who was in H5), the following morning. He had been pushing for ages to get a visit with him but the NIO had refused. He spoke of his hometown of Bellaghy and how he would love to live there again, to get married and invite all the neighbours to a big, outdoor reception. Everyone would be invited he said and this would show to the Protestants of the area that Republicans meant them no harm and that the Ireland Republicans wanted was one in which Protestants would realise they were treated as equally as everyone else – not the way Catholics had been treated in the North.

After about an hour or so he became very weak and said he would go back to his cell but would see us all the following morning. We bade him 'oíche mhaith'.

As I looked across at him that morning, he appeared to be in the best of form. I shouted into him on my way out for my regular morning check-up and weighing and when the doctor finished his rounds, I went out to the yard with a couple of the other lads. Pat Beag was one of them and we sat on a couple of chairs. It was a brilliant morning, very sunny, and I could feel the heat beam down on me; I love the sunshine and as it had been so long since I last felt these rays, I sat on enjoying them. The next thing I knew I was being carried into the ward by one of the orderlies. He had caught me as I blacked out and just put me across his arms and walked in with me. I was probably about 8 stone at this time. Just before we reached my cell, I spotted Fr Toner walking down the ward; we spoke and he made some joke about no better way to travel – me being carried. The orderly then carried me to my cell and layed me on the bed where I fell asleep immediately, feeling totally drained.

Awaking at noon, I reached out and switched on the radio, more so to get the right time than listen to music. The news was just ending on Downtown and I caught the headlines '. . . this brings to nine the number of those who have died on hunger strike . . .' I knew then that Tom must have died that morning.

I discovered later that he had been sitting up smoking and talking to Fr Toner. At one point Toner went out of the cell for a few minutes. When he returned he found Tom dead. It had been as sudden as that, occurring just as I was being carried up the ward.

Shortly after Tom died, Benny arrived for his visit with him. He was asked to identify the body.

JOHN THOMAS . . .

Father Tom Toner, while openly hostile to us and generally disliked, told us about Tom McElwee's death in a very reverential voice. He told us how Tom had asked him for a cigarette and told him how tired he was; 'I'm just tired, Tom, very tired' was how Toner described Thomas's last words. From his demeanour I could see the 60 or so days that Thomas McElwee had spent on hunger strike had made a tremendous impression on the man and while I was shattered for Thomas and his family, I also had a degree of compassion and sympathy for Fr Toner, as it was clear he was quite distressed also. Everyone at mass that day was deeply moved and we all knew it as there wasn't a sound to be heard until the mass ended, and then we went back to our cells with a quiet resignation that there would be more stories like Thomas McElwee in the near future.

TOM HOLLAND . . .

The deaths, in quick succession, of Kieran Doherty, Kevin Lynch and Tom McElwee were a blow to us in every sense of the word. Our emotions were numb as the grief passed through every inch of our bodies. The close proximity of the three deaths added to and compounded our sorrow. The full effect of Kevin's death was just sinking in when news came through that Kieran had died; in despair and desperation we hoped against hope that Tom would last out longer than expected, even if it was only to give us a break from the tragedy unfolding around us.

The sum result of Tom's death in emotional terms was one of emptiness. We had nothing left in us. We could cry no more, curse no louder, pray no harder – a terrible sense of resignation to the inevitable prevailed.

12

The Hunger Strike Ends

8 August 1981 - 3 October 1981

I n spite of the blow to morale of three deaths in quick succession, volunteers continued to join the hunger strike at weekly intervals. On the outside, while people were weary after more than five months of marching and protesting, support on the ground remained solid. In the Fermanagh/South Tyrone by-election Sinn Féin's Owen Carron won the seat, increasing the majority which Bobby Sands had had over his Unionist opponent. On the very day of polling Micky Devine became the tenth and last hunger striker to die.

In the weeks following his death the hunger strike lost momentum. It became obvious to the prisoners that pressure was diminishing upon the British, and mounting upon themselves and the Republican Movement. Even in those circumstances hunger strikers were prepared to continue, but as September wore on, more families authorised medical intervention, and others made known that they would do the same when hunger strikers reached a critical stage. Having lost the initiative, the prisoners bowed to the inevitable, and on 3 October the hunger strike was ended.

After 217 days of hope, despair, suffering and resignation the prisoners were drained. They had lost 10 friends and comrades, and faced a very uncertain future. Yet, above all, was a determination that after five years of extraordinary protest, they would never accept the label of criminals. The fight would go on.

LAURENCE MCKEOWN ...

Throughout the course of the stailc I hadn't given too much thought to the actual experience of dying. I had thought of course of how people would feel about me dying, of how my family would take it, and thought of the things I would never do again and the people I would never see again. At the same time I realised that if I was dead, I wouldn't be thinking or expressing regret. I would be dead. At this time I would still have held religious beliefs and, though by no means a committed Christian or Catholic, I would still have prayed.

My experiences on the Blanket, with time to think, reflect and discuss many topics of social and political interest, had turned me very much against the Catholic Church as an organisation. However, I could still identify with the humanity of many of the individual priests who came in to say mass. Missionaries were usually of great interest and I found that often our politics would be very similar, they themselves having experienced at first hand the tyranny and brutal oppression of people in the Philippines, Guatemala, Uruguay, parts of Africa and elsewhere. Others closer to home were the monks of Portglenone Abbey and Fr Brian Brady, whose integrity was very apparent and encouraging.

I was surprised that the prison chaplains, Tom Toner and John Murphy, hadn't attempted to talk me off the stailc by saying it was a sin against God or in other ways using religion against me. Possibly they had gone over the merits of that with the previous hunger strikers, but at no time did they in any way attempt to dissuade me from what I was doing. I enjoyed their daily visits; they weren't religious occasions, more a bit of craic than anything else. Spud (Fr Murphy) spoke of Francie Hughes and how he enjoyed debating with him. They would also bring Communion with them each day which I received.

The food placed in the cell every day never bothered me. It's difficult to describe the feeling of not eating. Some had told me that after three days I would lose interest in food. Well, I never encountered that nor did any of the other stailceoirí I spoke to. I think after a few days the stomach reduced in size and the body began to adapt to not using the digestive process, but I still had thoughts of food. During the Blanket protest we often talked for hours about the enormous meals we would make ourselves once we got political status. These would be described in great detail and the smell of cooking was almost tangible, so descriptive were the accounts of preparing meals up in the Cages. This was at a time when it was possible to predict what meal we would get on which day up to three months away.

If you go for a considerable number of hours without food, or if you expect a meal then don't get it, you begin to think of food and what you are missing. A hunger strike is different. I knew I wasn't going to eat. It wasn't that I was denied food or missed a meal. I had decided I wasn't going to eat and I knew the reasons why I was doing that. The food sitting on my table therefore had no appeal to me and it wouldn't have mattered how delicious it was. The sense of hunger that would exist on other occasions didn't therefore arise. Of course there was a feeling of emptiness, but not hunger pangs. Often in the hospital when adverts for food would appear on the TV, we would joke about it. 'Would you beat that down your neck? Better fuckin' believe it!', and we would discuss it just as we had done prior to the fast.

The orderlies working in the hospital were very sensitive about it. They would be afraid to eat in front of us, though one evening Bobby H walked into the canteen absent-mindedly munching away at a hamburger before he realised we were all there. He was overcome with embarrassment and really angry with himself, even though we were all saying to him, 'Go ahead Bobby, for Christ's sake. It doesn't annoy us.' Every Thursday, meat and eggs were sent up from the kitchens and the orderlies would cook it when we were locked up. The smell of it frying was delicious and we would come out of the cells at half past five, swearing to have one of those dinners as soon as we got status.

One funny incident regarding food occurred while Paddy, Tom and I were still in D wing, H3. A couple of lads up the wing had got their grub handed in, then discovered that there was only half a fish on each plate. The orderlies had obviously been short for themselves so just halved the Blanketmen's grub, a not unusual occurrence. The two lads kicked up a racket and the screws were down to find out what was going on. The rest of the wing also started to shout over to find out what was happening. Bik then got to the door and asked what the craic was. When he found out it was a row over half a fish he told the lads to let the issue drop. He was raging that there was a row about small portions of food while there were three of us on hunger strike on the wing, but the lads were just right to complain and our presence should not have hindered them in demanding what was rightfully theirs. In reversed roles the three of us would have complained.

I received many letters and cards during the stailc and was grateful for every one of them. I knew people found it difficult knowing what to say in them, or whether or not for instance they should refer to the brilliant holiday they were having. The most they could do was wish me all the best and say how they were thinking and praying for me. It didn't really matter though what they wrote; it was just nice to receive them. I got a few from people I hadn't heard from since coming into jail, and one from a woman who had written several letters to me during the Blanket protest but which I had never received. It brought back many happy memories and made me laugh in some places, but I didn't write much myself and then only in the early stages of the fast. As time went on I couldn't motivate myself to put pen to paper.

At the beginning of the staílc my thoughts were very much focused on political events and what could have a bearing on the outcome of the fast. I read any paper I could get, listened to the news and current affairs programmes and discussed the situation with the others, but as time wore on I found I was becoming less interested. Not a case of losing hope, more a lack of enthusiasm, a settling down to just doing the fast, spending the days until something happened. At times there would be particularly high moments when things looked good, other times things would look more bleak, but my moods didn't change a lot. Probably I would just take less interest in some things than in others.

Time dragged by fairly slowly in the hospital, but the nights were the longest, though I looked forward to locking up at 8.30 just to be on my own. While my sight was still good, I read the newspapers and did the odd crossword. Apart from writing the occasional letter I listened to the radio most of the time, though it was more a case of the radio providing background music than me actually listening to it. As time went on I listened to the radio less and less, though a strange thing that occurred was a change in my taste in music. Normally I could enjoy most types of music, with the exception of Country and Western. I loathe it, yet during the latter part of the fast it was the only music I could listen to. The only thing I can figure is that it's so boring and repetitive that you don't have to think about it – just switch it on and let it drone away.

Most of the time was spent reminiscing and day-dreaming. I had thoughts of how the staílc would suddenly end with all our demands granted and the partying we would do afterwards. Now and again I thought of my death. I feared that it would be a painful one or one in which I had lost control of my senses for a time beforehand. I wanted to stay lucid at all times.

I thought of my family often and of how the hunger strike was affecting them. I knew my mother was the one bearing the brunt of the pressure. She was the one most in contact with me, the one who had visited me regularly since my imprisonment and the one who felt most deeply for me. She was not a Republican and I wondered how she now felt being to the fore in this form of Republican struggle. I knew that her thoughts would be with everyone on the staílc and especially so with their families. I regretted I hadn't more time and better circumstances to speak with her on the visits, but also realised that I was often avoiding talk of what she meant to me as it would be just too emotional for both of us. So I presented the jovial face and spoke of how well I felt.

I relived many exploits with old friends. In fact, because the years on the Blanket involved recounting old stories of our youth, the images were familiar to me. I had really nothing in common now with most of these people, having drifted apart over the years, but their earlier friendship was still dear to me. You could say really that after 8.30 at night I wasn't really in the hospital but off in either bygone days or living in a future H-Block with political status and all the freedom of movement and pastime that allowed for.

Sleep was not deep. I would sleep for a few hours, then suddenly find that I was wide awake staring at the ceiling. Bernadette, my first love from secondary school days, kept appearing in my dreams. I hadn't seen her in about 10 years and couldn't recall a time I had ever been reminiscing about her with any great depth of feeling, but for the duration of the stailc I felt very, very close to her. I don't know if she was thinking of me at the time or even knew I was on hunger strike.

Like the prison camp in general, the hospital ward is very, very quiet at night, and although I know it sounds like a cliché, often what I was doing was listening to the silence. At such times I felt very close to the ones in the Blocks. I knew they would be thinking of us, asking for scéal about us, writing to whoever they could on our behalf and in some cases preparing to join the stailc themselves. The nights were long, but I enjoyed the solitude.

Pat Finucane, the solicitor, came to see me one day to make my 'last will and testament'. It was a bit unreal, me, who did not even have a set of clothes, making a will. I'm not so sure how I felt about it - 'in the event of my death' - but I don't really think I took the whole process too seriously. It was all a bit abstract in a sense. My death was more real to me in other terms than in concern about who I should bequeath my belongings to. I enjoyed the visit, though. Pat was able to tell me what was taking place outside and give a general assessment of feelings among the people. He did a lot of work around the time of both hunger strikes and we much appreciated it.

As I grew progressively weaker and realised that death was something which faced me very soon, my thoughts were mostly about the manner in which I would die. I had already witnessed others dying and in different ways. I hoped it would be sudden like Big Tom and without sickness.

I thought about Tom's death a lot. Probably it was the most vivid to me, having spoken together the previous night and having seen him that morning. He had been relatively free from sickness throughout the stailc and my own health and rate of deterioration up until then had very much mirrored this. I therefore looked on Tom's death as the most likely example of how I would die. That is, I would be lucid right up to the very end, then suffer a coronary attack or some other instantaneous form of death. That wasn't a morbid thought at the time. It was relevant to my circumstances. I had witnessed other men suffering the pain of sickness and had listened to the torments of Paddy Quinn, knowing that Martin Hurson had endured the same pain before finally dying. So the manner in which Tom died was therefore very much to be desired and I viewed it in as pragmatic a form as that.

The actual fact of dying, of being no more, didn't occupy my mind a lot. Possibly there was a reluctance to dwell on that, as it would have seemed to rule out the possibility of victory. I would always think positively (as I am inclined by nature to be more of an optimist than a pessimist), just as I would, for as long as possible, get up each day and walk about for a while, or even sit in an armchair. I was assisted and encouraged in this by Paul who made sure we didn't allow ourselves to become lazy or dejected. If he thought we were, he would come in shouting about getting us out of bed.

In the last days of my fast, death took on a more real appearance and was now an inevitability rather than a possibility, but by then I was almost totally exhausted and to even think such things in any deep sense or for any length of time takes a lot of concentration, so I didn't dwell on it. I think it must be like someone who has been on their feet for days without sleep and who is exhausted, then gets the chance to lie down and sleep but is awakened to be told the house is on fire. They don't want to know; they just want to lie and sleep. Danger means nothing to them, they don't even think about it. All that matters is the craving for rest and sleep. That's how I would compare the last days of the hunger strike: a state of exhaustion, where all I wanted to do was close my eyes and sleep.

After I was moved to the hospital, my progress through the fast in terms of how it affected me physically was one of slowly weakening. My step became shorter and my pace slower. In the last couple of weeks I would hold onto a wall, a chair or bed when walking, or at least have my arms outstretched. After about 40 days my eyesight became distorted. I had double vision, which lasted a few days and then my sight became hazy. I found it very difficult to read and soon after this stopped even trying. Similarly, watching TV had become painful. Anything which was bright, such as the large light in the cell, was irritating, so mostly I had them switched off.

The weakness in the body seemed to be paralleled in the mind. After 50 days or so I found difficulty in maintaining interest in conversation. I wasn't the only one who appeared to feel this way, and all dialogue between us was of short comments interspersed with long periods of silence. It wasn't melancholy or depression; it was simply tiredness and a disinterest in most topics which we, or anyone, would normally be concerned about. I found that increasingly I had little in common with those I met other than the other hunger strikers. Others lived a different life from me. Or maybe it was that they lived a life, whereas I knew that mine would soon end. The things they seemed anxious about seemed ludicrous to me. It was difficult therefore to express any real interest in what was taking place around me. In the last days of the stailc this was also the case with the protest and fast itself. I certainly wanted to see it succeed but by this stage had accepted that I wasn't going to see that, and that what I had to fix my mind on was living out my last days as comfortably as possible. Death now began to appear more as a release from a weak and troublesome body.

A phenomenon I noticed which indicated that death was about two, no more than three, days away was that a hunger striker's bowels would open. I believe I first identified it in the case of Tom McElwee. Following it, there was a marked deterioration. Not that the bowel movement was the actual cause of deterioration, but was an indication that the person was in the very last stages of life. Then Red Mick told me one night in the canteen that he had diarrhoea most of the day. I already knew as one of the MOs had told me, so I didn't comment much other than to ask if he was OK, and he said he was. Both of us knew what it signalled. Mickey was already very weak by this stage, though because his features were less sharp he didn't appear as gaunt as others such as Big Doc, Kevin and Tom had. This was the last night we talked together. The following day he didn't get out of bed and his family were allowed to stay in the hospital on a permanent basis. I could hear them going in and out of his cell for the few days he lingered on, but didn't go in myself as I would've felt I was intruding. Amongst the hunger strikers there were no goodbyes said, only 'See you'. His death occurred silently. All that was heard was the stretcher knocking against the wall as it manoeuvred through the doorway.

Apart from the time of Gerry Adams's visit and that of the Red Cross delegation (the content of which I remember little about, as it was more or less a rehash of what took place with the ICJP), I met with Bik on a number of other occasions. One of these was following the intervention of Pat Beag's family and his removal from the stailc. Pat had been sick for a few days and I knew his condition had rapidly deteriorated. Pauline, his wife, was then allowed in to see him and when he became unconscious, she authorised medical intervention. I was locked in my cell next to his and could just hear the noise of the stretcher being wheeled in and out again, though I guessed what had happened as all went quiet soon afterwards. Fr Murphy, who had been present in the hospital that afternoon, came and told me what had happened and that Pat had been moved to Musgrave Park Hospital.

I can't recall much that happened after that except that Matt Devlin and myself decided to get Bik up the following day. I was to ask for him. When Paddy Quinn's fast had ended, I was relieved, as I had listened to his painful roars and cries, and it had occurred at a time when there was less focus on the families to intervene. In the meantime, Fr Faul had begun a moral crusade against the hunger strike and was encouraging families to end it by medically intervening once their relative went into a state of unconsciousness. I knew therefore that a lot would be made of Pat's family now taking him off it and that the Brits would regard it as a victory for them and a weakening of our position. I was concerned about the overall effect this would have on our strategy. I also wondered about my own family and what my mother would be thinking.

Bik came up the following morning. I don't think he was surprised at our request to see him as he figured we would want to discuss the overall situation. There had been a degree of reluctance in asking for him in case the administration saw it as a panic move on our part, but we knew such illusions would soon be dispelled anyhow.

We gathered together in the canteen and went over the whole situation. It's possible that the others then on hunger strike but still in the Blocks were also present because I did see them at one time, but am not definite exactly when it was. We all accepted that the Church and media were coming out strongly against the continuation of the staílc but that our support on the ground and internationally had not diminished. There were also others prepared to join the fast at any time despite the numbers they had witnessed dying. The chat was good and we all agreed that, whilst we had suffered a setback, it was one that would be weathered and which didn't ultimately affect our overall position. Bik relayed a few messages from the lads in the Blocks. As usual there were witty remarks, then we broke up and Bik and the others left.

I thought then, as I had done on a few occasions before, that Bik's role was a thankless one. I had some idea of how he must feel sitting down to talk to men, not having any answers to questions they might raise and some of whom he might not see again. I knew we all understood the pressure he was under and I think we did our best to ensure we didn't add to it by a careless word. There was a close bond between all of us which allowed men to firmly argue their position even though the result of that would most likely mean the deaths of some of those across the table from them. It had been our experience throughout the Blanket and it was how we intended to continue.

By this time I was very weak, though I was still getting up for a while each day. I was less interested in what was happening around me and I knew I was preparing myself for death as I had joined the stailc a week behind Mickey and was now the longest on it. Even when Matt Devlin's family authorised medical intervention when he became unconscious and was removed to an outside hospital, it didn't cause me any great concern. No doubt a degree of fatalism had set in.

Only in those last few days did they stop leaving food in my cell. I had complained to them before about the smell of it once it cooled, but they said they were legally obliged to provide me with food. At this stage though they conceded that I probably couldn't eat that type of food even if I did decide to eat. The cell door was still locked during the night and Paul kicked up about this. He said it was totally illogical, besides being dangerous. They agreed to leave it open. I was on hunger strike about 65 days at this stage and they had begun to give me a body rub every so many hours to improve circulation and stop sores from forming on the skin of my back and hips where my body's weight was pressing down. I was also given a sheepskin rug to lie on, which greatly helped. Extreme luxury.

Someone came in to visit me one day and I still don't know if he was a doctor or an NIO official. He was with a few others besides the prison doctor and he strutted around my bed asking a few questions about how I felt. Initially I was replying to his questions but, as his manner was noticeably abrupt, I began to look away and ignore him. He stopped at the end of the bed and in a loud clear voice told me what was happening to my body. 'These purple marks on your chest and arms are blood vessels which have broken down and collapsed, your eyesight has been permanently damaged; your vital organs are under intense strain at this moment. There are a number of ways you will possibly die: a brain tumour or a massive coronary attack; your kidneys or liver could collapse at any moment. Either way you can expect to die very shortly.' He turned on his heel and made for the door, apparently more upset at my impending death than I was.

I was more concerned with the practicalities of dying than with the actual event. I was becoming increasingly sick, the first time during the stailc that I had experienced sickness. I don't know if it was because I had cut down a bit on the water, finding it increasingly difficult to drink, but I made a determined effort to increase the intake of it and the sickness got no worse. What was worse was the hiccups which came after about 67 days. They remained with me almost constantly and just as a bout of them would stop and I was getting relief, I would move in the bed and they would begin all over again. I couldn't hear so clearly and was having headaches at times. Bright lights really annoyed me, so the cell light was left off.

When I had a bowel movement, I knew I had not long left to live. It was on a Friday afternoon and the sensation was no different from feeling the need to go to the toilet in normal circumstances. However, it became quite painful given that in my case it had been more than eight weeks since I last had a bowel movement. The MOs gave me suppositories which helped, I suppose. Nevertheless, I still spent about an hour in the toilet and was exhausted when I was finished. I was already in a very weak condition, but this spent my last reserves of strength. Bobby H assisted me back down to my cell and into bed. I didn't get out of it again. I knew that I had now no more than two days left to live if even that, but I was too tired to dwell on that thought. In fact in many ways it appeared inviting, more or less as a release.

Some hunger strikers' families had been with them for a long period of time before their deaths. They would sleep in an empty cell in the prison ward and one of them would always be with the man on hunger strike. In Big Doc's case his family had come in when he was 50 days on hunger strike because he took very bad at that time. However, he picked up again and lived for almost another three weeks, during which time his family were always with him. After this, families were not allowed in until it was very apparent the stailceoir was going to die or, as in the case of Big Tom, not in at all because he died suddenly. A Doctor Bell came to see me when I was 68 days on hunger strike and after he asked me a few questions about how I felt, Paul, who had accompanied him, strongly recommended that my family be allowed in. He said that medically it could not be said that I was on the point of death, yet everyone knew that I could die at any minute given the length of time I was on hunger strike and the history of those who had already died. Dr Bell seemed to consider it for a few moments, then nodded his head that he would give permission for my family to come into the hospital. They came that night.

My recollection of this period of the stailc is not so clear in terms of the order in which events occurred. I remember Mary, my sister, coming in with my mother. Mary was in a distressed state and asked me if I intended continuing with the fast. I said I did and she began sobbing loudly. My mother sat beside her looking over to me in an expressionless manner. I knew that out of them all she was the one who was most calm and would bear not only the burden of her own sorrow but the weight of comforting others. I talked about some neighbours and friends and generally tried to make some conversation to show that I was lucid and in good spirits. I knew it distressed them when I was sick, particularly when they saw how much the hiccups drained me. My da came in to see me but just stood in the corner of the cell for a while and went out again. He was unable to speak. Eugene, my brother, also visited and appeared to be handling it OK. On the Saturday I was dozing in and out of sleep. I kept dreaming that I was in some place totally surrounded by blackness and that I felt very, very tired and wanted to sleep, but kept saying to myself, 'You mustn't sleep, you mustn't sleep or you're a goner'. It seemed like the last fight to hold onto life.

Members of my family kept a constant vigil at my bedside. When I would wake, they would ask me if I was OK, and pass me a drink of water if I asked. I don't know when exactly I began to lose consciousness but the last time I recall coherently talking to anyone was on the Saturday night. That evening my mother had been at my bedside on her own. She had never said to me at any time since joining the hunger strike, or even when I had first told her that I could possibly be on it, not to do so. She had never discouraged me in any way but had worked in every way possible with anyone who wanted to help our protest. We had never discussed the likely consequences of my going on hunger strike, both knowing what could happen, and we left it at that. So much went unsaid between us. I knew that when she was out of my cell she was across the ward on her knees praying and when she would return to me, she would still have that calm face even though she was feeling her sorrow intensely. That evening I said to her, 'I'm sorry that all this had to come about for you.' She leaned across to me and whispered, 'You know what you have to do and I know what I have to do.' And I understood what she meant. If I was to die suddenly then that was how it was intended to be; it would be God's will. But if my life ended up in her hands and she had a decision over it, then she would give me life as she would see it. She did that early on Sunday afternoon when she authorised medical intervention after I had been delirious for some hours before falling into unconsciousness.

BERNARD FOX . . .

Ten men had already died when I began my strike (Mickey Devine died on 20 August and I began mine on 24 August). I hadn't put forward my name for the first hunger strike. The feeling then was one of high optimism and expectation that it would be successful, that the staff already knew who their volunteers would be and so it would be a safe bet if I put my name forward I wouldn't be required. But the second hunger strike was different and I volunteered when names were asked for. My feelings as I began my hunger strike were the same as when Bobby started on his; I knew what I had let myself in for and had thought it all out. I had known that a few men would have died before I'd be called upon to embark on mine. Therefore, when the time came, I blotted out of my mind everything apart from going on hunger strike and the inevitability of dying.

That's the way it was at that time; I just thought of the time I forwarded my name and the resulting comms asking if I knew what I was letting

myself in for. I remembered that and carried on - it was my duty. I had
volunteered to hunger strike and it was my time to do it. There was no way
I even thought of questioning its continuance. I was still confident that we'd
win. It was my turn and if I was second or 22nd, I had to stand by my
commitment to hunger strike.

It was always policy to put a hunger striker in a cell of his own once he
began the hunger strike, usually cell 2, but I always enjoyed company and
wanted to remain in my own cell with Tom Donaghy. In hindsight, it was
very unfair of me to suggest to Tom that I stay, but he was all for it then. I
stayed two days, but realised I was wrong because Tom was feeling terrible
eating his grub while I didn't.

I had no problems the first week. The lads in the wing were great. I went
through all the usual routines that a hunger striker went through: doctor,
weight, amount of water I drank and so on. All these were documented for
outside. I was going well then and I remember one day having to call the
screws to fill my water gallon again because I'd drunk eight pints in half a
day; it was said that the more water you drank the better, so I was rather
pleased then.

After just 10 days everything changed. I couldn't keep the water down;
every time I drank some it came up again. I would try and keep trying.
Sometimes I'd keep it down, then the next time I tried it would all come up
again. I would only pass a trickle of urine, which was also bad. It wasn't
long before I was up in the hospital - earlier than normal because of my
condition. I rallied a bit, possibly because I could drink the Scottish Highland
Spring water which they had there, but this was only for a couple of days. I
was able to meet and talk with the other lads: Jackie McMullan, Pat
Sheehan and Liam McCloskey. I had already met Matt Devlin and Lorney
McKeown at a previous meeting of hunger strikers. However, by now both
had been taken off the hunger strike by their families. That was the big
worry then, our families taking us off.

At the start, visits weren't too bad. My family and girlfriend (now my
wife) were 100% behind me and had promised they wouldn't take me off
hunger strike should I go into a coma. They did all the usual things,
travelling all over the country and Britain, speaking at marches and meeting
people. I couldn't have asked for more from them.

I have only seen my father cry twice in my life. Once when I was released
for five hours compassionate parole to attend my grandmother's funeral
while interned, he cried as I was returning to Long Kesh. And then when he
visited me while I was on hunger strike, he cried again as the visit ended.
I'll never forget those two times.

While I was in the hospital I got visits daily because of my condition. If I
looked terrible, my family didn't let me know it. However, I will always

remember my daughter Roisin's reaction on the visits. She was only three years of age but I know she was frightened of the way I looked. God help her, she didn't understand.

My health deteriorated very quickly; I couldn't keep any water down and by then wasn't passing any water. Several specialists as well as doctors came in daily to see all the hunger strikers; our policy was to let them examine us. Many came in to see me to try and diagnose what was wrong with me. They told me I was seriously ill, had kidney trouble and most likely an ulcer and hadn't long to live. Of course, at times like that you say to yourself that they're trying to get you off the hunger strike and exaggerating your condition. Also, in my own head I was saying, if I come off hunger strike I'd be letting down my comrades who had died before me. But I did realise that I was seriously ill.

I vividly remember Jackie and Pat shouting into me from the exercise yard of the hospital one afternoon. They were saying that Father Faul had been on the radio saying both me and Liam McCloskey were in a bad way and near to death and called on our families to take us off. This had a major effect on my family because up to then they didn't realise how bad I was, and they were very angry with Faul for not getting in touch with them before he went on the radio and told everyone. To this day I don't know where Faul got his information from; I certainly never saw him in the hospital.

At that time I was almost 30 days on hunger strike and I had another visit from the specialists, two of whom were named Love and Grant. It was a Thursday I think, and when they were leaving, they told me I would be dead before the weekend was out. Immediately after this my family got in for a visit. In turn, my mother and brother whispered into my ear, asking if I wanted them to take me off. It would have been easy for me to say 'yes' but I didn't. Although I was ill, I knew what was happening around me; I knew I had to see Bik as soon as possible.

We knew beforehand that Liam's family were taking him off and it was looking bad for the future of the hunger strike. All the hunger strikers had a meeting with Bik, and I told him that I might not be able to hold on for too much longer, that there was something seriously wrong with me, and that I might come off. He asked me to hold on until he got word to outside the next day and I agreed.

The next couple of days aren't too clear to me. After 32 days on hunger strike the Sinn Féin centre announced on radio that I was off hunger strike but the NIO was saying that I wasn't. I only know that people were coming in and out, asking me, shouting in my ear that outside it was being said that I was off. They put on a radio but I couldn't hear what it said. Finally, I did come off. It was my decision and I knew what I was doing at the time.

Bik McFarlane ...

Although we had ample volunteers eager to play their part on hunger strike, and had used numerous replacements, we now encountered an intervention which was to take control completely out of our hands. A number of families, following the example of Mrs Quinn who intervened to save Paddy's life when he lapsed into a coma, were indicating that they would do likewise. We discussed possible avenues around this but it was becoming increasingly obvious that we were facing an impossible task. Lorney's mother intervened after 70 days, as did Matt Devlin's family after 52 days, and Pat McGeown's wife sought medical intervention for him after 47 days. Barney Fox had to come off on medical grounds with a similar complaint as that which forced Brendan McLoughlin off in May.

The dilemma could not be overcome at all and we were told that most families would now seek medical intervention. Liam McCloskey, when he could not persuade his family otherwise, decided to terminate his hunger strike as he entered the critical stage. We discussed the situation back in the Block and realised that our hunger strike had finally come to an end, not because we were in any way defeated by Thatcher's government or because we lacked the will to continue. We had effectively been robbed of the only means we had of making our protest a real threat, and the element which robbed us did so out of deep concern and love.

Jackie McMullan ...

In September the issue which preoccupied those of us then on hunger strike was that of intervention by our families and what we could do to prevent it. As each hunger striker lapsed into a coma the doctor certified him no longer competent to decide whether or not he wanted medical treatment and legal power of attorney was handed over to the next of kin. It was done in such a way as to put the onus onto families to decide whether or not their loved one should live. This proved to be an enormous emotional pressure on relatives and, with each family that intervened, so grew the pressure on the next one to follow suit. Fr Faul must be singled out here because, using the credibility he had built up as the prisoners' friend to gain access to our families, he actively and energetically exploited their emotional vulnerability to undermine our hunger strike. He visited each of the families secretly and to those who showed any resistance to his pressure he posed the question, 'Are you going to be the one to let your son die?'

I think too that during the gap in time since the last death, that of Mickey Devine, the notion began to take root that we had lost the momentum and the question of whether or not anyone else would or should die started to arise. This was something I read or detected in the thinking of others but guarded against taking on board myself. When I'd put my name down for the hunger strike, it was with the conviction that I would see it through to the end and no way could I afford to entertain any thoughts of it ending and possibly weakening my preparedness to go the full way. Pat Sheehan was my companion at this time in the hospital; he'd joined the hunger strike a week before me and was now entering the period of danger. We were both agreed that, whatever about other people's opinions or speculations, we had to keep our feet on the ground and, as far as we were concerned, the hunger strike was continuing.

There was never any shortage of volunteers for the hunger strike, but when the point was reached where most of the families of the remaining hunger strikers had indicated they would seek medical intervention when their sons reached the critical point, it became apparent that it would be futile to continue. Like everyone else I suppose, there was a part of me that wanted to carry on. Ten of my comrades, some of them close personal friends, had died. They'd died for me, for us, for the struggle we'd shared and endured and fought with such intensity every single day for the past five years and which had bound us together in a bond of love and solidarity that was closer than many people ever have the privilege of experiencing in their lifetime. All the suffering, all the sacrifices - how would their families feel? How would the lads in the Blocks feel? And all the people outside?

It was with mixed feelings therefore that we announced the end of the hunger strike and the eventual statement reflected this. We were sad almost beyond words that ten of our comrades had died and angry at those who had had it in their power to do something about it but chose instead to direct their efforts towards undermining our just demands. And, although we didn't know exactly what lay ahead of us, there was an unspoken determination that we would never ever betray the memories of those men whose deaths had so profoundly affected us.

John Pickering . . .

On the morning the hunger strike ended, a screw opened my cell door and said I was to go to the hospital. This message created a stir around the wing. It was unexpected and could only mean one thing; a meeting of the hunger strikers and the Camp OC. Some of the lads shouted messages to pass on to the other hunger strikers, but my mind was preoccupied with thoughts of what was in store at this meeting. Already, repeated interventions by families had created a new and unsettling situation. This was making the morale and tactical justification of the continuation of the hunger strike extremely difficult, something that we did not wish to recognise but was now nevertheless the unpalatable reality. The objective of the hunger strike, to bring unbearable moral and political pressure on the British, appeared now to be in the process of reversing on to our families. Fr Faul, in particular, had facilitated this shift of focus, hoping to damage the Republican Movement in the process. For the previous two months or so the question of intervention had been the main feature in most of our discussions. Each discussion ended with the same conclusion - that intervention by the families posed a major obstacle to the future of the hunger strike. Our principle dilemma was unchanged, however. The criminalisation policy was still being pursued; our situation had not changed one iota. To end the hunger strike would mean entering the pre-hunger strike scheme of things: same system, same policies, same regime.

By late September a realisation was setting in that we were not persuading, and would not be able to persuade, our families not to intervene. Every argument, including even the threat of legally changing who could act as next of kin, had been tried. The families, however, had now convinced themselves that their prime concern was to save their sons' lives. This situation caused some tremendous personal strain between some hunger strikers and their families. It was a very emotional issue. Eventually a point was reached where only one family would give a commitment not to intervene. The dilemma facing us could not be more severe: continue the hunger strike to the point of going into a coma and then be revived as a result of the families authorising intervention or, look afresh at the reality facing us and cancel the hunger strike.

When I arrived at the prison hospital that morning, the hunger strikers were all escorted to the waiting room where the meeting was held. There were five of us present plus the Camp OC. The other hunger striker, Pat Sheehan, was too sick to attend. It was a sombre scene. We didn't want to come off the hunger strike. Bik outlined all the various obstacles facing us and we discussed the possible ways of circumventing them. In the end we accepted that none was feasible. Eventually we could do nothing other than confirm the Camp leadership's decision to terminate the hunger strike. Bik then left the room to consult with Pat who was immediately transferred to Musgrave Park Hospital. While the rest of us went in for medical examinations, Bik set out to inform the Block OCs of the situation.

BIK McFARLANE ...

In the hospital I explained our position to all those still on hunger strike and we quickly arrived at a decision to call a halt. We set a date for Saturday 3 October at 3.00pm - some days hence - to enable me to have a major statement drafted by the PRO for release on that afternoon. We had announced and controlled the beginning of the hunger strike, and we would likewise terminate it in a controlled and dignified manner. On Saturday morning I met with all Block and wing OCs to inform them of the decision. There was obvious disappointment that we had achieved no settlement, but immense relief that no one else would have to endure such a horrific ordeal, or die. I spent that afternoon in the hospital with the remaining hunger strikers and felt the tension begin to lift the moment we informed the authorities it was over.

In H3 I began to notice smiles on faces. There had been sombre looks from early in the year and I couldn't remember the last time I heard laughter in our wing. We were relieved at coming out of the nightmare, but the wounds at the loss of our truly courageous and selfless comrades were very deep. The healing process would take a long time but no one really believed that the scars of 1981 would disappear. I was completely drained myself and spent a considerable time winding down. We would have our own clothes within weeks and we could then enter a new phase of jail struggle. But in the meantime all I needed was rest - a long peaceful rest.

STATEMENT AT END OF SECOND HUNGER STRIKE

We, the protesting Republican prisoners in the H-Blocks, being faced with the reality of sustained family intervention, are forced by this circumstance, over which we have little control at the moment, to end the hunger strike.

After four years of continual protest, and after the failure of the Cardinal O'Fiaich/Humphrey Atkins talks, and having exhausted all other means of protest to bring about a settlement, we embarked on hunger strike on October 18th, 1980.

That hunger strike ended on 18 December 1980, when the British government intimated to the hunger strikers that they would implement a workable and just solution which was forwarded to the hunger strikers on 18 December 1980.

In the course of the immediate post-hunger strike period it became increasingly clear that the British government had reneged on their commitment to implement that solution and so we were back in a pre-hunger strike predicament and thus forced to go back on hunger strike.

On 1 March 1981 Bobby Sands embarked on hunger strike.

On 23 April 1981, 30,492 people in the Fermanagh/South Tyrone constituency elected him as their MP and by doing so, they recognised him as a political prisoner and demanded that the British government respect the mandate given by them and by the entire nationalist community on the streets by implementing the five demands.

The British government, caught in the hypocrisy of their own 'democracy' jargon, ignored the people's wishes and mandate.

On 23 April 1981 Charles Haughey, then Dublin premier, met relatives of Bobby Sands and, by playing on their distress, convinced them that the intervention of the ECHR (European Commission on Human Rights) could, and would, solve the issue. Bobby's sister, Marcella, acted on Haughey's advice and signed an intervention document.

The ECHR delegation came to Long Kesh and Bobby Sands said he would meet them providing Brendan McFarlane, OC of the prisoners, Mr Gerry Adams and Mr Danny Morrison were present. This reasonable proviso was refused and the ECHR left Long Kesh. Bobby released a statement that night attacking Haughey for unscrupuously exploiting his family's anxiety to cover his own inactivity.

On 5 May 1981 Bobby Sands died on hunger strike, murdered by British callousness and vindictiveness.

Frank Hughes, Raymond McCreesh and Patsy O'Hara were soon to follow Bobby to the grave, and still the British government remained steadfastly and inhumanly inflexible.

On 11 June nine prisoners stood in the Southern general election. Of these, Paddy Agnew topped the poll in Louth, and Kieran Doherty was elected for the Cavan/Monaghan constituency. In the other seven areas the prisoners polled exceedingly well considering the lack of organisation and the short period of time there was to organise the election campaign.

The ordinary people of the South cast their votes in thousands. In Cavan/ Monaghan, Kieran Doherty polled first preference 9,121 (15%); Paddy Agnew, Louth, 8,368 (18%); Joe McDonnell, Sligo/Leitrim, 5,634; Martin Hurson, Longford/Westmeath, 4,573 (10%); Sean McKenna, Kerry North, 3,860; Kevin Lynch, Waterford, 3,337; Tony O'Hara, Dublin West, 3,034; Mairead Farrell, Cork North Central, 2,751 and Tom McAllister, Clare, 2,120.

On 4 July 1981 we issued a major policy statement outlining our five demands, and emphasising the fact that we wanted our five demands to be available for all prisoners (rejecting an assertion to the contrary, made by the British, which we regarded as nonsense and a red herring to justify the barbarity of the British government). This statement was almost universally accepted as 'remarkably conciliatory'.

On the same day, the ICJP (Irish Commission for Justice and Peace) entered the prison and put proposals to the hunger strikers. They put the same proposals to Brendan McFarlane the next day.

On 8 July Joe McDonnell died and the British government issued their policy statement.

We released a statement rejecting the government's statement and ambiguous proposals as even less than what we were originally led to believe was offered via the ICJP. We also rejected the ICJP's proposals which totally evaded the crux of the issue and we expressed our belief that the government had used the ICJP to foster the impression that a settlement was imminent.

The government's renegal on their own commitment to the ICJP compounded our belief that the ICJP were being used, and the ICJP dismissed the government's proposals as not a genuine attempt at a settlement.

On 13 July we were shocked and dismayed to hear that Martin Hurson had been violently ill and had died unexpectedly and prematurely.

The next significant development was the British government-sponsored intervention of the IRC (International Red Cross). The IRC tried to initiate direct dialogue between the Brits and ourselves, but the British rejected this and suggested mediation based on their July 8th statement, which was aimed at defeating us and unproductive, and we rejected this as futile.

We pointed out to the IRC that, as the Brits were not interested in an honourable settlement, their interest in the IRC must logically be to use them. A Red Cross delegate asked for a further breakdown of our 4 July statement and was initially refused. However, after discussion, we compiled and issued our 6 August statement and asked the British government, the Dublin government, the SDLP and the Catholic Church to respond to our statement.

Soon Kieran Doherty, Kevin Lynch and Thomas McElwee were to be murdered by Britain.

The British government, having been exposed for the hypocrites they are at the first Fermanagh and South Tyrone by-election, had instigated and passed legislation which erased our right to participate in elections and, this done, they fixed the by-election for Bobby Sands' seat for 20 August.

By this time, a new, active, treacherous, and vigorous campaign was under way to break the strike. This campaign was orchestrated by clerics who received approval from the Catholic Church. On occasion other individuals were involved also.

Attempts were made to discredit the prisoners and the National H-Block/Armagh Committee. More damaging was the promotion of the 'hopeless' syndrome. The projection of this 'hopeless' syndrome, plus the private lobbying of relatives to effect intervention when strikers were going into a coma, was proving to be a serious threat to the continuation of the hunger strike.

On 20 August 1981 Owen Carron was elected with an increased majority as proxy political prisoner MP for Fermanagh and South Tyrone. Even so, the British premier, Thatcher, again spurned this mandate for us prisoners and with encouragement from Dr Fitzgerald went further, by refusing even to meet with him to discuss the continuing spiral, and gruesome spectre, of death.

On 20 August Mickey Devine was the tenth hunger striker to die.

Mounting pressure and cleric-inspired demoralisation led to further intervention and at present five strikers have been taken off their fast. We accept that it is almost a physical and psychological impossibility to recommence hunger strike after intervention. Also, two men ended their fast to avoid a premature, non-hunger striking death.

The situation exists at present that a considerable majority of hunger strikers' families have indicated that they will intervene and under these circumstances we feel that the hunger strike must, for tactical reasons, be suspended.

We feel that it is of paramount importance that the political revelations, lessons and consequences of the hunger strike are recognised and perpetuated in the minds, the hearts and demeanour of the nationalist population of Ireland.

One of the primary lessons to emerge from this second hunger strike is that the nationalist community is politically inconsequential and impotent in the context of the six-county statelet.

Despite the electoral successes, despite the hundreds of thousands at hunger strikers' funerals, despite massive and unprecedented displays of community support and solidarity, the British government adhered rigidly to the precept that 'might is right' and set about hammering home that nothing has really changed since the fall of Stormont or from the inception of this state. That is, that nationalist Ireland must always be subjected to the British and Loyalist veto.

On the same theme, the lesson of Fermanagh and South Tyrone is that the self-exalted 'British Democracy' is an expediency manufactured - again from the setting up of the border (the 'first and biggest gerrymander') - to preserve a continued British presence in Ireland.

When defeated by their own rules at the polls the British government's concept of democracy altered and the rules were changed to suit them. When they are defeated even by their own rules, they ignore the democratically expressed voice of the electorate and thus undermine the entire principle and purpose of using their 'democratic' processes to effect social or political change.

The logical conclusion of this analysis is that nationalist pacifism in the Northern Ireland context dooms the nationalist population to subserviency, perpetuates partition, and thwarts the quest for a just and lasting peace in Ireland.

Another facet of this hunger strike was to expertly expose the true face of the present Irish Establishment, consisting of the Catholic Church, the Dublin government and the SDLP.

From the outset the Catholic hierarchy opposed the hunger strike even though they offered no alternative course of action.

We contend that their position has at all times been established by political consideration rather than the Christian values of truth and justice. Therefore, their stance has been extremely immoral and misleading.

At no time did the Church publicly support the five demands or for that matter reject them. Equally, when specifically asked to respond to our 6 August statement, they kept silent - even though hunger strikers were dying virtually on a weekly basis.

We contend very strongly that the reason that the British didn't respond to our 6 August statement is that the prison regime we proposed was inarguably superior and better than the present Victorian regime and that the Church accepted this, but to support our demands would be to oppose the British government.

And the logical conclusion, again, would be to consciously incite the Irish Catholic population to oppose the British policy. Therefore, they remained ambiguous on the entire issue and the reason, as we stated, is that they are intricately immersed in the field of politics and deceit.

It was the Catholic clerics, more than anyone, who were involved in the back door and public pressuring of families to get them to intervene.

We believe that the Dublin bloc of Fianna Fail, Fine Gael and Labour are accessories to the legalised murder of ten true and committed Irishmen who died heroically in the long tradition of republican resistance to British occupation, oppression and injustice in Ireland. They are accessories to murder by virtue of the fact that they sat idly by and thus encouraged the British to continue with the death policy.

The sheer hypocrisy of their position is that at no time did any of these three parties unequivocally or even tacitly support our demands, even though our five demands are implemented in their entirety (even more than we were looking for) in jails in Southern Ireland.

Well may they hang their heads in shame, for they are a pathetic reflection of republicanism and the spirit that traditionally earmarked the Irish patriot's pursuit of nationhood and justice, and by their cowardly collaborationist and quisling stand on the H-Block issue they have debased the memory of generations of Irish freedom fighters who fought for a separatist Ireland.

If John Bull doesn't actually rule the twenty-six counties physically, he still rules it in spirit.

And it must not be forgotten that Garret FitzGerald's concept of democracy parallels with Maggie Thatcher's.

There was only one positive injurious action available to the SDLP which would help to save lives in the H-Blocks and that was to isolate the British administration by withdrawing from the council chambers. This they consistently refused to do, preferring instead to cling tenaciously to their role of imperialist lickspittle.

Rather than take action to secure an honourable solution and save lives, they occupied their time trying to make political gain by attacking those who did genuinely endeavour to end the issue honourably, namely the National H-Block/

Armagh Committee and those councillors who answered our call to withdraw from the councils.

This party should now be recognised for what it is, an amalgamation of middle class Redmondites, devoid of principle, direction and courage. This party is spineless and weak and is very capable of selling out to unionist intimidators for imperialist perks. Their whole leadership combined do not possess a fraction of the moral fibre demonstrated so valiantly by our comrades.

There were several reasons given by our comrades for going on hunger strike. One was because we had no choice and no other means of securing a principled solution to the four year protest. Another, and of fundamental importance, was to advance the Irish people's right to liberty. We believe that the age old struggle for Irish self-determination and freedom has been immeasurably advanced by this hunger strike and therefore we claim a massive political victory. The hunger strikers, by their selflessness, have politicised a very substantial section of the Irish nation and exposed the shallow, unprincipled nature of the Irish partitionist bloc.

Our comrades have lit with their very lives an eternal beacon which will inspire this nation and people to rise and crush oppression forever and this nation can be proud that it produced such a quality of manhood.

We pay a special tribute to the families of our dead comrades. You have suffered greatly and with immense dignity. Your loved ones, our comrades and friends, were and would be very proud of you for standing by them. No tribute is too great.

Also, we give a special mention to those families who could not watch their loved ones die in pain and agony. We prisoners understand the pressure you were under and stand by you.

We thank the National H-Block/Armagh Committee, the H-Block movement, the nationalist people of Ireland, and all those who championed our cause abroad. We are indebted to you and ask you to continue your good work on our behalf.

Lastly, we reaffirm our commitment to the achievement of the five demands by whatever means we believe necessary and expedient. We rule nothing out. Under no circumstances are we going to devalue the memory of our dead comrades by submitting ourselves to a dehumanising and degrading regime.

FELIM O'HAGAN . . .

When the hunger strike was finally called, off my dominant feeling was one of relief. But unlike the ending of the first hunger strike, there was no sense of shattered defeat; while the way forward was by no means clear, there was a determination that the deaths of the 10 did not signal the end of our struggle in prison.

PEADAR WHELAN . . .

I was relieved that no one else would die. I hadn't any single thought or set of thoughts that would have dominated. It wasn't a clear-cut sense of relief because it wasn't a clear-cut set of circumstances that brought the hunger strike to an end. Thatcher's objective to stand firm against us was no less than murder. Faul, who had made a name for himself as a human rights campaigner on the back of republican POWs, followed the British line and did everything he could to undermine the hunger strike by using emotional blackmail to get families to take their sons, fathers, brothers off the strike. My resentment for Faul and Thatcher was as great as my relief.

Despite my relief that no one else would die I still felt gutted because 10 men had died and we had not won our demands. My morale was never as low. I don't believe I was capable of thinking further than the next day. Rumours were rife, but I dismissed them. Talk of this or that concession just seemed meaningless, although it wasn't long before we heard we would be allowed to get our own clothes in. This meant we would get out of our cells for association and exercise which made it the focus of events because, once we got out of the cells, we could weigh up the situation to see where we could go. A feature of the immediate post-hunger strike period was constant discussions and meetings to find answers to the questions we faced. It boiled down to two choices: should we stay on protest or go into the system to see how we could work it to our advantage?

Epilogue

Any account of life on the Blanket or of the hunger strikes inevitably throws up names which have now become familiar to many who have never set foot in Long Kesh. Hundreds of others, however, played an equally significant role in the stand against criminalisation. All endured the same extreme conditions, suffered the same brutality, felt the same fears and shared the same anxiety and concern for parents, families and loved ones on the outside. No less, all sensed the same rage at both the system which held us in such conditions and the people who brutalised and attempted to degrade us at every opportunity.

Although the Blanket was passive in nature, the story of the H-Block protest is essentially the story of defiance, no better exemplified than in the aftermath of some of the roughest wing shifts. Men bruised, battered and out of breath would stand at their cell doors and sing Republican songs at the top of their voices. This was the Blanketmen at their rawest and most defiant. To the screws it was a reminder that they could try in whatever way to break us; they could hurt us individually; they could knock us down again and again – but we would keep getting up, and together, we would win through in the end.

It would be all too easy in retrospect to present the history of the Blanket struggle against the backdrop of careful prior analysis on our part. Such was not the case. The average age of those on the protest was 20. We found ourselves, all too suddenly, thrown into the middle of Britain's attempts to criminalise our struggle. Our response was more instinctive than analytical. We knew only that we would not be criminalised, and so began our protest.

Our recollections of 1981 are painful but, nonetheless, precious. Time numbs little of the sorrow and the sense of loss we experienced as, one by one, our friends and comrades died on hunger strike. Nor does time diminish in any way the value of their sacrifice.

The protest by the Blanketmen in the H-Blocks and the women POWs in Armagh Jail stood as a line of stubborn resistance to Britain's criminalisation policy. The sacrifice of the men who died on hunger strike all but killed that policy off completely. The hunger strikers focused the eyes of the world on the political conflict in Ireland, and our struggle increased in legitimacy both at home and abroad as a consequence. Britain's hold on Ireland was severely weakened.

Within the jail the hunger strikers won us initially the right to wear our own clothes. The NIO's abandonment of the insistence that Republican prisoners wear the prison's uniform was more than a symbolic defeat of the outward badge of criminalisation. It afforded us room to manoeuvre, to reorganise and to plan for further action in pursuit of our objectives. Whilst not immediately obvious at the time, the hunger strikes had done much more than prise open the door to future gains. In the damage done to the criminalisation policy in the broader political sense, they sapped the will of the NIO to pursue its previous strategies within the prisons with any deep commitment to, or belief in eventual success.

From 1981 to the present day the legacy of the hunger strike, and the credibility we gained, has been the bedrock of our strength. That strength has combined with the same patient determination which characterised the Blanket protest as, one by one, our five demands were achieved. Today, the inheritance of our dead comrades is all around us as we pursue the new goals which we have set ourselves.

The Republican POWs
H-Blocks Long Kesh
March 1994